WITHDRAWN

CHINA
COMPETING IN THE GLOBAL ECONOMY

Edited by
Wanda Tseng and Markus Rodlauer

With
**David Robinson
Thomas Dorsey
Jahangir Aziz
Paul Heytens
Christoph Duenwald
Paul Gruenwald
Thomas Richardson
Raju Singh
George Tsibouris
Harm Zebregs
James Daniel
Cem Karacadag
Nicolas Blancher
Yongzheng Yang**

INTERNATIONAL MONETARY FUND

© 2003 International Monetary Fund

Cover design: Lai Oy Louie
Typesetting: Choon Lee

Library of Congress Cataloging-in-Publication Data

China, competing in the global economy : edited by Wanda Tseng and
Markus Rodlauer.
    p. cm.
    Includes bibliographical references.
    ISBN 1-58906-178-0
        1. China—Economic policy—2000– . 2. China—China—
Economic policy—1976–2000. 3. Competition, International.
I. Tseng, Wanda. II. Rodlauer, Markus.

HG427.95.C437 2002
338.951—dc21   2002038867

Price: $26.00

Please send orders to:
International Monetary Fund, Publication Services
700 19th Street, N.W., Washington, D.C. 20431, U.S.A.
Tel.: (202) 623-7430   Telefax: (202) 623-7201
E-mail: publications@imf.org
Internet: http://www.imf.org

recycled paper

Foreword

China's economic performance in recent years has been impressive by most standards. The country was able to weather the storm of the Asian crisis relatively unscathed and has sustained rapid growth in the face of last year's global downturn. These achievements have added to the visible success of economic transformation that two decades of market-oriented reforms have brought to China, including large gains in income per capita, the creation of a vibrant nonstate sector, and major inroads into poverty. One of the key driving forces of this growth and transformation has been the progressive opening up of the economy to foreign competition and investment, culminating in China's recent accession to the World Trade Organization (WTO).

At the same time, analysts point to problems in state-owned banks and enterprises, medium-term fiscal pressures, growing unemployment and income disparities, and weak governance. How will China be able to compete successfully in the global economy with these problems weighing on its economy, especially as WTO accession has set the stage for a further and decisive round of opening up?

The key task facing policymakers in China today is thus to push ahead with the unfinished reform agenda, to ensure sustained rapid growth and social stability, and to prepare the economy for increased global competition resulting from WTO accession. This book looks at those challenges and China's efforts to meet them, issues that have been at the center of the IMF staff's work on China in recent years.

The book brings together material and analysis prepared during 2000–01 by IMF staff working on China under the direction of Wanda Tseng. The team of authors was led by Markus Rodlauer and David Robinson and included Thomas Dorsey, Jahangir Aziz, Paul Heytens, Christoph Duenwald, Paul Gruenwald, Thomas Richardson, Raju Singh, George Tsibouris, Harm Zebregs, James Daniel, Cem Karacadag, Nicolas Blancher, and Yongzheng Yang.

YUSUKE HORIGUCHI
Director
Asia and Pacific Department

Acknowledgments

The authors acknowledge the valuable input and comments provided by many present and former colleagues at the IMF, including John Anderson, Ray Brooks, James Gordon, Aasim Husain, Russell Krelove, Bernard Laurens, Doug Laxton, Jun Ma, Ichiro Otani, and Sunil Sharma. Special thanks are due to Tarhan Feyzioğlu who saw to the completion of the book. The IMF staff's work on China has also bene-fited greatly from collaboration with our colleagues at the World Bank, in particular Deepak Bhattasali and Albert Keidel. Jieyan Yin of the Bank of Communications in China provided the elegant calligraphic work for the cover of the book. Anna Maripuu and Bin Zhang provided excellent research assistance, and we are indebted to Pihuan Cormier, Abdul Majeed Mahar, and Lakshmi Sahasranam for assisting with numerous drafts. The authors are also grateful to Michael Treadway, who edited the book, and Gail Berre of the External Relations Depart-ment, who coordinated its production.

The opinions expressed here, as well as any errors, are the sole responsibility of the authors and do not necessarily reflect the views of the Chinese authorities, the Executive Directors of the IMF, or other members of the IMF staff.

Contents

Tables

The following conventions are used in this volume:

. . .   to indicate that data are not available or not applicable;

—   to indicate that the figure is zero or less than half the final digit shown;

–   between years or months (for example, 2001–02 or January–June) to indicate the years or months covered, including the beginning and ending years or months;

/   between years or months (for example, 1991/92) to indicate a fiscal or financial year.

"Billion" means a thousand million; "trillion" means a thousand billion.

"Basis points" refer to hundredths of 1 percentage point (for example, 25 basis points are equivalent to ¼ of 1 percentage point).

Minor discrepancies between constituent figures and totals are due to rounding.

1

Introduction and Overview

MARKUS RODLAUER AND PAUL HEYTENS

China has received much attention in recent years as its economy has performed exceptionally well by most standards: after a soft landing from an episode of overheating in the mid-1990s, the Chinese economy managed to weather the Asian crisis of the late 1990s largely unscathed and has been able to sustain rapid growth in the face of the recent global downturn.[1] At the same time, however, analysts point to serious structural weaknesses in China's economy, such as problems in the state-owned enterprises (SOEs) and banks, growing unemployment and income disparities, weak governance and corruption, medium-term fiscal pressures, and environmental degradation. There is concern that these challenges, if unmet, could undermine sustained rapid growth and stability. The key task facing policymakers in China today is how to sustain the economy's growth and development while spreading the benefits more widely across society. This book looks at those challenges and China's efforts to meet them—issues that have been at the center of policy analysis and discussion by IMF staff working on China in recent years.

Background

More than two decades of market-oriented reform has brought visible success and economic transformation to China. Since the start of

---

[1]Throughout this book, "China" refers to the Chinese mainland, and "provinces" refers to the set of 28 provinces, autonomous regions, and municipalities listed in Table 3.1 in Chapter 3.

1

reforms in 1978, GDP growth has averaged over 9 percent a year, raising real income per capita fivefold, and more than 200 million people have been lifted out of poverty. The nonstate sector, comprising the private sector, urban collectives, and township and village enterprises, now accounts for nearly two-thirds of GDP, and China has become more integrated into the global economy: its share in world trade is now over 4 percent, compared with near zero in 1978. China's recent accession to the World Trade Organization (WTO) has set the stage for further opening of the economy and acts as an impetus for accelerated reforms.

Recent Macroeconomic Developments

The Asian crisis accentuated the slowdown of growth that had followed the boom of the early 1990s. Falling demand for exports compounded weakening domestic consumption, and concerns about the continued stability of China's currency, the renminbi, fueled capital outflows and a sharp drop in the balance of payments surplus. In response, the authorities acted promptly to support economic activity and reduce external vulnerabilities. An easing of fiscal and monetary policies was accompanied by measures to encourage exports, address rampant smuggling, and intensify enforcement of foreign exchange and capital controls, while exchange rate stability was maintained. These policies, aided by the still-limited openness of the economy and the strong external position built up before the crisis, helped limit contagion from the regional financial turmoil, sustained annual growth above 7 percent, and set the stage for a rebound in a more favorable external environment.

Starting in mid-1999, growth regained momentum, sparked by a strong pickup in exports and then sustained by rapid domestic demand growth. Domestic demand continued to be supported through increased fiscal spending, especially on public investment projects; in addition, private consumption was buoyed by housing reforms, an increase in civil service salaries, and higher social spending. Rising budget expenditure, however, was increasingly matched by rapidly growing revenue, attributable to the pickup in activity as well as to improvements in tax administration, permitting a gradual reduction in the overall budget deficit from its peak in 1999.

Growth in China held up relatively well in the face of the global downturn in 2001. Although the external slowdown dampened activity, the impact was muted by continued robust domestic demand growth and rising foreign direct investment (FDI). Thus, despite sharply declining export growth, GDP still grew by over 7 percent in 2001, thanks to strong growth in investment (mainly by the state) and buoyant private consumption. Reflecting the high import content of exports, import growth also dropped, limiting the negative external contribution to growth. Strengthened foreign investor confidence (partly related to WTO accession) boosted FDI inflows, aiding the economy's resilience against the external downturn.

Structural Reforms

Building on the fundamental reforms accomplished during the 1980s,[2] recent years have seen continuous progress in China's transformation into a market economy. Reinvigorated by Deng Xiaoping's famous tour of southern China in 1992, reforms over the past 10 years have completed the dismantling of the planned-economy apparatus (controlled prices and quantitative plans); fostered an increasing role for the private sector in the economy;[3] opened the economy further to foreign trade and investment; enhanced the autonomy of state-owned banks and enterprises; and established the basic building blocks of a modern tax system and indirect monetary policy. The experience of the Asian crisis and the landmark decision to join the WTO have given further impetus to these efforts, focused on improving the performance and financial condition of the SOE and banking sectors.

Nonetheless, the 1990s saw growing evidence of the costs of unreformed corporate and financial sectors. Despite greater autonomy and decentralization of management decisions, SOE performance has suffered from deeper problems rooted in the lack of tight budget constraints, weak management, and the requirement to provide job security and a range of social services. Growing competition, lower subsidies, and tighter credit (especially for smaller enterprises) revealed the poor performance of many SOEs in the 1990s and prompted new approaches to reform. The strategy included moving small enterprises out of the state sector and reforming some 1,000 large state firms that would be the pillars of China's industry. Reforms were stepped up beginning in 1998, and some progress has been made in introducing modern management systems, shedding excess labor, and lowering the social welfare burden. However, many of the fundamental problems in establishing effective outside governance and financial discipline remain to be solved, especially in the larger SOEs.

---

[2] For a comprehensive review of reforms during this period, see Bell and others (1993).

[3] Symbolized, for example, by an amendment to the Constitution in March 1999 putting private ownership and private enterprise on an equal footing with the state sector.

Reform of China's financial sector has also moved up the policy agenda in recent years, and the authorities have become increasingly frank about the problems in this area. The strategy has been to relieve the state commercial banks (SCBs) of the responsibility for policy lending, while placing their operations on a commercial footing and holding them accountable for new lending decisions. In pursuit of these goals a wide range of measures have been taken, including moving policy lending to newly created policy banks, restructuring the People's Bank of China, abolishing the credit plan, partially recapitalizing SCBs and transferring part of their nonperforming loans to asset management companies (AMCs), strengthening the prudential framework, and closing many small, insolvent financial institutions. AMCs have started to dispose of their assets, including to foreigners and with the assistance of international investment banks. These steps have been complemented by the SCBs' own efforts at such reforms as revamping internal controls and risk management, reducing staff, and rationalizing the branch network. Despite these efforts, however, the financial position of the SCBs remains very weak, and much remains to be done to prevent the emergence of new nonperforming loans.

In tandem with liberalization and SOE reforms, the social dimensions of the transition have become increasingly apparent. Some 16 million layoffs from SOEs during 1998–2000 indicate the huge social challenge facing China as the "iron rice bowl" system of the past is dismantled. The goal is to shift responsibility for social services (including education, health, pensions, and unemployment) from the SOEs to the private sector or to local and provincial governments.[4] Regional income disparity has also become a significant problem: the coastal regions have benefited much more from China's opening than the poor western and central regions and those with a high concentration of SOEs. In response, the authorities have expanded their economic opening policies nationwide, directed public investment to the western and central regions, and used discretionary transfers from the budget to ease the social burden on the poorer regions. However, a more systematic revamp of the current, regressive system of interregional budget transfers is needed to address the growing imbalance between the richer provinces and those with fewer resources yet large social safety and investment needs.

More generally, the transition from a centrally planned economy to a more open and market-oriented system has been accompanied by

---

[4]Experiments with such reforms are under way in a number of regions and localities, and a formal pilot program of social security reform was launched in Liaoning province in 2001.

rising governance problems and corruption. China's political leadership recognizes that addressing corruption is a top priority. Sustained success in improving governance and fighting corruption will require a broader effort to build the legal and judicial framework for a market economy, along with increased transparency and public accountability of government.

China's recent entry into the WTO marks a watershed for reform. A new push is needed to complete the unfinished reform agenda. WTO accession promises to stimulate such progress by increasing FDI, removing protection from inefficient industries, and spurring the development of the legal and regulatory framework necessary for a market economy. The authorities are aware that the benefits from WTO accession depend on the successful implementation of reforms to deal with the resulting increase of competition, and they have launched a major new effort to advance the reform agenda.

The Plan of This Book

The chapters that follow bring together recent analysis by IMF staff of these issues, focusing on four broad areas: China's growth dynamics, macroeconomic stability, SOE and banking sector reform, and global integration. In reviewing China's experience in these areas, the book highlights the elements behind the strong performance in recent years as well as the key items on the reform agenda:

- *Growth dynamics.* Chapter 2, "How Fast Can China Grow?" looks at the factors behind China's remarkable growth performance over the past two decades and whether it can continue in the future. The analysis suggests that rapid growth in the past has been underpinned by large-scale reallocation of agricultural labor to more productive uses and other productivity-enhancing structural changes. Looking forward, the chapter concludes that potential output should continue to grow at 7–8 percent a year provided critical structural reforms (mainly in the SOE and financial sectors) are implemented. Chapter 3, "Provincial Growth Dynamics," examines whether incomes across China's provinces are converging. It finds that the poorer provinces are indeed catching up with the richer ones, but that convergence weakened in the 1990s. It also finds that the incomes of the various provinces are stratifying into a bimodal distribution, and that economic structure and policies (such as the concentration of SOEs and openness to trade) are significant factors in explaining these distributional dynamics. Chapter 4, "The Growth-Financial Development Nexus," complements this analysis by showing that bank lending to SOEs has not significantly boosted growth among the provinces, highlighting the importance of channeling a larger share of China's saving to the more dynamic nonstate sector. The next two chapters review China's success in attracting FDI (Chapter 5, "Foreign Direct Investment in China: Some Lessons for Other Countries") and its significant contribution to growth (Chapter 6, "Foreign Direct Investment and Output Growth").

- *Macroeconomic stability.* Chapter 7, "China and the Asian Crisis," reviews China's passage through the storm of the East Asian financial crisis of 1997–98. It concludes that despite weak financial and corporate sectors—factors common to the crisis-affected countries—the Chinese economy was shielded mainly by high reserves, low debt, and limited capital mobility. Equally important, timely countercyclical policies were implemented to support domestic demand. However, the chapter points to policy challenges ahead with regard to fiscal sustainability, the vulnerability of banks and SOEs, and resource allocation, all of which are important for China's growth potential and sustained financial stability. The interlinkages among the banks, the SOEs, and the government budget are highlighted in Chapter 8, "Medium-Term Fiscal Issues," which indicates that the fiscal position could be an important source of vulnerability going forward. The chapter concludes that, to manage this vulnerability, although the budget deficit should be lowered gradually over the medium term, the key issue will be to curtail the flow of new nonperforming loans in the banking system.

- *SOE and banking sector reform.* As the preceding chapters suggest, the main risks for the future emanate from the unfinished reform agenda in the SOEs and the banking sector. From a review of progress on SOE reform since the mid-1990s, Chapter 9, "State Enterprise Reforms," argues that recent reforms have resulted in some efficiency gains but have been unable to substantially improve corporate governance and impose financial discipline, especially in the large SOEs. Similarly, Chapter 10, "Financial System Soundness and Reform," shows that, despite stepped-up reforms in recent years, serious weaknesses persist in the financial system. The chapter concludes that the reform process needs to be accelerated further, especially by rehabilitating the SCBs, creating a credit culture, and establishing a strong prudential framework. Finally, Chapter 11, "The Finances of China's Enterprise Sector," finds that the financial situation in the enterprise sector is weak, limiting the sector's capacity to service its substantial debt to the banks. Both Chapter 9 and Chapter 11, therefore, point to the need to strengthen SOE reform to improve corporate governance and financial discipline, harden budget constraints, and minimize the noncommercial activities of the SOEs.

- *Global integration.* Chapter 12, "The Impact of WTO Accession," describes China's accession to the WTO as a potential watershed for the reform process. Accession promises to increase FDI, remove protection from inefficient industries, and spur the development of the legal and regulatory framework necessary for a market economy. The overall macroeconomic impact for China is expected to be positive, although unemployment pressures are likely to increase in the short run. Finally, Chapter 13, "Exchange Rate Policy," makes the case for moving toward more flexible exchange rate management. Although the policy of maintaining the stability of the renminbi served China and the region well during the Asian crisis, a gradual move toward greater exchange rate flexibility will help China manage the structural changes under way and the country's growing integration into the global economy.

Reference

Bell, Michael W., Hoe Ee Khor, Kalpana Kochhar, with Jun Ma, Simon N'guiamba, and Rajiv Lall, 1993, "China at the Threshold of a Market Economy," Occasional Paper No. 107 (Washington: International Monetary Fund).

2

How Fast Can China Grow?

PAUL HEYTENS AND HARM ZEBREGS

Over the past two decades, China has been one of the fastest-growing countries in the world.[1] Growth in real GDP per capita has exceeded 8 percent a year on average, an impressive achievement even by East Asian standards. China's exceptional growth performance has been spurred by market-oriented structural reforms introduced since the late 1970s, which have also resulted in sizable productivity gains. However, annual GDP growth has declined since 1993, to 7–8 percent in 1999–2001, raising questions about to what extent China's impressive track record can be sustained in the future. Although most analysts believe some slowdown is inevitable, it is difficult to assess China's future growth potential given the deep structural reforms under way, the vast scale of the Chinese economy, and the complexities of its growth dynamics.

This chapter examines the dynamics of China's growth performance and attempts to shed light on how fast the country might grow in the future. In contrast with earlier empirical work, it seeks to identify and estimate the contributions of the sources of total factor productivity (TFP) growth, which explains most of the increase in output growth during the reform period. The chapter shows that China's growth performance has been underpinned by a large-scale reallocation of agricul-

---

[1]There is considerable debate about the accuracy of China's official output statistics, and some observers believe annual growth rates are overstated by as much as 2 percentage points. Although many shortcomings are believed to plague the output statistics, most observers have focused on problems with the deflators used to measure real output. See also Box 4.1 of IMF (1998).

tural labor to more productive uses and by other productivity-enhancing structural changes.

The main policy implication that emerges is that China's growth prospects will continue to depend on structural reform. However, many of the earlier reforms had a one-time impact on productivity growth, which suggests that future growth is unlikely to match that of the past two decades. In addition, future structural reforms—involving considerable labor shedding by state-owned enterprises (SOEs) and the shutting down of nonviable enterprises and outdated production capacity—could cause some disruptions in the labor market and slow the absorption of agricultural labor in the short term. Nevertheless, potential output should be able to grow at 7–8 percent a year over the medium term, provided reforms of the SOEs and the financial sector accelerate following China's entry into the World Trade Organization (WTO).

Structural Reform

Overview of the Reform Period

China's reform strategy over the past 20 or more years can best be described as incremental. Reforms followed a dual-track approach in which a market track was established in parallel with the preexisting tracks of the centrally planned economy, with the former gradually increasing in importance over time.[2] This dual-track approach was initiated in late 1978 with the rapid and comprehensive liberalization of the agriculture sector.

The agricultural reforms quickly allowed a substantial proportion of economic activity and of the labor force to move outside of central planning. The main feature of the agricultural reform was the replacement of the commune-brigade system of collective farming with a system in which communal land was leased to individual peasant households. Although households remained responsible for delivering a portion of their farm output to the state, they were allowed to sell any production above the state procurement quota on the free market. The quota was essentially a lump-sum tax, so that rural households effectively faced market-determined prices in making their production decisions.

---

[2]Many observers have also emphasized the importance of China's economic structure at the start of the reform process in the late 1970s—a large population heavily concentrated in low-wage agriculture, creating a situation conducive to labor-intensive, export-led growth like that in other parts of East Asia—as a major explanatory factor in the success of the subsequent reforms.

The impressive growth of agricultural output resulting from the initial market-oriented reforms also facilitated the liberalization of the industrial and services sectors in rural and urban areas that followed in the 1980s. The growth of the nonstate sector was also allowed to spread well beyond the communes themselves. The regulations governing the registration and supervision of nonstate enterprises were progressively liberalized beginning in 1984, and the result was rapid industrialization, particularly by community-owned enterprises in rural areas, which came to be known as township and village enterprises (TVEs). Thus the dismantling of the communes and the emergence of the TVEs exposed nearly 800 million rural inhabitants (some 80 percent of the population at the time) to market forces and provided a large proportion of them the opportunity to leave agriculture over a relatively brief time span.

Another purpose of the dual-track approach was to integrate China into the global economy. In 1980 four southern coastal cities—Shantou, Shenzhen, Xiamen, and Zhuhai—were designated as special economic zones (SEZs). They were provided certain discretionary powers over taxation and were given autonomy to experiment with new institutional forms, such as foreign-funded enterprises. In addition, SOEs operating in the SEZs were exempted from many elements of the central plan, such as certain labor regulations and the tax code. With the phenomenal initial growth of the SEZs, the privileges they were granted spread quickly to other areas, including Hainan, which became the fifth SEZ in 1988 (Chapter 5).

In contrast to reform in agriculture, the pace of reform in the SOE and financial sectors was initially more gradual. SOEs were not privatized, and indeed, they only became a key focus of reform in the mid-1990s. Instead the SOEs were the target of various attempts to introduce more market-based incentives to improve management and operational efficiency within the framework of state ownership. Beginning in 1984, decision-making power over production, marketing, and investment matters was incrementally devolved to SOE managers. However, it was not until Deng Xiaoping's celebrated tour of the southern provinces in January 1992 that the authorities formally embraced the view that the market system was not incompatible with socialism, and this change set the stage for a deepening of SOE and financial sector reform.[3] The initial focus was on moving small enterprises out of the state sector, placing large enterprises on a commercial footing, and shifting the burden of lending for policy purposes away from the state com-

---

[3] The position of the SOE sector in the economy had also begun to erode by that time as a result of the emergence of the more dynamic nonstate sector.

mercial banks. Following the Fifteenth Party Congress in September 1997, these reforms were expanded and accelerated.

China's reforms have facilitated a profound transformation of the country's economic structure and social development:

- The proportion of the labor force engaged in agriculture has fallen from nearly three-fourths in the late 1970s to less than half, and the proportion of industrial output produced by SOEs declined from nearly 80 percent to about one-quarter over the same period.
- Total trade (imports plus exports) rose from less than 10 percent of GDP in the late 1970s to just over 40 percent, and foreign direct investment (FDI) inflows have risen from virtually zero at the beginning of the 1980s to over $40 billion a year in recent years.
- Human development indicators—including life expectancy, literacy, infant mortality, and income per capita—have also improved dramatically. Indeed, the rapid growth and structural change witnessed in China over the past 20 years have delivered perhaps the greatest reduction in poverty in recorded history: 200 million people have ceased to be poor, where poverty is measured by China's official poverty line; the corresponding figure based on the World Bank's criterion (living on $1 or less a day) is considerably higher.

Although China's gradual approach to economic reform has had considerable success, some analysts have pointed out that it has also incurred significant costs (Lardy, 1998). In particular, the slow pace of SOE reform, although arguably necessary to maintain social stability, has contributed to growing SOE losses. These have largely been financed through the banking system and have led to a sharp deterioration in asset quality, reflected in rising nonperforming loans. In the past several years, owing to mounting problems in these areas and lessons learned from the Asian crisis, reform of the SOEs and the financial sector have moved to the top of the authorities' policy agenda (Chapters 9 and 10).

The Contribution of Structural Reform to Output Growth

Although little empirical work has been done to estimate the contribution of structural reform to growth directly, a number of growth accounting studies have attempted to measure this contribution indirectly.[4] Three main channels have been identified:

- *Raising TFP growth directly.* The literature agrees on the strong linkage between structural reform and the rapid productivity

---

[4]See, for example, Borensztein and Ostry (1996), Chow (1993), Chow and Li (1999), Hu and Khan (1996), Maddison (1998), Wang (1999), Woo (1998), and World Bank (1996).

growth over the past two decades. TFP growth was found to be particularly high following the liberalization of the agricultural sector in the early 1980s, and in the early 1990s after market-oriented reforms were accelerated, and to have been well above that of the prereform period (1952–78).[5] Estimates of TFP growth during the reform period range between 2 and 4 percent a year.[6]

- *Raising aggregate TFP growth through facilitating a more efficient allocation of labor.* A reallocation of labor from agriculture to other sectors increases aggregate output if the marginal product of labor is lower in agriculture than in the other sectors. A study by Chow (1993) indicates that there was indeed scope for efficiency gains through labor reallocation at the beginning of the reform period: Chow estimated that, in 1978, the marginal product of labor was only 63 yuan in agriculture but Y 1,027 in industry, Y 452 in construction, Y 739 in transport, and Y 1,809 in commerce. The empirical estimates of the impact of labor reallocation on TFP growth generally fall into a range of ½–2 percentage points, or up to about half the estimated productivity growth.
- *Enhancing the efficiency of capital accumulation and knowledge spillovers.* An economy that is more efficient at mobilizing and transforming savings into physical and human capital can realize higher growth rates. The increased marketization and opening of the Chinese economy are widely believed to have improved the efficiency of capital accumulation during the reform period. The rapid increase in FDI is considered to be a particularly important explanatory variable, as is the substantial spillover of technology and managerial know-how from the large number of joint ventures and wholly owned foreign enterprises (Chapters 5 and 6).

Potential Output and Its Components

This section reports the results of several different empirical approaches to identify the main determinants of China's potential out-

---

[5]Most researchers, for example Chow (1993), Hu and Khan (1996), and Maddison (1998), found little or no evidence of TFP growth during this earlier period.

[6]The variation in the empirical estimates found in the literature stems mainly from differences in the underlying data used, which in some cases result from corrections for the apparent underdeflation of industrial output in the official data, from different methodologies employed to construct time series of the capital stock, and from the use of different capital and labor shares.

put growth over the period 1970–98.[7] Because TFP growth has been identified as a major contributor to the increase in output growth during the reform period, it is important to examine its determinants, in particular, structural reform and labor migration from agriculture to other sectors.

The Hodrick-Prescott Filter

A commonly applied approach to decomposing actual output into its long-run potential and cyclical components is the Hodrick-Prescott (HP) filter. This is a statistical method that does not use any information regarding the determinants of each of the components, but is a useful first approximation of potential output growth. Let Y_t and $\hat{Y}_t$ be the logarithms of, respectively, actual and potential output at time t; then the cyclical components are given by $\varepsilon_t = Y_t - \hat{Y}_t$. Hence HP filtering decomposes Y_t into $\hat{Y}_t$ and ε_t.

When applied to China's real GDP, the HP approach reveals that potential output growth picked up strongly during the reform period (Figure 2.1). It peaked at 9.6 percent in 1985–87 and then slowed somewhat in the late 1980s. In the first half of the 1990s, when the reform process was reinvigorated, potential output growth rebounded, peaking at 9.9 percent in 1994–95, but it has since tapered off again.

However, the HP approach suffers from what has been called the endpoint problem: future potential output growth may be overestimated if actual output growth was comparatively high (or underestimated if it was comparatively low) at the end of the sample period. In the case of China, this could mean that the slowdown in potential output in the second half of the 1990s was actually more pronounced than the HP filter suggests. This would also imply that the estimated output gap is smaller.

The Production Function Approach

Another approach that is often used to determine potential output is the production function approach, which makes use of information regarding the sources of growth, namely, factor accumulation and TFP growth. The production function approach is described in Appendix II and can be represented as follows:

---

[7]Although longer time series are available, the earlier data are not comparable because of the dislocating nature of the events that took place before 1970 (the Great Leap Forward and the Cultural Revolution). See also Chow (1993), Hu and Khan (1996), and Borensztein and Ostry (1996) for a discussion of the problems pertaining to the pre-1970 data. Appendix I describes the sources of the data used in this study.

Figure 2.1. Actual and Potential Output Growth and the Output Gap
(*In percent*)

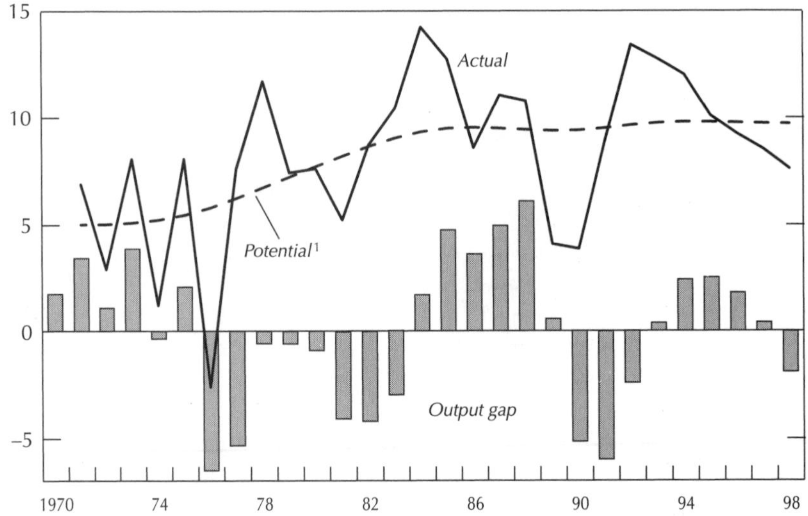

Source: Authors' calculations.
[1]Calculated using Hodrick-Prescott filtering.

$$Y_t = A_t + \beta_t z_t + \varepsilon_t,$$

where A_t represents TFP, β_t is a coefficient vector, and z_t is a vector of factor inputs, all measured at time t. Potential output is given by $\hat{Y}_t = A_t + \beta_t z_t$. Often, z_t contains only capital and labor, and when constant returns to scale are imposed, the elements in β_t must sum to 1.

Neither A_t nor β_t can be directly observed, but there are several ways to calculate TFP and the other parameters of the production function. If constant returns to scale are imposed and the only factor inputs are capital and labor, the parameters can be directly obtained from the national accounts by calculating the share of labor income in GDP; 1 minus this share is then the capital share parameter. The next step is to substitute these parameters into the production function and calculate the Solow residuals: $Y_t - \beta_t z_t = A_t + \varepsilon_t$. These residuals are the sum of TFP and the cyclical components in actual output. The time series of Solow residuals can be decomposed into A_t and ε_t through filtering or by regression on a set of variables, x_t, that are sources of TFP growth.

Hu and Khan (1996) constructed a time series of labor shares using Chinese national accounts data and a translog production function to calculate TFP growth for the 1953–94 period. Extending their series of

Figure 2.2. Potential Output Growth and the Output Gap: Estimates from a Translog Production Function
(In percent)

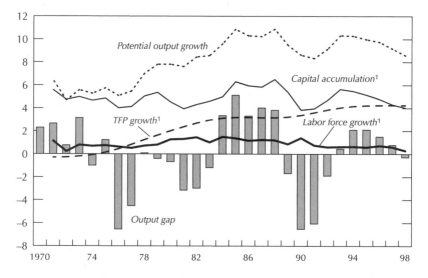

Source: Authors' calculations.
[1]Contribution to potential output growth.

labor shares to 1998, we calculated the contributions to potential output growth of capital accumulation, labor force growth, and TFP growth for 1971–98 (Figure 2.2; Table 2.1). In the prereform period, capital accumulation was the main contributor to potential output growth. The contributions of labor force growth and TFP growth were small and negative, respectively. However, TFP growth picked up strongly during the reform period and explains much of the increase in potential output growth during this period. Output gaps were also calculated on the basis of the production function approach, the pattern of which is very similar to that of the output gaps derived with the HP filter.[8]

Another way of calculating β_t and TFP is by regressing Y_t on z_t and x_t. In this case, direct estimates of A_t, as a function of x_t, and ε_t are obtained. A simple version of this approach is to estimate

---

[8]The output gaps have been calculated by HP-filtering the Solow residuals and therefore may also be affected by the endpoint problem. If the trend of TFP has slowed in recent years, this would not be fully picked up by the HP filter, and the output gap would be overestimated (that is, the actual shortfall of demand would be less than suggested by the calculated output gaps).

Table 2.1. Contributions to Output Growth

(In percent of GDP)[1]

Model	1971–78	1979–89	1990–98
Translog production function[2]			
Potential output	5.7	9.2	9.3
Capital accumulation	4.8	5.2	4.7
Labor force growth	0.7	1.2	0.7
TFP growth	0.2	2.8	4.0
Output gap	–0.3	–0.2	0.2
Cobb-Douglas with exogenous TFP growth[3]			
Potential output	5.7	9.2	9.5
Capital accumulation	4.7	5.6	6.3
Labor force growth	0.7	1.1	0.5
TFP growth	0.3	2.5	2.7
Output gap	–0.3	–0.1	–0.0
Cobb-Douglas with endogenous TFP growth[4]			
Potential output	4.9	9.3	9.5
Capital accumulation	4.8	5.7	6.4
Labor force growth	0.7	1.0	0.5
TFP growth	–0.5	2.5	2.6
Output gap	0.5	–0.2	0.0
Memorandum:			
Actual output growth	5.4	9.1	9.5

Source: Authors' regressions.
[1]Period averages.
[2]Based on national accounts-based factor shares from Hu and Khan (1996) supplemented with authors' estimates for 1995–98.
[3]Based on constant factor shares from Chow (1993).
[4]Based on coefficients from the regression estimated in Table 2.2.

$$y_t = C + \alpha_t k_t + \delta t + \varepsilon_t,$$

where y_t and k_t are the logarithms of output per worker and capital per worker, respectively; C is a constant; and t represents a linear trend. In this specification $A_t = C + \delta t$. Chow (1993) and Chow and Li (1999) used this approach and found a capital share, α, of 0.63. This direct estimate of the capital share parameter exceeds that derived from the national accounts, which is estimated to have been 0.56 on average during 1970–98. Although both estimates are high compared with capital share parameters found in industrial countries, they are not outside the range found in other developing countries.[9] Nevertheless, the possibility that they are biased upward cannot be ruled out. This may be the result

---

[9]In a growth accounting study of seven Latin American economies, Elias (1992) found capital share parameters ranging from 0.45 for Brazil and 0.52 for Chile to 0.66 for Peru and 0.69 for Mexico. Young (1995) found capital shares in East Asian economies between 0.29 for Taiwan Province of China and 0.53 for Singapore.

Figure 2.3. Potential Output Growth and the Output Gap: Estimates from a Cobb-Douglas Production Function with Exogenous TFP Growth
(In percent)

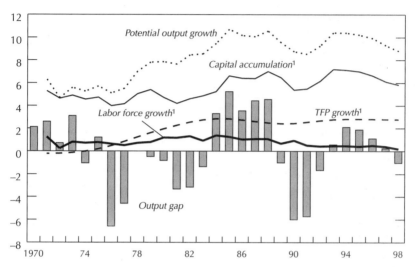

Source: Authors' calculations.
[1]Contribution to potential output growth.

of omitted variables, in particular human capital, or of measurement error in China's national accounts. The latter tend to overestimate output in the capital-intensive manufacturing sector and underestimate the output of more labor-intensive private and individual enterprises. It is also possible that the high capital share is a legacy of the previous plan system, which was strongly biased toward investment in capital -intensive heavy industries and was perpetuated through the continuation of state control of the banking system during the reform period.

When China's output growth is decomposed under the assumption that $\alpha = 0.63$, the contribution of capital accumulation is larger than when the implicit capital shares from the national accounts are used (Figure 2.3). The Solow residuals are therefore also sensitive to the relative magnitudes of the factor shares. In the case of China, a higher capital share reduces the residual and hence the contribution of TFP growth; during the reform period, TFP growth was 2–2¾ percent a year assuming a constant capital share of 0.63, and 3–4 percent assuming the average capital share from the national accounts of 0.56 over 1970–98 (Table 2.1).

Although the two approaches yield different conclusions about the level of TFP growth, both indicate that TFP growth picked up during

Table 2.2. Estimated Aggregate Production Function for the Chinese Economy

Variable[1]	Coefficient	Standard Error	t-Statistic
Constant	3.089	0.674	4.585
Capital stock per worker[2]	0.643	0.070	9.196
Structural reform index[3]	0.200	0.066	3.035
Percent of labor force in primary sector	−0.019	0.003	−6.677
Trend	−0.033	0.005	−6.059
Trend dummy, 1979–98	0.031	0.003	9.690

Summary statistics
$R^2 = 0.999$
Durbin-Watson = 1.83

Source: Authors' regressions.
[1]The dependent variable is real GDP per worker (in logarithms); the sample period is 1970–98.
[2]At constant prices (in logarithms). Variables are nonstaionary but cointegrated: the time series of the residuals is I(0).
[3]In logarithms.

the reform period and made a large contribution to the increase in output growth. However, neither approach can explain what caused the pickup in TFP growth. For this it is necessary to estimate an aggregate production function for the Chinese economy that, besides capital and labor, includes explanatory variables for TFP (Table 2.2). Apart from a trend and a trend dummy, explanatory variables in the regression include a structural reform index and a proxy for labor movements out of the primary (largely agricultural) sector.[10] The reform index, discussed in Appendix III, is constructed from four variables—the nonstate share of industrial output, the share of total trade in output, the level of urbanization, and the rate of capital formation—that together capture the impact of structural reform on the economy.

Table 2.3 shows the estimated contributions to TFP growth of structural reform, labor migration, and technological progress. What stands out is that labor migration has been a dominant factor in TFP growth both before and during the reform period. On an aggregate level, efficiency-enhancing labor migration shows up in TFP, whereas on a more disaggregated level it would be reflected in the contribution of labor to sectoral output growth. Hence, although the contribution of labor force growth has been small at the aggregate level (Figure 2.4), the reallocation of labor across sectors has been a significant contributor to output

[10]Because multicollinearity among the explanatory variables could not be ruled out a priori, this was tested for, but no convincing evidence of a significant bias in the estimation results was found.

Table 2.3. Contributions to TFP Growth

(In percent of TFP)[1]

Contributor	1971–78	1979–84	1985–89	1990–94	1995–98
TFP growth	–0.53	2.78	2.11	2.81	2.30
Structural reform	0.38	0.94	0.76	0.83	0.39
Labor migration out of primary sector	2.34	2.01	1.52	2.15	2.08
Exogenous trend	–3.25	–0.17	–0.17	–0.17	–0.17

Source: Authors' regressions.
[1]Period averages, based on estimation results in Table 2.2.

growth in the manufacturing and services sectors. This source of TFP growth has not yet been exhausted—the proportion of workers in the primary sector, 50 percent in 2000, is still high compared with more advanced economies—but it will certainly become less important in the long run. The contribution of structural reform has been positive and has added, on average, ¾–1 percentage point to TFP growth and hence to output growth.[11] The exogenous trend has been negative but has become less so during the reform period, and it might be reflecting aspects of structural reform that the reform index does not capture. These results, together with the estimate of the capital share parameter of 0.64, which is close to Chow's (1993) estimate of 0.63, suggest that capital accumulation and efficiency improvements from labor reallocation and structural reform have been the main engines of growth in China. Because part of TFP growth was driven by one-time level adjustments, and because capital accumulation will taper off in the future as the Chinese economy matures, potential output growth can be expected to decline over the medium term.

The Growth Outlook

Most analysts, as well as the Chinese authorities themselves, who are projecting average annual growth of 7 percent in the current five-year development plan (2001–05), believe that some slowdown in GDP growth is inevitable. The empirical findings described above provide

---

[11]Note that the reform index measures the *result* rather than the *implementation* of structural reform. Hence the relatively low contributions to TFP growth during 1971–78 and 1995–98 reported in Table 2.3 should not be interpreted as if the structural reform effort in the second half of the 1990s were as low as it had been in the prereform era. One interpretation is that the easy structural reforms have been completed and that China has now entered a phase of more difficult reforms that lack an immediate payoff.

Figure 2.4. Potential Output Growth and the Output Gap: Estimates from a Cobb-Douglas Production Function with Endogenous TFP Growth
(In percent)

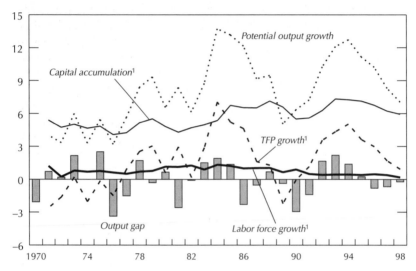

Source: Authors' calculations.
[1]Contribution to potential output growth.

support for this view. At the same time, however, China is still a relatively poor country and is likely to be able to continue catching up for many years to come. As neoclassical theory suggests, countries such as China that are relatively less developed and distant from the technological frontier in the industrial countries have a capacity for rapid growth if they mobilize and allocate physical and human capital effectively, adapt foreign technology to their factor proportions, and make good use of the opportunities for specialization that come from closer integration with the global economy.

Structural Policies for Future Growth

The discussion thus far in this chapter points to the necessity of intensifying and broadening economic reforms as a necessary condition for sustaining future growth of 7–8 percent a year. The reform areas most critical to China's growth outlook are the following:

- *Reform of the financial and SOE sectors.* Much remains to be done to strengthen the performance and financial health of the SOEs and the commercial banking system. In particular, extensive reforms to upgrade operational efficiency and product quality, to harden budget constraints, and to improve corporate governance in the SOEs are needed in the coming years. Similarly, bank rehabilitation will require far-reaching reforms, including the operational restructuring of the state commercial banks, the elimination of policy lending, and the development of a credit culture. The closely intertwined reforms of the SOEs and the financial sector must deepen if the efficiency of capital allocation in the Chinese economy is to be improved on a durable basis. SOE reform will also lead to scrapping of excess capacity, reflected in temporarily higher depreciation rates and slower output growth, but will result in a pickup in TFP growth over the medium term as the modernization of enterprises progresses and more productive capital is installed. Structural reform is expected to accelerate as a result of WTO accession.

- *Development of the nonstate sector.* Realizing the nonstate sector's potential to absorb workers laid off by SOEs, the authorities are attempting to foster the development of this sector, including by elevating the constitutional role of the private sector to one of parity with the state sector, and by taking some initial steps to improve nonstate firms' access to bank credit and the stock market. Continued efforts to encourage private sector development will be necessary in the years ahead, for example reducing sectoral barriers to entry and providing better protection of private property rights by deepening the rule of law.

- *Increased factor mobility.* The level of urbanization in China is very low, partly because of controls on the movement of labor from rural to urban areas. Some tentative steps have been taken recently to encourage the development of medium-size cities and towns, and the controls on the movement of labor into urban areas have been relaxed. However, China's labor market will need to become considerably more flexible, and medium-size cities and towns will need to be developed, in order to facilitate the continued reallocation of the rural labor force to more productive uses. In addition to limiting the mobility of labor, government policies have also had a dampening impact on the mobility of capital across provinces (Zhao, 1998). Capital is likely to become more mobile in the future as internal barriers to trade and investment are dismantled following WTO accession and as financial sector reforms proceed.

A Future Growth Scenario

The empirical results of this chapter suggest that future TFP growth and rates of capital accumulation will be below their averages over the

Table 2.4. Contributions to Output Growth, Actual and Projected
(In percent of GDP)[1]

Item	1990–94	1995–99	2000–05	2006–10
Potential output	9.7	8.7	7.2	7.5
Capital accumulation	6.4	6.4	5.7	5.9
Labor force growth	0.5	0.4	0.3	0.2
TFP growth	2.8	2.0	1.2	1.4
Output gap	0.4	–0.3	0.1	0.0
Memorandum:				
Actual output growth	10.1	8.4	7.3	7.5

Source: Authors' regressions.
[1]Period averages; the model is the Cobb-Douglas production function with endogenous TFP growth reported in Table 2.1.

past two decades. In addition, the next steps in the reform process, which involve more labor shedding by SOEs and the shutting down of nonviable enterprises and outdated productive capacity, will cause somewhat greater disruption in the short to medium term than did the earlier reforms. Accordingly, the deceleration of TFP witnessed since the mid-1990s is likely to continue over the next several years as reforms, in particular the restructuring of SOEs, intensify. The average rate of investment is also likely to decline somewhat in the next few years as excess capacity is scrapped and the effective rate of depreciation of the capital stock increases.

The direct contribution of labor to output growth, which has been modest throughout the reform period, will become even more so as population growth continues to slow as a result of China's population control policies. In addition, the further slowing of labor force growth and the rapid aging of China's population will push up the dependency ratio, particularly after 2010, and cause the saving rate to fall. Labor's indirect contribution to growth (reflected in TFP growth) through reallocation of workers from rural (agriculture) to urban areas (industry and services) should remain substantial for some time to come, although perhaps not quite as significant as in the past. However, an intensification of reform—in particular, labor shedding by SOEs—will reduce the capacity of urban areas to absorb labor from the countryside in the short and the medium run.

Although the effects of future reform are difficult to quantify, a possible growth scenario based on the estimates in this chapter is summarized in Table 2.4. Under this scenario, TFP growth remains below past levels as a result of a slowing of the outflow of labor out of agriculture (proxied by a slower decline in the primary sector's share of the labor force), as layoffs increase further as a result of enterprise restructuring. Nevertheless,

TFP growth should gradually pick up over the medium term as the positive effects of structural reform begin to prevail. Growth of the capital stock is projected to decline somewhat below historical levels because of a temporarily higher depreciation rate. The growth rate of potential output is projected to be 7 percent over the next few years.

Over the medium term, continued structural reform would eventually give new stimulus to TFP growth—not least by facilitating a pickup in the flow of labor out of agriculture into industry and services—and lay the foundation for faster TFP growth in the future, as the experience of other Asian countries suggests. The resulting improvement in efficiency as well as the updating of the capital stock should also sustain faster growth with lower rates of investment than in the past. Accordingly, the growth rate of potential output is projected to rise to 7½ percent on average during the second half of this decade, underpinned by the recovery in TFP growth to almost 1½ percent a year.

Conclusions

Labor migration out of agriculture, structural reform, and the partial reversal of the negative time trend are found to have raised TFP growth significantly during the reform period, and faster TFP growth in turn explains the substantial pickup in GDP growth in comparison with earlier periods. However, because many of these earlier reforms reflected one-time level effects, it is unlikely that future GDP growth will be able to match the levels witnessed during the reform period. China nevertheless remains a relatively poor country, and the scope for continued catching up with the industrial leaders will remain substantial for many years to come.

Capital accumulation will continue to be the largest contributor to economic growth in China. Whether TFP growth will also continue to play a pivotal role depends on the success of the next round of structural reform, and in particular on the progress with enterprise restructuring and banking system reform. Once the scope for further labor migration recedes, the pace of TFP growth will have to be sustained by the adoption of new technologies in the enterprise sector. To fulfill this role, SOEs need to be technologically upgraded and restructured according to market principles. Future technological progress will also require that the potential of China's rapidly growing nonstate sector and the benefits of opening to the outside world be fully realized. The empirical results suggest that growth in the 7–8 percent range could therefore still be sustained over the next decade, provided the pace of structural reforms is intensified.

Appendix I: Data Sources and Description

Data on the capital stock and real GDP were taken from Chow and Li (1999), who derived their data from source data taken from various issues of the *China Statistical Yearbook*.

Data on the labor force and the proportion of the labor force employed in the primary sector were taken from the 1999 edition of the *China Statistical Yearbook*. The labor force series was adjusted for a break in the time series in 1989–90.

Appendix III describes the computation of the structural reform index. The underlying source data on imports and exports, saving and investment, nonstate and total industrial output, and urban and total population were taken from various issues of the *China Statistical Yearbook*.

Appendix II: Aggregate Production Functions and TFP Growth

The methodology used in this chapter is based on the familiar notion of an aggregate production function:

$$\hat{Y} = f(z), \tag{1}$$

which relates GDP ($\hat{Y}$) to a vector of inputs (z). The production functions employed in this chapter satisfy the properties of a linearly homogeneous neoclassical production function $f(\cdot)$, which

- exhibits positive and diminishing marginal products with respect to each input $z_t \in z$:

$$\frac{\partial f(\cdot)}{\partial f_i} > 0,\ \frac{\partial^2 f(\cdot)}{\partial f_i^2} < 0, \quad \text{for all } z_i \in z;$$

- exhibits constant returns to scale:

$$\lambda \hat{Y} = f(\lambda z) = \lambda \cdot f(z), \quad \text{for all } \lambda > 0;$$

- satisfies the Inada conditions, which state that for each input the marginal product approaches infinity as the input goes to zero, and vice versa:

$$\lim_{z_i \to 0} = \frac{\partial f(\cdot)}{\partial z_i} = \infty, \quad \lim_{z_i \to \infty} = \frac{\partial^2 f(\cdot)}{\partial z_i} = 0, \quad \text{for all } z_i \in z.$$

Equation (1) can easily be expanded to incorporate an index of the level of technology in the economy, so that $\hat{Y} = f(z, A)$. In addition, the technology index, A, can be a function of time and of a vector, $\mathbf{x}$, of other relevant variables. In this chapter the focus is on two inputs (capital and labor) and TFP. Equation (1) can thus be specified as

$$\hat{Y} = f(K,L,A), \tag{2}$$

where K is capital, L is labor, and A is TFP.

In the remainder of this appendix all variables are defined in logarithms. Next, equation (2), which can be thought of as a potential output relation, is assumed to be related to actual output in the following way:

$$Y = \hat{Y} + \varepsilon,$$

where Y is the logarithm of actual GDP and ε is a cyclical disturbance term, or the output gap. To calculate TFP growth, potential output growth has to be decomposed into the contributions of capital and labor and a cyclical disturbance term. The first step in this calculation is to take time derivatives of both sides of equation (2) to obtain the growth rate of potential output:

$$\dot{\hat{Y}}/\hat{Y} = \frac{f_A}{\hat{Y}} \cdot \dot{A} + \frac{f_K}{\hat{Y}} \cdot \dot{K} + \frac{f_L}{\hat{Y}} \cdot \dot{L}, \tag{3}$$

where f_Q is the first derivative of $f(\cdot)$ with respect to $Q = A, K, L$, and a dot over a variable represents a derivative with respect to time. Under the assumption that technological progress is Hicks-neutral, that is, output augmenting, $f_A = f(\cdot)/A$, and equation (3) can be rewritten as

$$\dot{\hat{Y}}/\hat{Y} = \dot{A}/A + \frac{Kf_K}{\hat{Y}} \cdot \dot{K}/K + \frac{Lf_L}{\hat{Y}} \cdot \dot{L}/L. \tag{3}$$

The next step is to assume that factor markets are perfect, which implies that each input is paid its marginal product. Hence $Kf_K/\hat{Y}$ and $Lf_L/\hat{Y}$ are, respectively, the shares of capital and labor income in GDP. Furthermore, the property of constant returns to scale implies that the sum of both factor income shares equals 1. Depending on the specification of the production function, the factor income shares are constant or a function of relative factor endowments and technological progress.

Two specifications of the neoclassical production function are utilized in this chapter: the translog production function and the log-linearized Cobb-Douglas production function. The translog specification, which is the more general of the two in that it does not impose constant factor shares, has the following form:[12]

---

[12] See Christensen, Jorgensen, and Lau (1973).

$$Y = \alpha_0 + \alpha_K K + \alpha_L L + \alpha_t t + \tfrac{1}{2}\beta_{KK}K^2 + \beta_{KL}KL + \beta_{Kt}tK$$
$$+ \tfrac{1}{2}\beta_{LL}L^2 + \beta_{Lt}tL + \tfrac{1}{2}\beta_{tt}t^2,$$

In this translog specification, factor income shares are not constant, and TFP growth is only a function of time t. The translog production function satisfies the property of constant returns to scale if and only if the following parameter restrictions are imposed:

$$\alpha_K + \alpha_L = 1, \ \beta_{KK} + \beta_{KL} = 0, \ \beta_{KL} + \beta_{LL} = 0, \ \beta_{Kt} + \beta_{Lt} = 0.$$

It can be shown that, under the translog specification, the growth rate of the Solow residual (V) takes the following form in discrete time:[13]

$$dV_t = dY_t - \bar{\alpha}_t dK_t - (1 - \bar{\alpha}_t)dL_t, \quad \text{with } \bar{\alpha}_t = \tfrac{1}{2}(\alpha_t + \alpha_{t-1}),$$

where d is the first-difference operator and α_t is the share of capital income at time t. The final step in obtaining the growth rate of TFP is to decompose the Solow residual into TFP and cyclical components, which can be achieved by HP filtering.

In this chapter the labor income shares for the translog specification are obtained from the national accounts. Another way of obtaining the labor income share is through direct estimation of the production function. In this case a log-linear Cobb-Douglas specification is applied, which is assumed to have the following form:

$$Y = A + \alpha K + (1 - \alpha)L + \varepsilon. \tag{4}$$

Because of the property of constant returns to scale, equation (4) can be expressed in intensive form as

$$y = A + \alpha K + \varepsilon, \tag{5}$$

with $y \equiv Y/L$ and $k \equiv K/L$. This approach also allows for a direct estimation of TFP growth, as both A and ε are estimated individually. As mentioned above, TFP can be defined as a function of time and a vector of other variables. In the simplest specification A is just a constant, which assumes no TFP growth. Whether this is a valid assumption can be tested by adding a linear time trend, in which case equation (5) becomes

$$y = C + \delta t + \alpha k + \varepsilon,$$

where C is a constant and δ the rate of Hicks-neutral technological progress. Hence in this case, $A = C + \delta t$, but the analysis in this paper also considers $A = C + \delta t + x$, where x is a vector of variables (labor migration and structural reform) that contribute to TFP.

---

[13]See, for example, Hu and Khan (1996) for this derivation.

Appendix III: Measuring the Progress of Structural Reform

In this appendix an index is constructed to measure the progress of structural reform in China. The general approach to constructing the various indices of economic freedom, such as those compiled by the Fraser Institute,[14] are useful in this regard. Four indicators, which capture the broad spectrum of structural change in the Chinese economy over the past 20 years, have been selected to construct the index.[15] In addition, it is the combination of these variables rather than the variables individually that is considered to be the relevant measure of the progress of structural reform.[16] The four indicators are the following:

- *The nonstate share of industrial output.* One of the most notable features of the reform process has been the rapid growth of nonstate economic entities: the TVEs during the 1980s, and private (including individual) enterprises during the 1990s. The rising share of nonstate output is also a good proxy for the increased marketization of the economy (that is, the proportion of transactions taking place at market-determined prices) as well as the rapid redeployment of labor from agriculture to industry. The nonstate sector's share of industrial output grew from just over 20 percent in 1978 to nearly 75 percent in 1999.
- *The share of total trade in output.* Another notable feature of the reform period was the opening of the Chinese economy to the world economy following the establishment of the SEZs in 1980. The share of total trade (imports plus exports) in GDP, which rose from less than 10 percent in the late 1970s to just over 40 percent in recent years, is used to proxy the progressive integration of China's economy with the rest of the world.
- *The level of urbanization.* Although the pace of urbanization has not been quite as dramatic as the absorption of agriculture labor by

---

[14]Although these indices include China, they are very data intensive and have been compiled for only a few years. European Bank for Reconstruction and Development (1996) constructs indices of economic transition for various Eastern European countries. However, this approach assigns numerical grades based on the status of reforms in several sectors in a particular country on the basis of qualitative assessments and thus does not readily translate into a single number, much less a time series.

[15]Such variables (including the various indices of economic freedom themselves) have often been used to proxy the progress of structural reforms in numerous cross-country growth accounting studies, the so-called Barro-type regressions, since the early 1990s.

[16]That is, the variables individually are not expected to be statistically significant or robust in a regression specification, but rather the index combining them is. Aziz and Wescott (1997), for example, argue that it is the package of structural reform policies and not the individual components that matter in transforming economic performance.

TVEs (which have created over 100 million jobs since 1978), some 80 million people have left the countryside to work in urban areas over the past two decades. China's level of urbanization (at 30.5 percent in 1998) is still well below the world average of 45 percent (75 percent in industrial countries) and according to the World Bank (1997) is about 13 percent below that in countries with comparable income per capita. Urbanization nevertheless has nearly doubled over the reform period, as controls on labor movements from rural to urban areas have slowly been relaxed.[17]

- *The rate of capital formation.* As noted in the text, the conversion of saving to fixed asset investment has become significantly more efficient during the reform period. However, the efficiency of capital formation is still quite low by international standards, given China's late start on SOE restructuring and continued state dominance of the banking system. Nevertheless, capital accumulation during the reform period still increased very rapidly because gross saving also grew rapidly.

Measuring each indicator on a zero-to-one scale and assigning an equal (one-fourth) weight to each yields an overall index of structural reform that slightly more than doubles—from 0.25 in 1978 to 0.53 in 1998—over the reform period.[18] Although this index points to a profound transformation of China's economic structure over the reform period, at the same time it suggests there is still considerable scope for further structural change toward a more open and market-oriented economy.

References

Aziz, Jahangir, and Robert Wescott, 1997, "Policy Complementarities and the Washington Consensus," IMF Working Paper 97/118 (Washington: International Monetary Fund).

Borensztein, Eduardo, and Jonathan D. Ostry, 1996, "Accounting for China's Growth Performance," *American Economic Review Papers and Proceedings,* Vol. 86, No. 2 (May), pp. 224–28.

Chow, Gregory C., 1993, "Capital Formation and Economic Growth in China," *Quarterly Journal of Economics,* Vol. 108, No. 3 (August), pp. 809–42.

---

[17]Zhang (2000) estimates that for each 1-percentage-point increase in urbanization during the 1990s, an additional 6 million to 7 million rural workers were absorbed in productive employment in urban areas.

[18]Most industrial economies would fall in the 0.7–0.8 range on the basis of the criteria employed in the index.

————, and K. Li, 1999, "Accounting for China's Economic Growth: 1952–1998" (unpublished; Seattle: APEC Study Center).

Christensen, Laurits, Dale W. Jorgenson, and Laurence J. Lau, 1973, "Transcendental Logarithmic Production Frontiers," *Review of Economics and Statistics,* Vol. 55, No. 1 (February), pp. 28–45.

Elias, Victor J., 1992, *Sources of Growth: A Study of Seven Latin American Economies* (San Francisco: ICS Press).

European Bank for Reconstruction and Development, 1996, *Transition Report 1996* (London: European Bank for Reconstruction and Development).

Hu, Zuliu, and Mohsin Khan, 1996, "Why is China Growing So Fast?" IMF Working Paper 96/75 (Washington: International Monetary Fund)

International Monetary Fund, 1998, *World Economic Outlook and Capital Markets Interim Assessment* (Washington: International Monetary Fund).

Lardy, Nicholas R., 1998, *China's Unfinished Economic Revolution* (Washington: Brookings Institution).

Maddison, A., 1998, *Chinese Economic Performance in the Long Run* (Paris: Organization of Economic Co-Operation and Development).

Wang, X., 1999, "Incentives for Economic Growth: Prospects Across the Millennium" (unpublished; Beijing: National Economic Reform Institute and the Chinese Academy of Social Sciences).

Woo, W., 1998, "Chinese Economic Growth: Sources and Prospects," in *The Chinese Economy,* ed. by Michel Fouquin and Françoise Lemoine (London: Economica).

World Bank, 1996, *The Chinese Economy: Fighting Inflation, Deepening Reforms* (Washington: World Bank).

————, 1997, *China 2020: Development Challenges in the New Century* (Washington: World Bank).

Young, Alwyn, 1995, "The Tyranny of Numbers: Confronting the Statistical Realities of the East Asian Growth Experience," *Quarterly Journal of Economics,* Vol. 110, No. 3 (August), pp. 641–80.

Zhang, J., 2000, *Solving the New Urgent Problems of China* (Beijing: Economic Daily Publishing House).

Zhao, R., 1998, "Capital Mobility and Regional Integration: China 1978–95" (unpublished; Washington: IMF).

3

Provincial Growth Dynamics

JAHANGIR AZIZ AND CHRISTOPH DUENWALD

The rapid pace of growth of China's economy masks substantial differences in growth rates and levels of income per capita across different provinces in China. The issue of uneven regional development has recently moved to the top of the policy agenda in an effort to share the benefits of economic reform more broadly.

This chapter seeks answers to the following three questions:

- Are the relatively poor provinces in China catching up with the rich ones?
- If they are, what are the characteristics of the catch-up process?
- On current trends, what will the provincial income distribution look like in the future?

In the empirical growth literature, these questions have been broadly classified as relating to the study of *convergence* of income levels among economic units—countries or provinces within a particular country. However, "convergence" has been used in the literature to refer to several different phenomena. In this chapter, convergence is defined as the phenomenon of income levels in poorer provinces catching up in relative terms with those in the rich provinces.

The subject of income disparities within China has of late been the focus of several studies. Generally speaking, three main results emerge from these studies:

- If one looks only at the incomes per capita in China's provinces, there is little evidence that, since 1978, the initially poorer provinces have on average grown faster than their richer counterparts: what the growth literature calls *absolute* (*or unconditional*) *beta-convergence*. However, if provincial incomes per capita are adjusted for differences in economic structure, economic policies, demographics, and geography, there is evidence that, on average, the initially poorer provinces have indeed grown faster: what the literature calls *conditional beta-convergence*.

- Forces of conditional convergence were stronger in the pre-1990 era—the early reform period—and weaker in the 1990s.
- The dispersion in relative incomes per capita of the provinces fell in the early reform period and rose in the 1990s. A decline in this dispersion is referred to as *sigma-convergence*.

However, virtually all these studies provide only a partial view of the convergence process. They tend to focus exclusively on the average (in the case of unconditional and conditional beta-convergence) or the standard deviation (in the case of sigma-convergence) of the relative income distribution of provinces and, based on the behavior of these two statistics, draw inferences about whether relative incomes in China's provinces are converging or not. Although these two statistics provide valuable insights into the convergence process, as shown in many studies both theoretical and empirical, inferences based solely on the behavior of these two statistics are incomplete. In particular, the answer to whether or not the poor provinces are catching up with the rich ones depends on how the shape of the entire provincial relative income distribution has changed over time, and not simply on the behavior of two statistics of the distribution.

The approach taken in this chapter is to exploit more fully the information contained in the shape of the relative income distribution and how it has changed over time. To do this, in the spirit of Quah (1997), kernel estimates of the relative income distribution of China's provinces are computed and their intertemporal properties characterized. The results from this exercise suggest the following:

- Incomes per capita in the initially poor provinces are catching up with those in the initially richer provinces.
- However, this overall tendency masks significant differences across provinces. On the one hand, the coastal provinces are growing relatively faster than the rest, including the initially richer provinces. On the other hand, many of the initially poorer provinces, after improving their relative rankings in the 1980s, fell behind in the 1990s. The initially richer provinces have been losing their standing in the relative income ladder quite rapidly.
- As a result, the relative income distribution seems to be stratifying into a bimodal distribution, with the coastal provinces gravitating toward one mode and the remaining provinces toward the other.
- Provinces' economic structure and policies, in particular the concentration of state-owned enterprises (SOEs) and the openness of

Figure 3.1. Income per Capita by Province
(Shanghai, 1997=100)

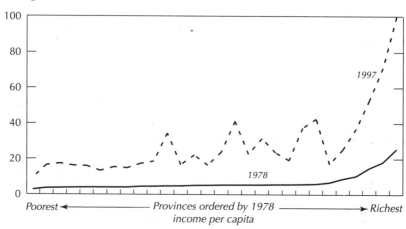

Sources: National Bureau of Statistics; and IMF staff estimates.

the province to external trade, have been significant factors in these distributional dynamics.

Recent Evidence on Convergence

This section summarizes existing evidence on convergence among China's provinces, first by reviewing the record of economic performance across provinces and then by distilling the results of past studies of convergence in China.

Economic Performance of China's Provinces

Economic performance has varied widely across China's provinces.[1] Between 1978 and 1997, incomes per capita grew in all Chinese provinces in absolute terms, and both initially rich and initially poor provinces experienced a significant increase in living standards (Figure 3.1). However, the extent of improvement in living standards differed substantially from province to province. Although real GDP per capita has grown by at least 5 percent on average during the reform period,

---

[1]This section draws on Husain (1998), Jian, Sachs, and Warner (1996), and Dayal-Gulati and Husain (2000).

some provinces—notably those along the coast—have grown more than twice that fast.[2] Indeed, the variation in economic performance has displayed some distinct geographical patterns. Coastal provinces have tended to outperform the central provinces, which in turn have surpassed the western provinces. For example, coastal provinces such as Guangdong, Fujian, and Zhejiang each grew at an average annual rate of around 12 percent in real per capita terms during 1978–97, while central provinces like Hubei, Henan, and Jiangxi grew by about 9 percent a year. Western provinces such as Gansu, Qinghai, and Ningxia grew at rates between 5 and 7 percent.

Significant variation in relative economic performance over time is also a feature of the provincial data (Table 3.1). Shanghai and Guizhou were China's richest and poorest provinces, respectively, both in 1978 and in 1997. However, there were considerable changes in the rankings (in terms of the level of real GDP per capita) of the other provinces between those two years. For instance, the coastal province of Zhejiang moved from 15th in the rankings in 1978 to 5th in 1997; the western province of Qinghai dropped from 6th to 20th over the same period. More broadly, in 1978 the most affluent provinces tended to be in the northeast, but by 1989 some of the coastal provinces had joined the northeastern region among the most affluent in the country. By 1997 the coastal provinces were clearly the most affluent (apart from the metropolitan areas of Shanghai, Beijing, and Tianjin), followed by the northeastern region.

Studies of Convergence in Growth Regressions

One of the key predictions of the neoclassical growth model is the convergence hypothesis: the tendency of poor countries, or regions within a country, to catch up with richer countries or regions.[3] In the literature, the most common approach to identifying such a phenomenon is to conduct a beta-convergence exercise, which amounts to verifying whether the neoclassical (standard Solow or augmented endogenous growth) model is a good description of a country's develop-

---

[2]As noted in Chapter 2, some observers believe that China's GDP growth rates are overstated by as much as 2 percentage points. This issue is not relevant to the present study, which focuses on relative provincial GDP levels and growth rates, under the assumption that there is no systematic tendency for growth in some provinces to be overstated more than in others.

[3]More precisely, and as argued by Barro and Sala-i-Martin (1995), the neoclassical model leads to conditional rather than absolute convergence as these terms were defined in the introduction to this chapter.

Table 3.1. Real GDP per Capita Relative to Shanghai, by Province

(Index, Shanghai = 1.00)[1]

Province	1978	Province	1989	Province	1997
Shanghai	1.00	Shanghai	1.00	Shanghai	1.00
Beijing	0.70	Beijing	0.79	Beijing	0.69
Tianjin	0.57	Tianjin	0.57	Tianjin	0.53
Liaoning	0.41	Liaoning	0.46	Guangdong	0.41
Heilongjiang	0.35	Guangdong	0.35	Zhejiang	0.41
Qinghai	0.29	Heilongjiang	0.33	Jiangsu	0.37
Guangdong	0.23	Zhejiang	0.32	Liaoning	0.36
Jilin	0.22	Jiangsu	0.32	Fujian	0.35
Shanxi	0.22	Shandong	0.28	Shandong	0.31
Jiangsu	0.22	Xinjiang	0.28	Heilongjiang	0.25
Hebei	0.21	Jilin	0.27	Hebei	0.24
Shandong	0.21	Fujian	0.27	Jilin	0.23
Xinjiang	0.21	Qinghai	0.25	Hubei	0.22
Ningxia	0.21	Hubei	0.24	Xinjiang	0.22
Zhejiang	0.20	Shanxi	0.23	Shanxi	0.19
Hubei	0.19	Hebei	0.23	Inner Mongolia	0.18
Hunan	0.19	Ningxia	0.23	Anhui	0.17
Fujian	0.18	Inner Mongolia	0.22	Guangxi	0.17
Inner Mongolia	0.18	Shaanxi	0.20	Hunan	0.16
Guangxi	0.18	Yunnan	0.19	Qinghai	0.16
Gansu	0.16	Hunan	0.19	Henan	0.16
Yunnan	0.16	Anhui	0.18	Ningxia	0.16
Shaanxi	0.16	Henan	0.17	Jiangxi	0.16
Sichuan	0.15	Sichuan	0.17	Yunnan	0.15
Anhui	0.15	Gansu	0.17	Sichuan	0.15
Jiangxi	0.15	Jiangxi	0.17	Shaanxi	0.14
Henan	0.14	Guangxi	0.16	Gansu	0.13
Guizhou	0.11	Guizhou	0.13	Guizhou	0.09

Source: National Bureau of Statistics.

[1]Hainan and Tibet Autonomous Region were excluded because income per capita data are not available before 1985. Data for Chongqing, which became a municipality in 1997, are included in the data for Sichuan.

ment experience.[4] In this context, as already noted, a distinction between absolute and conditional beta-convergence is typically made. If economies vary in their saving rates and initial capital stocks, then the neoclassical model predicts conditional convergence, a situation in which incomes per capita converge, conditional on each economy's steady state.[5] That is, among economies that are similar in preferences,

---

[4]Examples include Mankiw, Romer, and Weil (1992), Cashin and Sahay (1996), and Dayal-Gulati and Husain (2000).

[5]Convergence in this case arises from the assumption of diminishing returns to capital. Since the rate of return on capital is lower in economies with more capital per worker, there are incentives for capital to flow from rich to poor economies, boosting growth in the latter relative to the former, and thus causing convergence.

Table 3.2. Selected Previously Reported Tests of Convergence for China's Provinces

Study and Period	Type of Convergence Found
Jian, Sachs, and Warner (1996)	
1978–93	Absolute
1978–85	None
1985–93	None
1990–93	None
Chen and Fleisher (1996)	
1978–93	Conditional
Raiser and Nunnenkamp (1997)	
1978–85	Conditional
1985–92	Conditional
1978–92	Conditional
Li, Liu, and Rebelo (1998)	
1978–95	Absolute
1978–95	Conditional
Dayal-Gulati and Husain (2000)	
1978–82	Conditional
1983–87	Conditional
1988–92	None
1993–97	None

Source: Literature cited.

technologies, saving rates, and other structural characteristics, the lower the initial level of output per capita, the higher the growth rate.

Testing the hypothesis of beta-convergence commonly involves regressing growth in output per capita during a given time interval on a constant, initial income per capita, and a set of conditioning variables. Empirical studies differ in the conditioning variables included, but investment ratios, educational characteristics, population growth, and (in the case of China) dummy variables for coastal effects have typically been used. The conditional convergence hypothesis predicts a statistically significant negative coefficient on initial income (holding the conditioning variables constant).

In the case of China, several studies have shown that, in general, the relative dispersion of provincial incomes per capita fell in the 1980s but rose subsequently. This observation suggests that the evolution of China's regional income dynamics can be roughly divided into two time periods: 1978–89 and 1990–97, with the former period characterized by convergence and the latter by divergence, as measured by sigma-convergence.

A number of studies have also tested the beta-convergence hypothesis using Chinese provincial data. Table 3.2 provides a selected survey of these studies, whose main findings are the following:

- Jian, Sachs, and Warner (1996) find that China's regional disparities narrowed between 1978 and 1990 but that, subsequently, the
  coastal and interior regions of China began to diverge, reflecting
  in part the special privileges given to the coastal regions. These
  authors explain the divergence in regional incomes by an increase
  in the variance between the coastal provinces and the interior
  provinces, rather than by an increase in the variance within either
  the coastal region or the interior. They conclude that China is on
  a dual track, with a prosperous coastal region that is growing
  rapidly and a poor interior that is growing more slowly.
- Chen and Fleisher (1996), using an augmented Solow growth
  model, find evidence that convergence was conditional on coastal
  location. Their result suggests that convergence is occurring
  within the coastal and inland regions but not between these
  regions.
- Raiser and Nunnenkamp (1997) find evidence in support of conditional income convergence among China's provinces; however,
  they also show that the rate of convergence in the 1985–92 period
  was markedly slower than that for 1978–85.
- Li, Liu, and Rebelo (1998), using the augmented Solow-Swan
  model, find support for the conditional convergence hypothesis
  and estimate the convergence rate to be a relatively high 4¾ percent a year.[6] However, they also note an increase in income
  inequality after 1990, and they point out that although economic
  reforms in China have facilitated convergence of each province
  toward its steady state, they have also widened the gap between
  the steady states of different provinces. The authors also present
  evidence in support of unconditional convergence during the sample period, so that regional economies converge even though they
  have dissimilar steady states.
- Dayal-Gulati and Husain (2000) show that regions are converging, but to different steady-state levels of income. They find that
  the pattern of foreign direct investment flows, as well as structural
  characteristics of the regions—including total investment, the
  concentration of SOEs, and bank loan-deposit ratios—are important factors determining growth and convergence.

Using a representative set of the same conditioning variables used in
the above studies, similar beta-convergence exercises were performed
for this chapter for the period 1978–97 and the subperiods 1978–89 and

---

[6]By comparison, estimates of the rate of convergence for other economies center
around 2 percent a year. See Mankiw, Romer, and Weil (1992), for example.

Table 3.3. Results of Provincial Growth Regressions

Variable[1]	1978–97		1978–89		1990–97	
	(1)	(2)	(3)	(4)	(5)	(6)
Initial income per capita (in logarithms)	–1.24	–3.57**	–2.49***	–5.62***	2.77*	–1.56
Population growth (in percent)		–0.52		–2.01		0.3
Domestic investment-to-GDP ratio		0.027		0.07*		0.02
Foreign direct investment-to-GDP ratio		0.14		0.27***		0.05
Government revenue-to-expenditure ratio		–0.001		0.003		–0.004
M2-to-GDP ratio		–0.007		–0.001		–0.014
Share of SOEs in industrial output		–0.045***		–0.02		–0.09***
Coastal dummy variable		1.83***		1.3*		1.97
Summary statistics						
Adjusted R^2	0.03	0.79	0.09	0.61	0.02	0.84
Standard error of the regression	3.03	0.8	1.48	0.97	2.48	1.01

Source: IMF staff estimates.
[1]The dependent variable is the growth rate of real GDP per capita.
***Indicates statistical significance at the 1 percent level.
**Indicates statistical significance at the 5 percent level.
*Indicates statistical significance at the 10 percent level.

1990–97. The results, summarized in Table 3.3, generally confirm those from the earlier studies.

Dynamics of Convergence

The results summarized in the previous section, although useful, do not provide a complete picture about the shape of the relative income distribution or how it has evolved over the years. To obtain such a picture, the *kernels* of the actual relative provincial incomes in different time periods are estimated so that their shapes and intertemporal dynamics can be studied. A *kernel estimator* of a set of observations—in this case the relative rankings of provincial income per capita—is an estimate of the distribution function from which the observations are likely to have been drawn (for details, see Silverman, 1986). Mathematically, the kernel estimator $f(x)$ is defined as

$$f(x) = \frac{1}{Nh} \sum_{j=1}^{N} K\left(\frac{x - X_j}{h}\right),$$

where X_j are the individual observations, N is the number of data points, h is a window width or smoothing parameter,[7] and K is a kernel or weighting function (assumed here to be the normal distribution).

Provincial Income Distribution

Figure 3.2 displays the kernels of provincial relative incomes in 1978, 1989, and 1997. In each panel the kernel was estimated in the following three steps:

- In each year the real income per capita of each of China's 28 provinces was rescaled as a fraction of Shanghai's income per capita,[8] such that the range of the distribution is restricted to lie between 0 and 1. Since, by construction, Shanghai's relative income is always 1, it, too, was excluded from the sample.
- For a suitably large number of points spanning the interval from 0 to 1,[9] the relative frequency (that is, the unconditional probability) with which each of these values could have occurred was estimated. The probability of each point was computed as the weighted average of the distance of that point from the given relative incomes of all the 27 provinces, with the weights drawn from a normal or Gaussian distribution centered at that point.
- The relative frequencies of these points were filtered for noise using the procedure in Silverman (1986). The collection of the filtered relative frequencies formed the kernel of the relative provincial incomes in that year. The area of the distribution was normalized to 100.

One interpretation of the kernel estimators is that, based on the actual growth experience of China's provinces, they tell us how likely it is that a province's income per capita, on average, was a certain fraction of Shanghai's income per capita in a particular year. For example, in the top panel of Figure 3.2, the unconditional probability that a province's income per capita in 1978 was one-fifth of Shanghai's was 14 percent. This probability declined to 10 percent in 1989 and then rose to 12 percent in 1997 (middle and bottom panels).

---

[7]The window width was chosen following the suggestion in Silverman (1986) that it be given by $0.9AN^{-1/5}$, where A = min(standard deviation, interquartile range/1.34).

[8]The choice of Shanghai as the numeraire is arbitrary and has little impact on the analysis. Hainan and the Tibet Autonomous Region were excluded from the sample because data on income per capita are not available before 1985. Data for Chongqing, which became a municipality in 1997, are included in the data for Sichuan.

[9]For these exercises, the interval from 0 to 1 was divided into equally spaced 50 subintervals.

Figure 3.2. Gaussian Kernels of Provincial Relative Income Distribution
Relative frequency (percent)

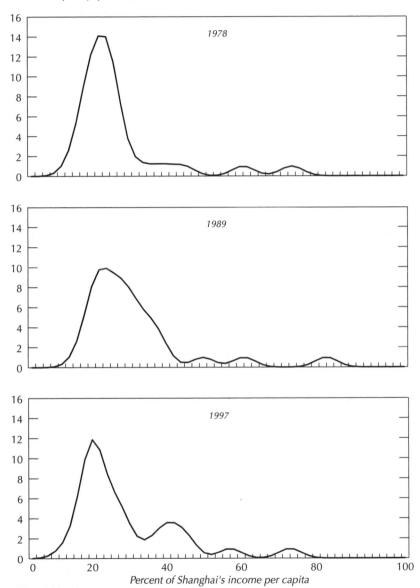

Sources: National Bureau of Statistics; and IMF staff estimates.

An examination of the provincial income distributions over the period 1978–97 reveals the following stylized facts:[10]

- Most of the mass of the income distributions for all three periods remained below two-fifths of Shanghai's income per capita, indicating that, throughout the last two decades of reform, on average, a province's income per capita was most likely to have been less than 40 percent of Shanghai's.
- In the early reform period there was some decline in the mass of provinces in the first quintile of the distribution, but this was partly offset by an increase in the second quintile.
- In the late reform period, the shift to the second quintile was reversed, as the proportion of provinces in the first quintile rose.

These stylized facts are consistent with some of the results of the convergence exercises. It shows that there was a tendency in the early reform period toward unconditional beta-convergence, which disappears in the later reform period. It is also consistent with a decrease in the standard deviation of provincial relative incomes in the 1980s (sigma-convergence), followed by a rising trend in the 1990s.

However, the relative income distributions tell us little about whether the poor provinces became richer or poorer in relative terms in the early and late reform periods. Figure 3.3 provides various examples of movements of provinces over time that preserve the overall shape of the distributions in Figure 3.2 but reflect dramatically different growth dynamics. In particular, it is possible that a province at point A in 1978 (at one-fifth of Shanghai's income per capita) moved to point B in 1989 and then to point C in 1997. Alternatively, the province at point A could have moved to point D in 1989 and then fallen back to point E in 1997. These examples suggest that an answer to the question requires carefully tracking the positions of each province in the relative income distributions in 1978, 1989, and 1997.

Growth Dynamics in China's Provinces

The intradistributional dynamics among the Chinese provinces is displayed in Figure 3.4. In each panel the kernel of the joint distribution of relative incomes in the initial and terminal years is shown.

---

[10]In the remainder of this chapter the terms "kernel" and "distribution" will be used interchangeably. In the figures the income distribution is referred to as the Gaussian kernel, because the weights used were drawn from a Gaussian distribution. Weights drawn from an Epanechnikov distribution, the other frequently used weighting method, did not seem to make any material difference to the shape of the estimated kernels.

Figure 3.3. Examples of Distribution-Preserving Movements Within Gaussian Kernels
Relative frequency (percent)

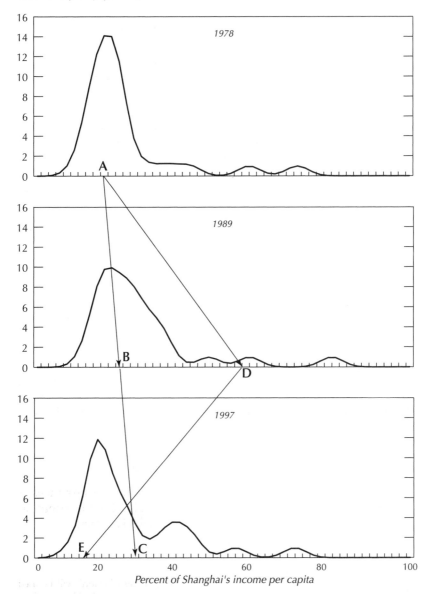

Percent of Shanghai's income per capita

Sources: National Bureau of Statistics; and IMF staff estimates.

Figure 3.4. Distribution Dynamics Across the Reform Period and in Subperiods[1]

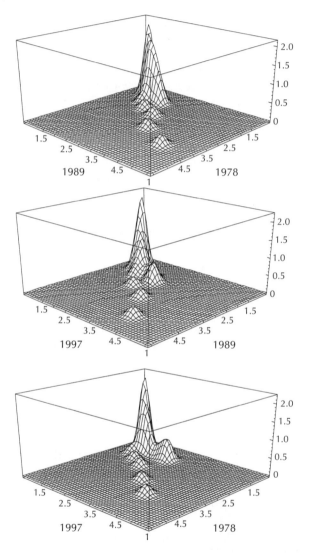

Sources: National Bureau of Statistics; and IMF staff estimates.

[1]The figures depict Gaussian kernels of the joint distribution of provincial relative income. The area under the entire distribution is normalized to be 100. Horizontal axes measure provincial income per capita as a fraction of Shanghai's, and the vertical axis the relative frequency in percent. Movement to the right of the north-south diagonal indicates improvement in the relative ranking, and movement to the left a worsening, between the initial and the terminal years.

The horizontal axes measure the relative incomes in the initial and terminal years, and the vertical axis measures the frequency with which a particular growth experience occurred between the two periods. Points of the distribution that lie along the north-south diagonal represent unchanged relative incomes, whereas points to the right of the diagonal represent a rise in relative incomes between the two periods plotted, and points to the left represent a decline.

In the first panel of Figure 3.4, the kernel shows that the dominant experience among China's provinces was that relative incomes were between one-fifth and two-fifths of Shanghai's income in 1978 and remained in that interval in 1989; for a small number of provinces relative income was higher in 1978, but they remained around the same levels 11 years later. Put differently, based on China's actual provincial growth experience during 1978–89, the probability that a province in the interval between one-fifth and two-fifths of Shanghai's income in 1978 remained in that interval at the end of the period was fairly high, and that of reaching, say, three-fifths or more of Shanghai's income was virtually zero.

This picture of apparent immobility, however, is not entirely correct. Along the north-south diagonal of the panel, the entire distribution is skewed to the right. This implies that although most provinces remained in the second quintile between 1978 and 1989, many shifted closer to the upper end of the interval during the period. The same was true for those in the fourth quintile in 1978; they moved up into the fifth quintile in 1989. Consequently, in the early reform period, not only was there considerable intradistributional mobility across provinces, but the poor provinces did in fact become richer in relative terms.

This trend seems to have been somewhat reversed in the later reform period (second panel of Figure 3.4). The kernel of the joint distribution between 1989 and 1997 shows a distinct leftward skew along the north-south diagonal at both the lower and the upper end of the range. This implies that although the provinces in the second quintile shifted toward the lower end of the interval, so did those in the upper quintiles. More interestingly, however, a set of provinces in the second quintile in 1989 broke out of that range to move into the third and fourth quintiles in subsequent years. Some of the relatively better-off provinces whose relative positions worsened were Heilongjiang, Liaoning, Qinghai, Tianjin, and Beijing, while provinces such as Guizhou, Yunnan, Gansu, and Shaanxi, which were already relatively poor, became relatively poorer. The provinces that gained the most in relative terms were those in the coastal region: Guangdong, Jiangsu, Zhejiang, and Fujian. Thus, while the coastal provinces gained in rank, some of the relatively rich provinces and many of the low-income provinces fell behind.

What do the intradistributional dynamics for the entire 1978–97 period look like? The third panel of Figure 3.4 shows the kernel of the joint relative income distribution between 1978 and 1997. The distribution has two distinct features: although the bulk of the distribution is shifted to the left of the north-south diagonal, there is also a significant mass skewed to the right. It would seem as if the coastal provinces are gravitating rightward and forming their own cluster, while the remaining regions—both the relatively rich and the relatively poor—are gravitating to the left to form a separate cluster. In other words, there is an emerging tendency for the distribution to be stratified into a bimodal distribution.[11]

These results provide somewhat firmer ground on which to answer the questions raised in the introduction:

- The relatively poor provinces are catching up with the rich ones, but this is occurring in a somewhat complex manner. Some of the coastal provinces, which were relatively poor at the beginning of the reform period, have been growing at a considerably faster pace than the erstwhile rich provinces of the rust belt, especially in the 1990s. As a result, the gap between the coastal provinces and the initially rich provinces is closing in relative terms. On the other hand, the other initially poor provinces are falling behind in relative terms, such that the dispersion among these initially poor and initially rich provinces is also declining—the provinces seem to be clustering toward two separate relative income clubs.

- Furthermore, there has been considerable mobility in the relative rankings. This raises a whole new set of questions, which are explored in the next section. If labor and capital were relatively immobile in China, as conventional wisdom suggests, what explains the intradistributional churning? Is it due to the structure of these economies, or to differences in the policies adopted by these provinces? The next section provides partial answers to these questions.

- To answer the question about the future shape of the regional income distribution, the relative income rankings based on the relative growth differentials among the provinces in the 1990s were projected to 2010. Figure 3.5 shows the kernel of the joint

---

[11]Quah (1997) termed this bimodality "twin peaks" in the context of cross-country growth experience. In that study the twin peaks lay along the north-south diagonal, implying little mobility in relative rankings. In the case of China's provincial growth, the emergent twin peaks would lie across the north-south diagonal, implying significant mobility in the rankings. This is a specific example of what Baumol (1986) termed "club convergence."

Figure 3.5. Projected Distribution Dynamics on Current Trends[1]

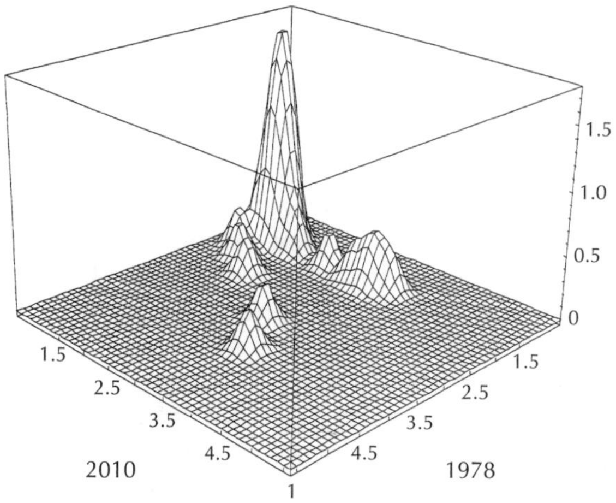

Sources: National Bureau of Statistics; and IMF staff estimates.
[1]The figures depict Gaussian kernels of the joint distribution of provincial relative income. The area under the entire distribution is normalized to be 100. Horizontal axes measure provincial income per capita as a fraction of Shanghai's, and the vertical axis the relative frequency in percent. Movement to the right of the north-south diagonal indicates improvement in the relative ranking, and movement to the left a worsening, between the initial and the terminal years.

distribution of relative incomes in 1978 and that projected for 2010. The stratification into two peaks has become more pronounced, underscoring the earlier conclusion about emerging club convergence.

Explaining Provincial Growth Dynamics

The analysis so far has not made a distinction of the kind commonly made between conditional and unconditional beta-convergence. Recall that this distinction was based on the notion that different provinces could be converging to different steady states, depending on the specific features of their economic structure and economic policies, and thus converging at different rates. This section focuses on whether the growth dynamics observed and inferences made in the previous section, which were based only on the growth experiences of the provinces and thus unconditional in nature, are affected by economic structure and policies.

The methodology used was the following:

- For each province, "conditioned" growth rates for the periods 1979–89 and 1990–97 were constructed using the fraction of the growth rate explained by the variables in regression equations (4) and (6) in Table 3.3: the population growth rate, the foreign direct investment-to-GDP ratio, the domestic investment-to-GDP ratio, the government revenue-to-expenditure ratio, the M2-to-GDP ratio, the share of SOEs in industrial production, and a dummy variable for the coastal provinces.[12]
- Residual growth rates were then computed by subtracting the conditioned growth rates from the realized growth rates. Using these residual growth rates, conditioned relative incomes for 1989 and 1997 were computed.
- Finally, based on actual relative incomes in 1978 and the conditioned relative incomes in 1989 and 1997, kernels of the conditioned joint distribution of relative incomes between 1978–89, 1989–97, and 1978–97 were computed.

The noticeable feature of the conditioned distributions for 1978–89, 1989–97, and 1978–97 (Figure 3.6) is that they are all skewed to the right of the north-south diagonal. By comparing the conditioned joint distributions with the unconditioned ones (Figure 3.4), the following inferences can be drawn:

- For the period 1978–89, the skew in the unconditioned joint distribution is not very different from that in the conditioned distribution; thus, economic structure and policies had little influence on interregional convergence.
- However, for the period 1989–97, the conditioned distribution shows a more marked skew toward the right of the north-south diagonal than does the unconditioned distribution. This underscores the strong presence of convergence forces after the influence of policies and economic structure has been filtered out. Importantly, the coastal regions no longer show the previous strong shift to higher rankings. The absence of the marked shift was largely due to the strong explanatory power of the coastal dummy in the growth regression for the later reform period. As noted previously, the coastal dummy acts as a proxy for the external openness of the provinces, albeit a very weak one. This suggests that external trade was a strong factor behind the growth of the coastal provinces in the 1990s.

---

[12]Except for population growth, all the other variables were chosen on the basis of results in Dayal-Gulati and Husain (2000).

Figure 3.6. Conditioned Distribution Dynamics Across the Reform Period and in Subperiods[1]

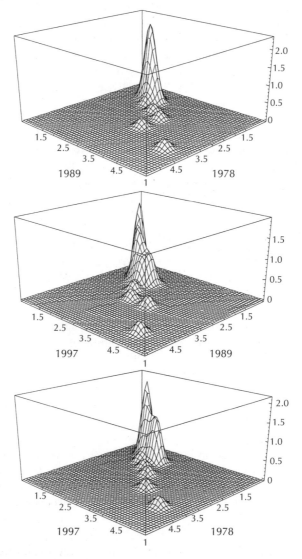

Sources: National Bureau of Statistics; and IMF staff estimates.

[1]The figures depict Gaussian kernels of the joint distribution of provincial relative income. The area under the entire distribution is normalized to be 100. Horizontal axes measure provincial income per capita as a fraction of Shanghai's, and the vertical axis the relative frequency in percent. Movement to the right of the north-south diagonal indicates improvement in the relative ranking, and movement to the left a worsening, between the initial and the terminal years.

- For the period as a whole, the conditioned distribution shows an almost uniform tendency toward convergence. In contrast, the unconditioned distribution showed more complex dynamics, with an emerging tendency toward twin-peakedness. Consequently, it would appear that the economic structure and policies of the provinces have played an important role in increasing stratification.[13]

The variation in economic performance across provinces has been a function of the timing, sequencing, and targeting of economic reforms and the associated structural shifts. China's pre-1978 development strategy had emphasized balance and equity, but this gave way to the pursuit, in the 1980s, of the objective of rapid growth based on gradual and incremental reforms.[14] This new strategy shifted the focus of state investment from the interior to the coastal regions and granted the latter preferential treatment. Beginning in 1980, the coastal region was opened to foreign investment through the creation of special economic zones and open cities. Combined with this region's other advantages, such as a relative abundance of human capital and favorable geographical location, this resulted in a sharp pickup in growth along China's southern coast. The resulting narrowing gap between the southern coastal provinces and the eastern coastal provinces served to reduce regional disparities during the 1980s. As the government's pro-coastal policy orientation strengthened further in the late 1980s, the interior provinces became increasingly cut off, and income disparities started to rise. This led the government to adjust its policies during the Eighth Five-Year Plan (1991–95) and to increase support to the less developed regions in the central and western parts of China in the Ninth Five-Year Plan (1996–2000). More recently the government has redoubled its efforts to reduce regional disparities.

The northeastern provinces, including Liaoning and Heilongjiang, were initially the most affluent (except for the largely metropolitan areas of Shanghai, Beijing, and Tianjin), reflecting large-scale investment in the industrial sector under central planning. As a result, on the eve of the reforms, provinces with relatively large industrial sectors

---

[13]The major factors, however, are mainly structural, because the coefficients on the structural variables in regressions (4) and (6) in Table 3.3 are statistically significant whereas those on the policy variables are not.

[14]During the Sixth Five-Year Plan (1981–85), a pro-coastal policy program was adopted, and this orientation became even more pronounced in the Seventh Five-Year Plan (1986–90). The idea was that reforms should be conducted on an experimental basis in certain regions first. If these experiments were successful, their influence would eventually spread to other regions (see Wang and Hu, 1999).

tended to be the most affluent. However, the associated high concentration of SOEs in the eastern provinces subsequently became a drag on growth, with most of these provinces recording relatively low growth rates.

Apart from the selective opening during the 1980s, the other major area of reform in the post-1978 period was in the agricultural sector. A shift in agricultural production from the commune system to the household responsibility system led to a rapid increase in agricultural productivity, raising incomes per capita in those central and western provinces where agriculture was a relatively large share of provincial GDP. In addition, rural areas benefited from the emergence of township and village enterprises, which operated outside of the central plan and absorbed excess labor from agriculture. These reforms, which took place for the most part between 1979 and 1985, resulted in relatively strong growth in income per capita in those provinces where agriculture was the dominant sector and where there was a high concentration of township and village enterprises, contributing to a reduction in regional income inequalities during the 1980s.

Conclusions

Conventional convergence studies, which use regression techniques to determine the existence of convergence, do not provide a complete answer to whether poor provinces in China are catching up with richer provinces. A better approach is to examine the entire distribution of relative provincial incomes, because this sheds light on the intertemporal dynamics that lie behind China's development and growth experience. The distributional dynamics suggest that China's poor provinces are catching up with the rich ones. This catch-up, however, is occurring in a complex manner, with the gap between the coastal provinces and the initially rich provinces closing in relative terms. Moreover, the initially poor provinces, as well as the previously richer provinces, are both falling behind in relative terms (the latter at a faster pace). Thus provinces in China appear to be clustering into relative income clubs of their own, which is causing the distribution of relative incomes to become stratified into a bimodal distribution. An extrapolation of current growth trends to 2010 reveals an even more pronounced bimodal stratification. Finally, this chapter finds that economic structure and policies have played an important role in bringing about this stratification.

China's entry into the World Trade Organization could accelerate the process of stratification. The coastal provinces and, to a lesser extent, those provinces' immediate hinterlands, could benefit from the expected growth in international trade. On the other hand, the relatively poor provinces, particularly those dependent on agriculture, could see a further slowdown in the growth of incomes per capita as prices for agricultural products fall. Moreover, the provinces with a heavy concentration of SOEs may see their former affluence erode even further as pressures mount to restructure the state enterprises.

As mentioned earlier, the Ninth Five-Year Plan (1996–2000) addressed regional disparities, and since then the Chinese authorities have intensified their efforts to narrow the income gaps among China's provinces. Indeed, about two-thirds of expenditure under the fiscal stimulus packages in 1998 and 1999 was targeted at the central and western provinces. Developing the central and western regions is also a cornerstone of the Tenth Five-Year Plan (2001–05), and a "Develop the West" initiative has recently been launched. Under this plan, efforts are focused on infrastructure investment, technological upgrading, and training and education. In addition, efforts are being made to equalize preferential tax policies between coastal and inland areas. With regard to the fiscal system more generally, although discretionary fiscal transfers have been used in the past to help offset large social safety net needs in poorer regions, concerns about regional disparities may necessitate a review of the entire system of intergovernmental fiscal relations at some point in the future.

References

Barro, Robert J., and Xavier Sala-i-Martin, 1995, *Economic Growth* (New York: McGraw-Hill).

Baumol, William, 1986, "Productivity Growth, Convergence, and Welfare," *American Economic Review*, 76 (December), pp. 1072–85.

Cashin, Paul, and Ratna Sahay, 1996, "Internal Migration, Center-State Grants, and Economic Growth in the States of India," *Staff Papers*, International Monetary Fund, Vol. 43 (March), pp. 123–71.

Chen, Jian, and Belton M. Fleisher, 1996, "Regional Income Inequality and Economic Growth in China," *Journal of Comparative Economics*, Vol. 22, No. 2, pp. 141–64.

Dayal-Gulati, Anuradha, and Aasim M. Husain, 2000, "Centripetal Forces in China's Economic Take-off," IMF Working Paper 00/86 (Washington: International Monetary Fund).

Husain, Aasim M., 1998, "Economic Performance and Business Cycles in China's Provinces and Regions," in *People's Republic of China—Selected Issues* (Washington: International Monetary Fund, SM/98/184).

Jian, Tianlun, Jeffrey D. Sachs, and Andrew M. Warner, 1996, "Trends in Regional Inequality in China," NBER Working Paper 5412 (Cambridge, Massachusetts: National Bureau of Economic Research).

Li, Hong, Zinan Liu, and Ivonia Rebelo, 1998, "Testing the Neoclassical Theory of Economic Growth: Evidence from Chinese Provinces," *Economics of Planning*, Vol. 31, No. 2–3, pp. 117–32.

Mankiw, N. Gregory, David Romer, and David N. Weil, 1992, "A Contribution to the Empirics of Economic Growth," *Quarterly Journal of Economics*, Vol. 107, No. 2 (May), pp. 407–37.

Quah, Danny, 1997, "Empirics for Growth and Distribution: Polarization, Stratification, and Convergence Clubs," *Journal of Economic Growth*, Vol. 2 (March), pp. 27–59.

Raiser, Martin, and Peter Nunnenkamp, 1997, "Die andere Seite Chinas—Strukturprobleme, Reformdefizite und verzögerte Aufholprozesse im chinesischen Binnenland," Kiel Working Papers 794 (Kiel, Germany: Kiel Institute of World Economics).

Silverman, Bernard W., 1986, *Density Estimation for Statistics and Data Analysis* (New York: Chapman and Hall).

Wang, Shaoguang, and Angang Hu, 1999, *The Political Economy of Uneven Development—The Case of China* (New York: M.E. Sharpe).

4

The Growth-Financial Development Nexus

CHRISTOPH DUENWALD AND JAHANGIR AZIZ

In recent years the empirical growth literature has refocused on the linkages between a country's economic growth and the level of development of its financial system. The observation that such a link exists dates back to Schumpeter (1911), who argued that the services provided by financial intermediaries—mobilizing savings, evaluating projects, managing risk, monitoring managers, and facilitating transactions—are essential for technological innovation and economic development. Although this notion was examined empirically to a limited extent in the 1970s, more sophisticated analysis of the link did not take place until the 1990s. These studies, which use cross-sectional data for large sets of countries, have tended to find a positive association between faster growth and more developed financial systems. This chapter examines this link more closely for China, through an analysis of data from China's 28 provinces.[1]

Although China's growth performance since the onset of economic reform in 1978 has been remarkable, this performance masks substantial differences in the growth rate and level of incomes per capita across different provinces. Indeed, empirical work on income convergence among China's provinces suggests that convergence weakened in the 1990s, with the coastal provinces tending to grow much faster than the interior provinces and making a commensurately greater contribution

---

[1]As discussed further below, data limitations have largely prevented China from inclusion in cross-country studies.

to China's overall growth (see Chapter 3). At the same time, the coastal provinces have the highest relative degree of nonstate sector involvement in the economy. However, almost two-thirds of domestic bank credit continues to go to the state sector, raising the question of how the nonstate sector is financing its rapid growth. More generally, after adjusting for other factors that contribute to variation in interprovincial growth, do differing degrees of financial development help explain differences in growth across provinces?

Data limitations prevent a rigorous examination of the growth-financial intermediation nexus for China as a whole; however, it is possible to analyze the issue by looking at data on China's provinces, autonomous regions, and municipalities. Accordingly, this chapter seeks to answer the following questions:

- What are the main characteristics of China's system of financial intermediation at the national level, and how do they compare with those of similar countries?
- Do differing degrees of financial development across China's provinces help explain differences in growth performance? In this context, how has China's growth been financed?
- What policy implications flow from the empirical results, especially as they pertain to China's financial sector reform program?

The main findings of this chapter are as follows:

- *Although the level of financial intermediation in China is relatively high, the financial system is generally viewed as inefficient at converting financial resources into productive investment.* China's large pool of savings—currently equivalent to 38 percent of GDP—has been almost wholly intermediated through the domestic banking system and, in large part, has been allocated to the state enterprise sector. Indeed, the nonstate sector appears to have financed itself mainly out of retained earnings or savings by the principal owner of the enterprise, or by foreign direct investment (FDI), rather than from bank credit or the capital markets.
- *Financial system development, as measured by bank loan-to-GDP ratios, has been much lower in the faster-growing provinces than in provinces that have grown less quickly than the average.* Not surprisingly, provinces with higher concentrations of state-owned enterprises (SOEs) had higher loan-to-GDP ratios.
- *Although total bank credit is not significant in explaining interprovincial growth differences, nonstate sector credit is.* Panel regressions suggest that, after conditioning on a number of variables including initial GDP per capita, population growth, investment, FDI, concentration of SOEs, and the ratio of fiscal revenue to expenditure, the level of financial development is not a statistically significant

explanatory variable for observed interprovincial differences in growth rates of GDP per capita. However, once bank lending is adjusted for lending to SOEs so as to construct a variable that measures nonstate credit (no direct measure is available in the Chinese statistics), variations in this variable were found to affect growth in income per capita to a statistically significant (but small) degree.

Theory and Earlier Findings

Financial intermediation can affect growth through any of three channels. It can increase the marginal productivity of capital by collecting information from which to evaluate alternative investment projects, and by sharing of risk. It can raise the proportion of savings channeled to investment through financial development, by reducing the resources absorbed by financial intermediaries (in the form of interest rate spreads, commissions, and the like), thus increasing the efficiency of financial intermediation. And it can raise the private saving rate.[2]

The positive correlation between growth and indicators of financial development was first documented by Goldsmith (1969), McKinnon (1973), and Shaw (1973). Since then, a flourishing body of empirical work has emerged.[3] These studies, which are typically based on regression analyses of large cross sections of countries (both advanced and developing), generally find that cross-country differences in financial development explain a significant portion of differences in average growth rates.

In testing for the link between growth and financial development, studies generally regress countries' growth rates on an indicator of financial development and a set of control variables, typically including initial income per capita, educational attainment, political stability, and population growth. Following King and Levine (1993) and Levine (1997), the following indicators of financial development have typically been chosen: the ratio of liquid liabilities of the financial system to GDP (a variable that measures the combined size of the country's financial intermediaries), the ratio of bank credit to the sum of bank credit and central bank domestic assets, the ratio of private credit to total domestic credit, and the ratio of private credit to GDP.

---

[2]However, the impact of financial development on private saving is ambiguous theoretically. Efficient risk sharing could lower the saving rate, reducing growth. For example, see the discussion in Pagano (1993).

[3]What follows is a partial review of the macroeconomic literature. There have also been numerous studies investigating the growth-financial development link at the industry and at the firm level. Levine (1997) and Khan and Senhadji (2000) provide more comprehensive surveys.

The main outstanding issues in the literature are threefold. What is the appropriate measurement of financial development, given that the empirical results are sensitive to the measure of financial depth used? What is the true direction of causality between financial development and growth; that is, do financial systems develop in tandem with or ahead of growth?[4] And is a bank-based or a securities market-based financial system superior in terms of maximizing finance's contribution to growth? This chapter will not explore the third issue further, but Levine (1999) and others have argued that the debate is probably misplaced: both sources of finance are important to growth, and financial development is best fostered through the establishment of a strong legal and regulatory system.

China's System of Financial Intermediation

Despite a large deposit base, China's system of financial intermediation is generally judged to be relatively underdeveloped and inefficient at converting financial resources into productive investment.[5] This view is based on a number of the system's characteristics:
- *Financial intermediation in China is largely bank based and dominated by four state commercial banks (SCBs), with securities (bond and equity) markets still relatively small* (Table 4.1).[6] The SCBs together account for two-thirds of financial system assets. Although a financial system dominated by state-owned financial institutions is not necessarily less efficient than one dominated by private firms, the state has been involved in China's financial system on a very large scale, with government budgetary grants having been replaced since the late 1970s by state bank credit as the main source of funds for SOEs.[7] Indeed, a large proportion of savings continues to be channeled to SOEs: state bank claims on SOEs still amounted to two-thirds of GDP at the end of 2000 (Table 4.2).
- *The resources intermediated through bank lending may have been misallocated.* Evidence of this is the excess capacity built up in the

---

[4]Econometrically, this is a problem of simultaneity bias and has been tackled using instrumental variables or related econometric techniques.

[5]For example, see Lardy (2000).

[6]Average stock market capitalization for China as shown in the table masks the fact that it has risen sharply in recent years—largely reflecting higher prices—to reach 55 percent of GDP in mid-2001. However, two-thirds of market capitalization is nontradable, and equity issuance is dominated by SOEs.

[7]Cull and Xu (2000) find that the shift of SOE financing from government transfers to bank credit increased the SOEs' productivity (at least in the 1980s).

Table 4.1. Indicators of Financial Development in Selected Countries and Country Groups, 1993–2000

(In percent)[1]

Ratio	China	India	Rep. of Korea	Japan	United States	Country Income Group High income	Middle income	Low income
Private sector credit to GDP	40.0	24.1	112.5	65.1	76.7	121.8	41.1	59.6
Domestic assets of deposit money banks to total domestic assets	80.0	77.3	93.5	87.9	90.2	. . .	. . .	. . .
M2 to GDP	121.7	47.5	113.3	48.0	59.1	. . .	39.3	73.5
Stock market capitalization to GDP	14.1	32.4	32.7	67.8	112.6	81.4	35.4	20.5
Memoranda:								
Annual growth in real GDP per capita	8.9	4.8	3.5	0.8	2.5	1.7	1.0	5.2
Ratio of FDI to GDP	4.8	0.5	0.6	0.1	1.4	1.1	1.8	3.1

Sources: *World Economic Outlook* and *International Financial Statistics* databases; World Bank, *World Development Indicators,* various years.
[1]Period averages.

1990s in the real estate and manufacturing sectors, which have contributed to over two years of deflation, and the weak performance of the banks themselves. Burdened by portfolios dominated by directed credit, the state banks have been weakly profitable. Substantial nonperforming loans remain in the banking system,[8] and capital adequacy needs considerable strengthening to meet international standards.

- *Despite its lack of access to domestic bank credit, China's nonstate sector has been the most dynamic part of the economy.* Thus the International Finance Corporation (IFC; Gregory, Tenev, and Wagle, 2000) estimates that, between 1990 and 1997, new jobs created in the private sector accounted for 56 percent of new formal employment in urban areas. This rapid growth has occurred despite relatively few resources coming from the financial sector: in 1991–97 the share of private investment in national investment was in the range of 15–27 percent, because private investors had little recourse to formal bank loans (less than 1 percent of working capital loans went to the private sector, according to the IFC report). In addition, private firms' access to equity markets has been lim-

---

[8]Despite the transfer of a substantial portion (Y 1.4 trillion) of nonperforming loans to the asset management companies, the average ratio of nonperforming loans to total lending is officially estimated at 25 percent. Market estimates are substantially higher.

Table 4.2. Allocation of State Bank Credit
(In percent of GDP)

State bank claims	1993	1994	1995	1996	1997	1998	1999	2000
On nongovernment sector	97.5	89.5	88.3	94.0	102.9	112.2	121.8	124.6
of which:								
On non-SOE sector	35.7	32.6	31.8	35.4	37.4	41.2	48.8	57.0
On SOE sector	61.8	56.9	56.5	58.6	65.5	71.0	73.0	67.6

Sources: *International Financial Statistics,* various issues; People's Bank of China data; and IMF staff estimates.

ited. The same IFC volume reports that, of the 976 companies listed on the Shanghai and Shenzhen stock exchanges, only 11 are nonstate firms, and that in 1998 and 1999 only four initial public offerings of shares in nonstate firms took place. Based on evidence from a sample survey, the IFC finds that private firms in China tend to rely primarily on internal sources of financing—including retained earnings and principal-owner financing—for both start-up capital and subsequent investments.

Evidence from Provincial Data

In contrast to most other empirical analyses of this genre, which have been carried out in a cross-country setting, this chapter uses data from China's provinces, for several reasons:

- Differences in the level of economic and financial development among the provinces contain information that can be exploited.
- China's large population and limited labor and capital mobility between provinces make the study similar to a cross-country study of medium-size countries.
- Compared with cross-country studies, use of provincial data increases the likelihood of homogeneous data compilation methodologies.
- The use of provincial-level data expands the sample size considerably.

Although provincial-level data on "national" accounts are available for a relatively long period, information on financial variables in the provinces is more limited. As a result, much of the analysis is conducted for 1988–97, a period for which consistent data covering 27 provinces (listed in Table 4.3) are available.[9] Apart from the short time span, other shortcomings in the available information exist and are discussed below.

---

[9]The provincial data set used in this chapter was first compiled by Zhao (1998) and later updated by Dayal-Gulati and Husain (2000) and Chapter 3, this volume.

Table 4.3. Summary Financial and SOE Data by Province, 1988–97

(In percent)[1]

Province	Growth in GDP Per Capita	Ratio of Bank Loans to GDP	Ratio of Banking Sector to GDP	SOE Share of Industrial Output	Ratio of FDI to GDP	Ratio of SOE Operating Surplus to GDP
All China	8.2	70.5	6.0	43.4	3.3	22.6
Fujian	14.0	53.5	5.8	32.0	9.5	21.4
Guangdong	13.4	72.1	7.3	29.6	10.6	20.0
Zhejiang	12.6	45.3	4.4	21.2	1.8	27.8
Jiangsu	12.3	50.7	4.9	26.7	4.2	27.0
Shandong	11.7	51.0	5.8	34.2	2.6	25.4
Hebei	10.9	61.9	6.3	40.1	1.1	27.4
Shanghai	10.2	99.8	9.5	50.3	6.9	34.4
Guangxi	10.1	60.7	4.6	55.4	2.5	17.0
Jiangxi	10.0	77.2	6.6	55.1	1.2	20.1
Anhui	9.7	59.2	4.2	42.8	1.0	17.7
Henan	9.4	61.7	4.8	43.9	0.8	15.2
Hubei	9.2	77.8	4.2	50.9	1.3	22.4
Beijing	9.0	108.2	10.3	56.0	5.2	30.6
Tianjin	8.8	113.0	8.4	40.8	7.1	33.2
Yunnan	8.5	61.8	5.5	70.4	0.4	19.2
Sichuan	8.4	58.3	5.3	51.4	1.7	19.5
Jilin	8.2	111.1	6.2	65.8	1.4	17.9
Hunan	8.2	57.5	4.4	50.6	1.2	15.7
Inner Mongolia	7.8	83.9	5.5	66.6	0.4	21.8
Gansu	7.7	89.3	5.4	71.7	0.5	21.2
Xinjiang	7.7	86.8	5.4	77.9	0.3	23.0
Shanxi	7.6	83.9	7.8	51.0	0.5	22.8
Shaanxi	7.5	91.2	7.6	63.0	1.7	16.0
Liaoning	7.5	82.0	6.4	50.4	2.9	30.1
Heilongjiang	7.1	84.1	5.6	72.6	1.1	22.8
Ningxia	6.9	107.6	8.9	73.0	0.3	22.3
Guizhou	6.2	72.6	4.5	71.0	0.5	13.8
Qinghai	5.2	115.9	7.0	82.1	0.1	17.1

Sources: National Bureau of Statistics (1996); *China Statistical Yearbook*, various issues.
[1]Value added less depreciation, wages, and taxes.

Overall, the results suggest that the level of financial development has not played a key role in contributing to growth within China. Rather, bank loans appear to have been channeled to provinces with heavy concentrations of SOEs, which are also the provinces that have tended to grow relatively slowly, suggesting that the productivity of lending was relatively low. This picture appears to corroborate an often-told story about China's transition from plan to market: although things are changing with ongoing SOE and banking reforms, the banking system has been used to keep inefficient SOEs afloat so as not to produce excessive layoffs and raise the cost of the transition to levels that might threaten social stability.

Figure 4.1. Financial Intermediation and Growth
(In percent)[1]

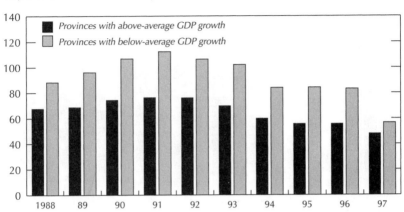

Sources: National Bureau of Statistics; Lardy (1998); *Almanac of China's Finance and Banking,* various issues; and IMF staff estimates.
[1]Financial intermediation is measured on the vertical axis as the ratio of bank loans to provincial GDP.

Preliminary Analysis

To get a sense of the role played by financial development in China's growth, provinces were grouped according to certain economic characteristics, and dummy variables were constructed for each group. Three groupings were made, as follows: provinces with above-average and those with below-average growth, those with above- and below-average levels of financial intermediation (as measured by the bank loans-to-GDP ratio), and those with above-average and below-average levels of SOE concentration. For the first grouping, the level of financial intermediation in the high-growth group was compared with that in the low-growth group, and similar exercises were conducted for the other groupings. This exercise produced the results presented in Figures 4.1 to 4.4 and summarized below:

- Those provinces with above-average GDP growth had bank loans-to-GDP ratios that were significantly lower—by up to 36 percent of GDP—than provinces with below-average growth (Figure 4.1).[10]

---

[10]Whether the large drop in the difference in 1997 is an anomaly is difficult to ascertain without an extension of the data base beyond 1997.

Figure 4.2. Growth and Financial Intermediation
(In percent)[1]

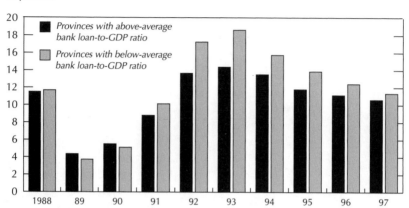

Sources: National Bureau of Statistics; Lardy (1998); *Almanac of China's Finance and Banking*, various issues; and IMF staff estimates.
[1]Growth is measured on the vertical axis as the growth rate of provincial GDP per capita.

- Correspondingly, provinces with above-average levels of financial intermediation experienced lower annual growth rates (by up to 4¼ percentage points) than provinces with below-average levels of intermediation (Figure 4.2).
- Provinces with above-average concentrations of SOEs had higher loan-to-GDP ratios than those with below-average concentrations (Figure 4.3).
- Provinces with above-average growth rates had relatively larger profit-to-GDP ratios, suggesting that firms in these provinces financed themselves out of retained earnings rather than with bank loans (assuming profits are a good proxy for corporate saving; Figure 4.4). Moreover, as discussed in the next section, firms in fast-growing provinces were able to avail themselves of foreign savings through FDI.

Regression Analysis

The methodology adopted in this section closely follows that established in previous studies. A series of fixed-effects panel regressions are estimated, with various combinations of control variables, to draw inferences about the role played by bank intermediation in growth, resource mobilization, and productivity. The general form of the panel regression equations is the following:

Figure 4.3. Financial Intermediation and SOE Concentration
(In percent)[1]

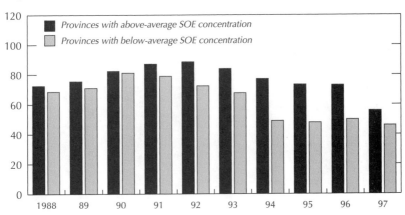

Sources: National Bureau of Statistics; Lardy (1998); *Almanac of China's Finance and Banking,* various issues; and IMF staff estimates.

[1]Financial intermediation is measured on the vertical axis as the ratio of bank loans to provincial GDP.

$$y_{it} = \alpha_i + \beta X_{it} + \gamma F_{it} + \delta K_{it} + \varepsilon_t,$$

where y is the dependent variable (growth, investment, or productivity), X is the standard set of neoclassical growth factors (lagged real GDP per capita, population growth, and investment), F is the financial intermediation variable of interest (total bank loans, bank loans to SOEs, or bank loans to the nonstate sector), and K is a set of other control variables (such as the fiscal surplus, the share of SOEs in industrial output, a dummy variable for coastal provinces, and FDI). Subscript i indicates a province and subscript t the time period.

This equation follows the practice elsewhere in the literature of supplementing a standard growth regression with variables measuring the level of financial development. The expectation is that the coefficient on the financial development variable is positive and statistically significant.

The following results pertaining to growth emerge from this exercise:

- *The expansion of bank credit during 1988–97 did not exert a statistically significant influence on growth.* This can be seen from regression equation (5) in Table 4.4, where, although the ratio of total bank loans to GDP has a marginally positive sign, it is not significant. This result formally confirms the preliminary analysis (Figure 4.1), which indicated that bank credit in the faster-growing

Figure 4.4. Profitability and Growth
(In percent)[1]

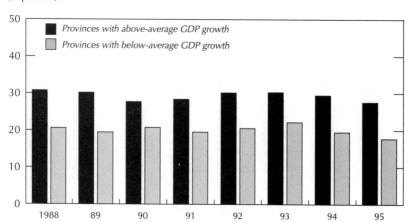

Sources: National Bureau of Statistics; and IMF staff estimates.
[1]Profitability is measured on the vertical axis as the ratio of profits to provincial GDP.

provinces was lower than that in the slower-growing provinces. In that discussion it was also pointed out that the likely reason behind this phenomenon was the large proportion of bank credit provided to the SOE sector, which was relatively less productive than the nonstate sector. This hypothesis is also confirmed.

- *Bank credit to the nonstate sector, however, exerts a positive and statistically significant influence on growth.* This result is borne out by equation (6), where the coefficient on bank loans to the nonstate sector—although small, possibly because it is a constructed variable—is significant at the 1 percent level. The small coefficient, however, could also reflect the limited importance of this source of financing for China's fast-growing nonstate sector enterprises.[11]

- *Apart from the financial sector results, the exercise also shows that FDI has played a significant role in China's growth process.*[12] Equations (4) through (6) display a remarkable consistency in the growth elasticity of FDI: regardless of the control variables used, a 1-percentage-point increase in the FDI-to-GDP ratio raises the per capita

[11]Since the nonstate credit variable was constructed by regressing total bank loans on the share of SOEs in industrial output, the latter variable is dropped from this regression to avoid multicollinearity.

[12]This finding is consistent with the results in Chapter 6, which provides a detailed analysis of the impact of FDI on GDP and total factor productivity growth.

Table 4.4. Results of Regressions of Output Growth on Financial Intermediation Measures

Variable[1]	(1)	(2)	(3)	(4)	(5)	(6)
Lagged real GDP per capita	1.29	1.57	−3.73***	−5.27***	−5.48***	−5.31***
Population growth (percent)	−1.46**	−1.45**	−1.44***	−1.42***	−1.41***	−1.42***
Ratio of total investment to GDP	0.28**	0.25**	0.25***			
Ratio of domestic investment to GDP				0.21***	0.21***	0.21***
Ratio of FDI to GDP				0.56***	0.57***	0.56***
Ratio of government revenue to expenditure				0.02***	0.03**	0.02**	0.03**
Share of SOEs in industrial output				−0.19***	−0.18***	−0.2***
Coastal dummy variable		−1.56			
Ratio of bank loans to GDP					0.03	
Ratio of bank loans to nonstate sector to GDP						0.002***
Summary statistics						
Adjusted R^2	0.43	0.41	0.49	0.50	0.50	0.51
P value of Hausman test[2]	0.00	0.00	0.00	0.00	0.05	0.01
No. of observations	280	277	277	277	277	277

Source: IMF staff estimates based on data from *China Statistical Yearbook*, various issues.
[1]The dependent variable is the growth rate of real GDP per capita; regressions are fixed-effects panel regressions on data from 1988 to 1997.
[2]Null hypothesis: random versus fixed effects.
***Indicates statistical significance at the 1 percent level.
**Indicates statistical significance at the 5 percent level.

growth rate by about ½ percentage point. This again corroborates the widely held view that FDI has been a critical source of financing for China's growth.[13]

Several previous studies have also pointed out that financial intermediation helps growth in two ways: by facilitating resource mobilization, and by helping to improve resource allocation, thereby enhancing total factor productivity (mostly of capital). To test this hypothesis, these studies measure the impact of financial intermediation separately on growth, investment, and productivity. Measures of productivity by province are not readily available for China, however. Following the literature, total factor productivity growth is therefore proxied as actual

---

[13]The results from the exercise also confirm the findings in Chapter 3 that incomes per capita are converging across China's provinces not in the absolute sense but only in the conditional sense. For details, see Dayal-Gulati and Husain (2000), who studied convergence using average cross-provincial regressions, and Chapter 3, this volume, which used nonparametric estimators.

Table 4.5. Results of Regressions of Investment on Financial Intermediation Measures

Variable[1]	Equation				
	(1)	(2)	(3)	(4)	(5)
Lagged growth of real GDP per capita	0.26***	0.27***	0.318**	0.24***	0.25***
Ratio of bank loans to nonstate sector to GDP	0.001	0.001	0.001	0.001	0.02
Ratio of government revenue to expenditure		−0.01	−0.02	−0.01	−0.01
Ratio of FDI to GDP			−0.398**	−0.3***	−0.27*
Ratio of lagged domestic investment to GDP				0.35***	0.34***
Share of SOEs in industrial output					1.95
Summary statistics					
Adjusted R^2	0.79	0.79	0.82	0.83	0.83
P value of Hausman test[2]	0.05	0.23	0.27	0.00	0.00
Number of observations	252	249	249	249	249

Source: IMF staff estimates based on data from *China Statistical Yearbook,* various issues.
[1]The dependent variable is the ratio of domestic investment to GDP; regressions are fixed-effects panel regressions on data from 1988 to 1997.
[2]Null hypothesis: random versus fixed effects.
***Indicates statistical significance at the 1 percent level.
**Indicates statistical significance at the 5 percent level.

growth less the fraction α of capital growth (net investment), under the assumption that about one-third of national income accrues to capital.

The level of financial development did not have a statistically significant impact on domestic investment (Table 4.5). In many developing countries the deepening of financial development generally raises the rate of investment by lowering the cost of matching the savings of households with the investment needs of the corporate sector. This does not appear to have occurred in China. Neither total bank credit nor nonstate bank credit exerted a significant influence on the rate of domestic investment.

On the other hand, nonstate bank credit appears to have exerted a positive and significant influence on productivity (Table 4.6). Thus the deepening of financial intermediation in China seems to have aided growth by allowing savings to be allocated more efficiently rather than simply making more savings available for investment purposes.

Data Issues

As noted above, regression analysis of the growth-financial development link is complicated by the paucity of data on financial variables. In particular, data on private credit, an indicator of financial development used extensively in the literature, are not available. At the provincial

Table 4.6. Results of Regressions of Productivity on Financial Intermediation Measures

Variable[1]	Equation				
	(1)	(2)	(3)	(4)	(5)
Lagged real GDP per capita	1.71	–3.73***	–5.28***	–5.49***	–5.32***
Population growth (percent)	–1.45***	–1.43***	–1.42***	–1.42***	–1.42***
Ratio of total investment to GDP	–0.05	–0.05			
Ratio of domestic investment to GDP			–0.09**	–0.09**	–0.09**
Ratio of FDI to GDP			0.26***	0.27***	0.26***
Ratio of government revenue to expenditure		0.028*	0.03**	0.02**	0.03**
Share of SOEs in industrial output		–0.19***	–0.18***	–0.2***	
Ratio of total bank loans to GDP				0.03	
Ratio of bank loans to nonstate sector to GDP					0.002***
Summary statistics					
Adjusted R^2	0.50	0.55	0.56	0.56	0.55
P value of Hausman test[2]	0.00	0.00	0.01	0.01	0.01
Number of observations	280	277	277	277	277

Source: IMF staff estimates based on data from *China Statistical Yearbook,* various issues.
[1]The dependent variable is total factor productivity; regressions are fixed-effects panel regressions on data from 1988 to 1997.
[2]Null hypothesis: random versus fixed effects.
***Indicates statistical significance at the 1 percent level.
**Indicates statistical significance at the 5 percent level.

level, only data on aggregate bank lending are available on a consistent basis. However, a significant portion of bank lending in China has gone to SOEs, so that using total bank lending as a proxy for nonstate sector credit is not appropriate. To circumvent this difficulty, a proxy for non-state sector credit was used in the empirical analyses in this chapter.

The proxy is constructed using the share of credit to SOEs predicted by a province's share of SOE value added in GDP. Formally, a fixed-effects panel regression of the total bank lending-to-GDP ratio on the share of SOEs in industrial output is estimated, with the error term following a first-order autoregressive process to correct for serial correlation. Loans to the nonstate sector are then proxied by discounting from total bank lending the proportion explained by the share of SOEs in industrial output in the estimated equation.

Conclusions

Contrary to the findings of most previous studies for large cross sections of countries, the results of this chapter suggest that financial development, as proxied by total bank lending, has not significantly boosted growth among China's provinces. This finding probably reflects the large proportion of lending channeled to the SOE sector. Nonstate credit, on the other hand, has had a statistically significant, although small, effect on growth.

This chapter also finds that nonbank sources of finance have played a significant role in financing China's growth. In particular, FDI was shown to have a large impact on provinces' income per capita: the coefficient on the FDI variable displayed remarkable robustness in the face of changing model specifications.

Anecdotal and survey evidence suggests that the internal savings of enterprises have played an important role in financing growth in China. However, this conclusion could not be corroborated empirically, reflecting the lack of consistent data on corporate savings in China's provinces.

The main implication for China's financial sector reform agenda is the importance of channeling a higher proportion of savings to the nonstate sector. This will allow China's financial sector to act as an efficient intermediary between savers and borrowers, and thus strengthen the positive link between financial development and growth. Some related conclusions can also be drawn:

- *It will be crucial to raise the efficiency of bank lending through the adoption of market-based lending principles.* The commercialization of banking, in turn, will require the establishment of an appropriate legal framework to protect creditor rights, as well as the gradual liberalization of interest rates.
- *The nonstate sector's access to equity and debt financing should be enhanced.* Again, strengthening the legal framework (bankruptcy and company laws, protection of shareholder rights) as well as the application of internationally accepted accounting rules and governance codes will be important in giving firms the incentives to finance themselves through the securities markets, and investors the incentives to participate in this process. Such enhancements to the investment environment would also promote a continued strong inflow of FDI.

References

Cull, Robert, and L.C. Xu, 2000, "Bureaucrats, State Banks, and the Efficiency of Credit Allocation: The Experience of Chinese State-Owned Enterprises," *Journal of Comparative Economics*, Vol. 28, No. 1, pp. 1–31.

Dayal-Gulati, Anuradha, and Aasim M. Husain, 2000, "Centripetal Forces in China's Economic Take-off," IMF Working Paper 00/86 (Washington: International Monetary Fund).

Goldsmith, Raymond W., 1969, *Financial Structure and Development* (New Haven, Connecticut: Yale University Press).

Gregory, Neil, Stoyan Tenev, and Dileep Wagle, 2000, *China's Emerging Private Enterprises—Prospects for the New Century* (Washington: International Finance Corporation).

Khan, Mohsin S., and Abdelhak S. Senhadji, 2000, "Financial Development and Economic Growth: An Overview," IMF Working Paper 00/209 (Washington: International Monetary Fund).

King, Robert G., and Ross Levine, 1993, "Finance and Growth: Schumpeter Might Be Right," *Quarterly Journal of Economics*, Vol. 108, No. 3 (August), pp. 717–37.

Lardy, Nicholas R., 1998, *China's Unfinished Economic Revolution* (Washington: Brookings Institution).

———, 2000, "When Will China's Financial System Meet China's Needs?" paper presented at the Conference on Policy Reform in China, Center for Research on Economic Development and Policy Reform, Stanford University, November 18–20, 1999.

Levine, Ross, 1997, "Financial Development and Economic Growth: Views and Agenda," *Journal of Economic Literature*, Vol. 35, No. 2, pp. 688–726.

———, 1999, "Financial Development and Growth: Where Do We Stand," *Estudios de Economia*, Vol. 26, No. 2, pp. 113–36.

McKinnon, Ronald I., 1973, *Money and Capital in Economic Development* (Washington: Brookings Institution).

National Bureau of Statistics, 1996, *The Gross Domestic Product of China, 1992–95* (Beijing: China Statistical Publishing House).

Pagano, Marco, 1993, "Financial Markets and Growth—An Overview," *European Economic Review*, Vol. 37, No. 2-3, pp. 613–22.

Schumpeter, Joseph A., 1911, *The Theory of Economic Development: An Inquiry into Profits, Capital, Credit, Interest and the Business Cycle*, tr. by Redvers Opie, 1934 (Cambridge, Massachusetts: Harvard University Press).

Shaw, Edward S., 1973, *Financial Deepening in Economic Development* (New York: Oxford University Press).

Zhao, Rui, 1998, "Capital Mobility and Regional Integration: China 1978–95" (unpublished; Washington: International Monetary Fund).

5

Foreign Direct Investment in China: Some Lessons for Other Countries

WANDA TSENG AND HARM ZEBREGS

A driving force behind China's exceptional growth performance has been the increasing openness of its economy, especially to trade and foreign direct investment (FDI). Indeed, attracting FDI has been a pillar of China's policies to increase its openness to the world economy, and it has resulted in China becoming the largest recipient of FDI among developing countries.

This chapter looks into several questions posed by China's success in attracting FDI. What explains that success? Can other countries replicate it, or is it unique to China? Has China benefited from the large inflow of FDI? And what lessons can China's experience with FDI offer for other countries?

Key Trends and Characteristics

FDI inflows to China have surged from almost nil at the start of reform in the late 1970s to between $40 billion and $45 billion a year (nearly 5 percent of GDP) in the second half of the 1990s (Table 5.1; Figure 5.1). The surge occurred in the early 1990s, following Deng Xiaoping's tour of the southern coastal areas, where he reaffirmed China's continued commitment to reforms and to opening the economy to the outside world. His tour ushered in an era of renewed confidence and entrepreneurship. Although FDI inflows declined slightly during the Asian financial crisis, they picked up again in 2000, partly in antic-

68

Table 5.1. Alternative Measures of FDI Inflows

Measure[1]	1984–89	1990–99	1990–94	1995–99
Billions of dollars	2.3	28.3	16.1	40.6
Percent of GDP	0.7	4.4	3.7	4.7
Percent of total FDI flows to developing countries	12.7	24.3	27.1	25.3
Memorandum: Growth in GDP (percent a year)	9.7	10.1	12.2	8.3

Sources: IMF, *Balance of Payments Statistics Yearbook* and *International Financial Statistics,* various issues; *China Statistical Yearbook.*
[1]Period averages.

ipation of China's accession to the World Trade Organization (WTO). By the 1990s China had become the second-largest FDI recipient in the world, after the United States, and by far the largest recipient among developing countries, accounting for about 25–30 percent of FDI flows to all developing countries.

However, part of China's success in attracting FDI may be exaggerated because of misreporting and round-tripping. The latter refers to capital originating in China that is sent to other economies and then returns disguised as FDI to take advantage of tax, tariff, and other benefits accorded to foreign but not domestic investment. The extent of this round-tripping is difficult to assess; estimates range from 7 percent

Figure 5.1. FDI Inflows
(In billions of dollars)

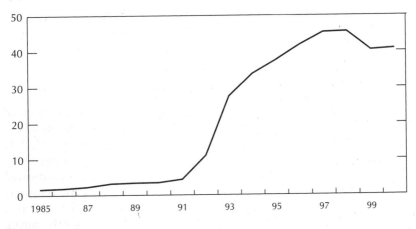

Source: *China Statistical Yearbook,* various issues.

Table 5.2. Sources of FDI
(In percent of total)

Source Economy	1991	1995	1999
Hong Kong SAR	55.3	53.4	41.0
Japan	13.1	8.5	7.2
Taiwan Province of China	10.1	8.4	6.5
United States	7.1	8.2	9.9
European Union	5.7	5.7	11.0
Singapore	1.2	4.9	6.2
Republic of Korea	0.0	2.8	3.0
Other	7.5	8.2	15.1

Source: *China Statistical Yearbook,* various years.

of inflows in 1996 to almost 25 percent in 1992.[1] Some FDI is actually better characterized as foreign borrowing, because the inflows in question (mainly for infrastructure) were guaranteed a specified rate of return. Misreporting may also be a problem, because local officials have an incentive to exaggerate their ability to attract FDI, and foreign investors have an incentive to overstate their actual investment in order to report lower taxable income.

Hong Kong SAR and Taiwan Province of China have traditionally been important sources of FDI in China (Table 5.2). Their importance diminished somewhat in the 1990s as multinationals from Europe, Japan, and the United States entered China, but these two economies still account for almost half of FDI inflows.

The largest share of FDI is destined for manufacturing, which took up almost 60 percent of total contracted FDI in 1998 (Figure 5.2). Next is real estate at 24 percent, followed by distribution (transport, wholesale, and retailing) at 6 percent. Among manufacturing industries, about half of FDI has been directed toward labor-intensive products such as textiles and clothing, food processing, and furniture. Technology-intensive manufacturing (for example, medical goods and pharmaceuticals, electrical machinery and equipment, and electronics) and physical capital–intensive manufacturing (for example, petroleum refining and chemical materials) share almost equally in the remainder. This suggests that an important motivation for foreign companies has been to take advantage of China's low labor costs.

The geographic pattern of FDI in China shows a huge disparity among regions. The eastern region accounts for 64 percent of GDP but took up nearly 88 percent of FDI entering China from 1983 to 1998,

---

[1]Harrold and Lall (1993); Lardy (1995); Wei (1998).

Figure 5.2. FDI Inflows by Sector, 1998
(In percent of contracted value)

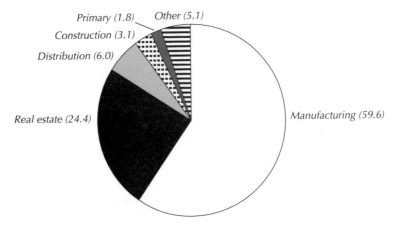

Primary (1.8)   Other (5.1)
Construction (3.1)
Distribution (6.0)

Real estate (24.4)

Manufacturing (59.6)

Source: OECD (2000).

while the central region (with 29 percent of GDP) took up 9 percent and the western region (with 23 percent of GDP) attracted only 3 percent (Figure 5.3). This pattern stems from the FDI policies pursued by the Chinese authorities and reflects the incremental nature of the reform process in China. Much of the early reforms consisted of experi-

Figure 5.3. FDI Inflows by Region, 1983–98
(In percent of total)

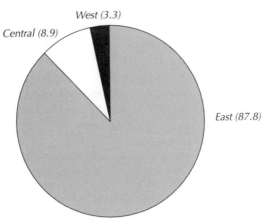

West (3.3)
Central (8.9)

East (87.8)

Source: OECD (2000).

ments in selected regions and sectors; this allowed the authorities to assess the results of these experiments before extending them to other parts of the country. The "open door" policy started with the creation of the special economic zones (SEZs; see below) in the southern provinces of Guangdong and Fujian at the outset of the reforms in the late 1970s, followed by the opening of another SEZ in Hainan and the designation of 14 cities in China's coastal regions as "open coastal cities" in the 1980s. This has resulted in an overwhelming concentration of FDI in the eastern part of the country. When the authorities adopted more broadly based economic reforms and open-door policies for FDI in the 1990s, FDI started to spread to other provinces.

Equity joint venture companies, cooperative joint venture companies, and wholly foreign-owned enterprises have been the main forms of FDI entering China.[2] Early in the reform period, China allowed FDI only in the form of joint ventures (except in the SEZs), for ideological reasons and because the authorities thought this form was better suited to tapping advanced foreign technology. It was not until 1986 that wholly foreign-owned enterprises were permitted outside the SEZs. Accordingly, equity and cooperative joint ventures accounted for the lion's share of FDI in 1990 (Figure 5.4). Recent trends, however, show that FDI is increasingly directed into wholly foreign-owned enterprises, which accounted for more than half of total commitments in 1999.

At the start of the reform process in 1978, China was not evidently better placed to attract large amounts of FDI than, for example, India, which at the time shared a number of characteristics with China. Both countries had relatively closed economies, with low average incomes and a large share of the population dependent on agriculture. Neither China nor India was then receiving significant amounts of FDI. This picture has since changed dramatically. India remains a fairly closed economy while China has become more integrated into the global economy. And as India's GDP per capita more than doubled between 1978 and 2000, China's GDP per capita quadrupled (in constant dollar terms).

China's increasing openness to the outside world can be seen in the rapid growth of its foreign trade. Exports and imports as a share of GDP rose from negligible amounts to about 25 percent in 2000. The average

---

[2]Under an equity joint venture, Chinese and foreign investors operate the venture and share the risks, profits, and losses jointly. All the parties agree on the equity share of each party, and profits are distributed in proportion to these shares. In a cooperative joint venture, the Chinese partner provides land, natural resources, labor, and equipment or facilities, while the foreign partner provides capital or technology, key equipment, and materials. Both parties decide on the proportions in which products, revenue, and profits will be distributed.

Figure 5.4. FDI by Type of Ownership Arrangement
(In percent of total contracted value)

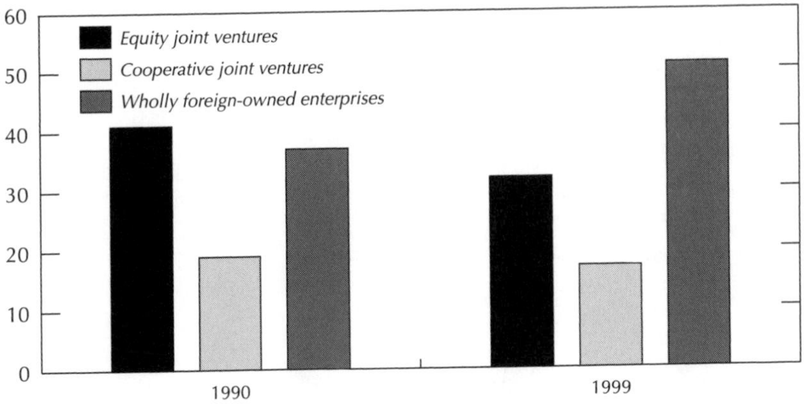

Source: OECD (2000).

tariff rate in China fell from well over 50 percent in the early 1980s to about 15 percent now, less than half that in India. Equally important, because China exempts so many goods entirely from import duties, and because a significant share of imports of goods subject to high tariffs are imported illegally, actual tariff collection as a percentage of total import value has been much lower. The effective tariff rate—that is, tariff revenue as a percentage of total imports—is only 3 percent in China, compared with 23 percent in India (Table 5.3). As a percent of GDP, net FDI inflows into China in 2000 were more than seven times those in India.

Main Determinants

Studies of FDI in China have shown that the determinants of FDI in China are not unique to China but have also been important in attracting FDI to other emerging market economies.[3] Two types of FDI flows can be considered: domestic market-oriented flows and export-oriented flows. Domestic market-oriented FDI is motivated mostly by the size and growth rate of the host country. Export-oriented FDI mainly looks for cost competitiveness. The factors that have been most important in influencing FDI in China can be grouped into three categories: eco-

---

[3]Cheng and Kwan (2000); Liu and others (1997).

Table 5.3. China and India: Selected Openness Indicators
(In percent)

Indicator	China	India
Share of world trade flows, 2000	3.7	0.7
Goods and services exports as share of GDP, 2000	25.9	13.1
Goods and services imports as fraction of GDP, 2000	23.2	16.0
Average tariff rate (years as indicated)	15.3[1]	32.9[2]
Effective tariff rate, 1998[3]	2.8	23.0
Tariff revenue as percent of total revenue, 1998	6.3	20.1
Net inward FDI flows as fraction of GDP, 2000	3.6	0.5

Sources: IMF, *Government Finance Statistics,* various issues; *International Financial Statistics,* various issues; and IMF staff estimates.

[1] In 2001.
[2] In 1999.
[3] Tariff revenue divided by the value of all imports.

nomic structure, liberalization and preferential policies, and cultural and legal environment.

Economic Structure

Market Size

Empirical studies at both the national and the provincial level have found a strong correlation between GDP and FDI inflows in China.[4] The causality between the two variables runs in both directions: FDI has been attracted by the enormous market potential that China has to offer, and has at the same time contributed to GDP growth through various channels (discussed below).[5] It appears that market size has been a more important determinant of FDI from Europe and the United States than of FDI from Hong Kong SAR and Taiwan Province of China, as the latter tends be more export oriented. In contrast, many European and American multinationals have set up factories in China with the aim of producing for the domestic market.

Abundant Supply of Cheap Labor

Although the empirical evidence is somewhat mixed, low wage costs appear to have played a significant role in attracting FDI to China and in the distribution of FDI flows across provinces.[6] Some analysts have

---

[4] Cheng and Kwan (2000); Liu and others (1997); Zhang (1999). See also Chapter 6 of this volume.

[5] Zhang (1999). See also Chapter 6 of this volume.

[6] Chen (1996); Cheng and Kwan (2000); Head and Ries (1996); Liu and others (1997).

Table 5.4. Infrastructure Indicators

Indicator	1990	1998
Electric power		
Consumption (in kwh per capita)	471	746
Transmission and distribution losses (in percent)	7.5	7.1
Transportation		
Air freight transported (in millions of ton-km)	818	3,345
Goods transported by road (in billions of ton-km)	336	548
Telecommunications		
Telephone mainlines per 1,000 population	5.9	69.6
Mobile phones per 1,000 population	0.02	19.0
Average cost of 3-minute telephone call to U.S. (dollars)	. . .	6.7
Average cost of 3-minute local call (dollars)	. . .	0.01
Internet hosts per 10,000 population	0.0	0.2

Source: World Bank, *World Development Indicators.*

suggested that low wage costs have been especially important in attracting export-oriented FDI from Hong Kong SAR and Taiwan Province of China, as a response to rising wage costs in those economies and others in the region. This has contributed to China's rapid emergence as an important global competitor in labor-intensive manufacturing. Although most empirical studies have not found the quality of labor to be a significant determinant of FDI in China—indeed, the shortage of highly qualified personnel is a problem often noted by foreign investors—this will likely change in the future as China's comparative advantage evolves toward higher-value-added manufacturing.

Infrastructure

Empirical studies confirm that those provinces with more developed infrastructure have tended to receive more FDI.[7] This partly explains the concentration of FDI in the eastern coastal areas with their superior infrastructure and transport links to external markets. The devolution of investment decisions to local governments, particularly in the open economic zones (OEZs),[8] allowed them to upgrade their infrastructure in an effort to attract FDI (Table 5.4). Of the increase in fixed-asset investment from the late 1980s to the late 1990s, which amounted to

---

[7]Cheng and Kwan (2000); Head and Ries (1996).

[8]Open economic zones include SEZs, the open coastal cities, and various development zones. For a taxonomy of the different types of zones see Box 5.2 and Wall, Jiang, and Yin (1996).

6½ percent of GDP, local governments accounted for about 3 percentage points; these were mainly in infrastructure, particularly electricity, gas, water, transport, and posts and telecommunications.

Scale Effects

Several studies have found a strong persistency in FDI flows.[9] This is the case not only for total FDI flows to China, but also for FDI flows to China's provinces. This suggests that once a province has attracted a critical mass of FDI, it finds it easier to attract more, as foreign investors perceive the presence of other foreign investors as a positive signal. In addition, economies of scale make it more efficient for foreign multinationals to locate in the same area, allowing them to share information and facilities, such as schools and health facilities, for expatriate workers. The coastal provinces, in particular the southern provinces of Guangdong and Fujian, which are close to Hong Kong SAR and Taiwan Province of China, have been the largest recipients of FDI and have acquired an important advantage over the inland provinces in attracting FDI over the past two decades.

Reduced Barriers and Preferential Policies

The reduction of barriers to FDI and policies to improve the investment environment have played a key role in attracting FDI to China. From the beginning of the reform process, the Chinese authorities considered attracting FDI an important goal, expecting that it would introduce new technologies, know-how, and capital and help to develop the export sector. However, they also recognized that it posed a risk to state control. In addition, the authorities had to overcome certain ideological obstacles to FDI that were rooted in the historical legacy of the Western powers' opening of Chinese port cities after the Opium War. This legacy had left a tendency to equate FDI with imperial colonialism and the exploitation of China by "Western capitalists." These factors affected the evolution of FDI policies in China. Initially, laws and regulations tended to be too restrictive, and many bureaucratic and legal problems were encountered. Over time, however, the authorities responded to the complaints of foreign investors, by clarifying the legal environment for FDI, relaxing governmental controls, and providing practical assistance as well as political and

---

[9]Cheng and Kwan (2000); Head and Ries (1996).

legal assurances (Box 5.1). What had begun as an experiment limited to a few localities and sectors at the outset of the reforms became accepted practice as more and more regions and economic sectors were opened to FDI by the 1990s.

The preferential policies used to attract FDI have been tax concessions and special privileges for foreign investors and the establishment of OEZs (Box 5.2). Tax incentives for foreign-funded enterprises (FFEs) are mostly in the form of reduced enterprise income tax rates and tax holidays (Box 5.3). These are available to all FFEs as well as domestic firms in the OEZs and to export-oriented and advanced-technology FFEs outside the OEZs. In addition, firms in the OEZs enjoy great autonomy in managing operations: they face minimal controls on the movements of goods and are allowed to export and import almost freely (Grub and Lin, 1991). These firms also benefit from more flexible labor relations and more liberal land use rights. Additional benefits are available for export-oriented and advanced-technology FFEs, including tax exemptions on profit remittances, additional tax benefits for reinvested profits, and larger reductions in land use fees.

OEZs have played a central role in the gradual opening of the economy to foreign investors. In the early reform period, one important difference between the OEZs and other areas in China was the administrative decentralization that permitted investment decisions in the OEZs to be made largely outside the state plan. Local authorities in the OEZs were allowed to attract foreign investors through preferential policies. They were also allowed to undertake their own infrastructure development and other investment as long as they could raise the funds from taxation, from profits of the enterprises they wholly or partly own, or from banks in the zones. Although the zones have provided favorable business conditions, a number of important constraints—such as restricted access to foreign exchange and domestic markets—remained in place in the early reform period. This largely limited the business scope of foreign enterprises to export-oriented activities. When these restrictions were eased in the second half of the 1980s, foreign investors gradually gained access to the domestic market, and, as a result, links with the domestic economy increased.

The international empirical evidence on the impact of preferential policies on FDI flows is mixed, and more work is needed to assess the impact in the case of China.[10] What is clear is that, in the context of the political economy of China's reform process, preferential policies

---

[10]See Chalk (2001).

Box 5.1. China's FDI Regime

FDI in China was heavily restricted before 1978. Since then the FDI regime has been liberalized gradually. A legal framework was progressively developed to facilitate and regulate FDI. China's accession to the WTO promises further liberalization of FDI.

Key Laws and Regulations

The legal framework for FDI has been progressively codified and clarified. The 1979 Law on Joint Ventures Using Chinese and Foreign Investment provided a basic framework for the establishment and operation of foreign economic entities. It specified a variety of incentives and terms for joint ventures. The 1983 Regulations for the Implementation of the Law on Joint Ventures Using Chinese and Foreign Investment provided greater detail on operations and preferential policies for joint ventures. The 1986 Law on Enterprises Operated Exclusively with Foreign Capital formally permitted the establishment of wholly foreign-owned enterprises outside the SEZs. The 1986 Notices for Further Improvements in the Conditions for the Operation of Foreign Invested Enterprises and Provisions of the State Council for Encouraging Foreign Investment provided further incentives, particularly for FDI using advanced technologies or producing for export. These provisions were subsequently codified in the 1988 Cooperative Joint Ventures Law. The 1990 Amendments to the Equity Joint Venture Law and Wholly Foreign-Owned Enterprise Implementing Rules provided a more complete legal structure to facilitate the operations of these enterprises. Notably, these rules abolished the stipulation that the chairman of the board of a joint venture be appointed by Chinese investors and provided for protection from nationalization.

Industrial Guidance

The Interim Provisions on Guiding Foreign Investment Direction (revised in 1997) classify four categories for FDI: encouraged, permitted, restricted, and prohibited. The regulations aim to encourage greater geographic dispersion of FDI inflows within China and to promote FDI inflows in targeted sectors and industries, such as export-oriented and high-technology industries, agriculture, and infrastructure.

---

provided a means for incremental experiments with economic reforms that was acceptable to the political leadership. Reforms were initially confined to certain localities and FFEs and gradually extended more broadly. In this environment the success of OEZs in China suggests that preferential policies were useful in catalyzing economic development and attracting FDI. In the absence of preferential policies, FDI would likely have been substantially less, given the restrictive environment in

In broad terms, projects are encouraged or at least permitted in designated industries that introduce new and advanced technologies, expand export capacity, raise product quality, and use local resources in the central and western regions. Restricted or prohibited are projects in designated sectors that make use of existing technologies, compete with domestic production or state monopolies, make extensive use of scarce resources, or are deemed to be a danger to national safety and the environment.

Sectoral Limits on FDI

Foreign participation in certain sectors and industries is limited. Regulations specify those industries where Chinese partners must play a leading role or have a majority share, and those where wholly foreign-owned enterprises are not permitted. These restricted industries include "strategically" important infrastructure projects, such as airports, nuclear power plants, oil and gas pipelines, subways and railways, and water projects, as well as projects in aerospace, automobiles, defense, high-technology vaccines, medical institutions, mining, petrochemicals, printing and publishing, shipping, satellite communications, and tourism (Foreign Investment Administration, 1998). About half of these industries are considered high-technology industries.

WTO Agreement on FDI

China has made substantial commitments to trade and investment liberalization as conditions for its accession to the WTO. General commitments include nondiscriminatory treatment of foreign and domestic enterprises, adherence to WTO rules on intellectual property rights, and elimination of various requirements on FDI, including foreign exchange and trade balancing, technology transfer, local content, and export performance. Sectoral commitments involve a significant expansion of market access, particularly in the services sector. These involve eliminating geographic and other restrictions in key sectors (such as motor vehicles) and increasing foreign ownership limits in telecommunications (to 50 percent by 2002), life insurance (to 50 percent on accession), distribution and retailing, and securities (to 49 percent by 2003), and giving full national treatment to foreign banks (by 2005).

which Chinese enterprises outside the OEZs had to operate. Thus it can be argued that preferential policies yielded a net gain to the economy by allowing reforms to take hold and by attracting FDI, which contributed to output growth. Over time, however, as the reform process advanced, preferential policies created distortions and inequities, and in particular a complex and biased tax system and regional income disparities, which now need to be addressed.

Box 5.2. Open Economic Zones in China

Since the beginning of China's economic reforms, a variety of open economic zones have emerged, which have offered a more liberal investment and trade regime than other areas, as well as special tax incentives. Although open to both domestic and foreign investors (indeed, most of the investment in the zones has come from domestic sources), these zones have played an important role in attracting FDI (IMF, 1997; Wall, Jiang, and Yin, 1996).

Special Economic Zones

SEZs were the first and, until 1984, only open economic zones in China. Four SEZs were established in 1980, three (Shenzhen, Shantou, and Zhuhai) in Guangdong Province near Hong Kong SAR, and one (Xiamen) in Fujian Province, close to Taiwan Province of China. In 1988 Hainan Province became the fifth SEZ.

SEZs have enjoyed considerable autonomy in their investment policies regarding both infrastructure projects (provided they can be financed locally) and investment approvals (for projects worth up to $30 million). They have offered preferential income tax treatment and exemptions from import licenses (for FFEs automatically, for domestic enterprises subject to approval) as well as tax and tariff concessions for raw materials and for intermediate and capital goods (concessions for the latter were rescinded in 1996). Within SEZs, sales of locally produced goods have been free from duties and taxes, and sales of imported goods have been subject to a reduced tariff, with full tariffs and duties applying to sales outside SEZs (except exports).

Open Coastal Cities

In 1984, 14 cities in the coastal regions with already established industrial bases and infrastructure were designated open coastal cities

---

Cultural and Legal Environment

Shared Cultural Background

It has often been argued that the unique phenomenon of a large Chinese diaspora has been key to China's success in attracting FDI. The fact that Hong Kong SAR, Singapore, and Taiwan Province of China together account for more than half of FDI inflows into China is usually used to support this argument. Although indeed few countries have such a large overseas ethnic community, it could be argued that the large share of nonresident Chinese in FDI flows into China is a reflection of distortions rather than a unique advantage. Cultural barriers, such as the language, that deter foreign investors from entering

(OCCs) and opened to foreign investment. Although not separate customs areas, and less independent than SEZs, OCCs have enjoyed greater flexibility in investment and tax policies than other regions in China. Several OCCs and the surrounding counties have created larger development areas, such as the Pearl River delta and the Yangtze delta (including Shanghai).

Economic and Technology Development Zones

Within the 14 OCCs, special areas were set aside for economic and technology development zones (ETDZs), offering tax incentives similar to those in SEZs. Further ETDZs in the Yangtze valley, as well as in border and inland cities, were subsequently approved by the State Council. The largest ETDZ, the Pudong New Area (Shanghai), opened in 1990.

High-Technology Development Zones

High-technology development zones (HTDZs) emerged in the early 1990s. Similar in most respects to ETDZs, HTDZs have placed particular emphasis on attracting investment in high-technology industries by providing additional tax concessions.

Free Trade Areas

The first two free trade areas (FTAs) were established in the early 1990s in Pudong and Shenzhen, and a number of others have been opened since then. Exports and imports can be traded freely within FTAs, and enterprises are free to engage in bonded entrepôt trade as well as export-oriented production.

China could be a sign that the investment climate is difficult for outsiders, which implies a cost, not an advantage.

Corruption and the Legal Environment

Two factors that have been found to be significant in explaining FDI to many countries are the degree of official corruption and the presence or absence of a strong legal environment.[11] In the case of China, many foreign investors perceive Chinese law as ambiguous, and legal disputes

---

[11]Wei (2000).

Figure 5.5. Transparency International Corruption Perceptions Index for Selected Countries, 2001
(Index, 10=least corrupt)

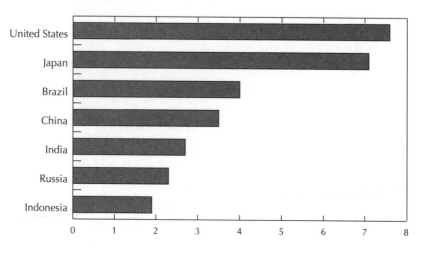

Source: Transparency International.

often are settled through personal contacts rather than formal contracts enforceable in the courts. The ambiguity in the law has, in turn, contributed to corruption. China scores relatively poorly on corruption and governance indicators in international comparisons (Figure 5.5). This situation has deterred foreign investment from Europe and the United States more than it has investment from Hong Kong SAR and Taiwan Province of China. Familiarity with the local culture helps in passing bureaucratic hurdles, and that is one reason why European and American investors have often sought local partners. One study found that China could attract more FDI from Europe and the United States were it not for the implicit tax imposed by bureaucratic hurdles.[12]

Impact of FDI

FDI flows to China have contributed to GDP growth in at least two ways (see Chapter 6):
- *Increased capital formation.* This effect is estimated to have contributed about 0.4 percentage point to annual GDP growth in the 1990s. The direct contribution of FDI to GDP growth has been

---

[12]Wei (1998).

highest in those provinces that have attracted the most foreign investment: it has ranged from almost 4 percentage points a year in Guangdong to negligible amounts in most inland provinces.

- *Higher total factor productivity (TFP)*. Empirical research suggests that FDI raised TFP growth in China by 2.5 percentage points a year during the 1990s. Again, this effect was found to be strongest in the provinces that have received the most FDI. Thus, in sum, FDI has contributed nearly 3 percentage points to potential GDP growth for China.

FDI has contributed to GDP growth both directly, through the establishment of FFEs, and indirectly, by creating positive spillover effects from FFEs to domestic enterprises. FFEs tend to be the most dynamic and productive firms in China's economy. Their output in the industrial sector expanded at four times the rate of other industrial enterprises during 1994–97, and labor productivity in FFEs is almost double that in public sector enterprises. In addition, empirical research has found that domestic enterprises appear to have benefited from the presence of FFEs, through both increased sales and positive spillovers. Such spillovers come about when FFEs introduce new technologies and management skills. They are thought to have become progressively more important as more links began to develop between FFEs and domestic enterprises in the 1990s.

The creation of employment opportunities—either directly or indirectly—has been one of the most prominent impacts of FDI in China. Employment in FFEs in urban areas quadrupled between 1991 and 1999, to a total of 6 million, accounting for 3 percent of China's urban employment.[13] This has been particularly important in ameliorating unemployment pressures stemming from ongoing reforms of state-owned enterprises. FFEs are particularly important employers in the coastal provinces, accounting for over 10 percent of urban employment in Guangdong, Fujian, Shanghai, and Tianjin as of 1999.

FDI has built a highly competitive and dynamic manufacturing sector for exports. The growth of China's trade since 1978 has been four and a half times that of world trade, and China's share of world trade quadrupled from 0.9 percent in 1978 to 3.7 percent in 2000—an achievement not matched by any other country.[14] FFEs played a key role in this achievement. Between 1985 and 1999 the share of exports accounted for by FFEs grew from 1 percent to 45 percent; FFEs accounted for half of overall export growth and one-third of import growth during this period.

---

[13]It is difficult to measure the indirect employment effects of FDI, which include the employment indirectly generated as a result of spending by FFEs, or as a result of linkages of FFEs with domestic enterprises, either as competitors or as suppliers and customers.

[14]Lardy (2000).

Box 5.3. Tax Incentives for FDI

China has extensively but selectively used tax incentives to guide FDI into designated regions, sectors, and industries. FFEs enjoy exemptions from and reductions in the national business income tax as well as other incentives including exemptions from custom duties and the value-added tax for imported equipment and technology, exemptions from and reductions in local business income tax, full refunds for income tax paid on reinvested earnings, and no restrictions on profit remittances or capital repatriation. Generally speaking, the tax incentives offered in the SEZs and economic and technology development zones in open cities are much more favorable than in other regions (see below). Also, the tax incentives are more favorable for technology- and export-oriented FFEs.

In 1994, China adopted a new taxation system that unifies the tax treatment of domestic enterprises and FFEs. At the same time, China decided to reduce gradually the preferential treatment of FFEs in order to establish a level playing field for both types of enterprises. With the implementation of this policy, the preferential policies, including tax incentives, will be gradually reduced and then abolished.

Standard Income Tax Rates

The standard income tax rate for domestic enterprises and FFEs is 33 percent. (This includes a 3 percent local government component on which local governments may grant reductions.) FFEs with contracts for operating periods of 10 years or more are exempt from income tax for two years after the first profit is realized, and eligible for a 50 percent reduction in their tax liability in the following three years. FFEs that export at least 70 percent of their annual output remain eligible for a 50 percent reduction after these five years. Advanced-technology FFEs receive a 50 percent reduction for three years after the initial five years.

Special Economic Zones

The income tax rate for domestic enterprises and FFEs in SEZs is 18 percent (again including the 3 percent local government component). FFEs receive the same two-year exemption and three-year reduction as under the

---

Conclusions

Although more work is needed to flesh out the lessons from China's experience with FDI, some tentative conclusions may be drawn. Factors important in attracting FDI to other countries have also been key to China's success. China's large domestic market, low wage costs, and improved infrastructure, complemented by open FDI policies (especially

standard income tax regime. Export-oriented and advanced-technology FFEs pay 10 percent (instead of 15 percent) after the initial five-year exemption and reduction period has expired. FFEs engaged in infrastructure projects in Hainan (for airports, harbors, docks, railroads, highways, power plants, and water conservation) and with contracts for operating periods of 15 years or more are eligible for a five-year exemption period followed by an additional five years at a reduced rate (10 percent instead of 15 percent) after the first profitable year.

Open Coastal Cities and Areas, Open Border Cities, Inland Provincial Capitals, and Yangtze River Open Cities

Domestic enterprises in these areas pay 33 percent and FFEs 27 percent (including the 3 percent local government component) and enjoy the same two-year exemption and three-year reduction as under the standard income tax regime. For projects with foreign investment of $30 million or more (registered capital) and a long recovery period, knowledge- or technology-intensive projects, and energy, transportation, or harbor construction projects, the 24 percent component may be reduced to 15 percent.

Economic and Technology Development Zones

Domestic enterprises and production-related FFEs in economic and technology development zones pay 18 percent (including the 3 percent local component), the latter with the same two-year exemption and three-year reduction as under the standard income tax regime. For export-oriented and advanced-technology FFEs, the same extended reductions as in the SEZs apply.

High Technology Development Zones

Domestic enterprises and FFEs pay 18 percent (including the 3 percent local component). The latter are entitled to the same exemptions and reductions as under the standard income tax regime for high- or new-technology enterprises.

the establishment of OEZs), seem to have been major factors in attracting FDI. But China could probably attract even more FDI if governance improved and if China's legal system became more effective in enforcing contracts.

A unique factor in China's success is the large presence of investors from two of the most dynamic economies in the region: Hong Kong SAR and Taiwan Province of China. Although part of the FDI flows from these economies may be induced by distortions, the fact remains that, together with Singapore, they have accounted for more than half of FDI flows to China.

Apart from the economic environment, political commitment is an important ingredient in attracting FDI. For example, India shares with China many of the structural factors that have been important determinants of FDI: a large market, abundant labor, and a large diaspora. So, a priori, there seems to be no reason why India could not become an attractive destination for FDI. There are, of course, important differences in how the two countries have made political choices. In China the political leadership imposed a vision of the country's path of growth and development. Nevertheless, these leaders had to overcome obstacles to FDI rooted in history and ideology. They did so by limiting the opening to a few localities initially, but even then a great deal of autonomy in economic decision making was given to the localities, allowing a market-based economy to develop alongside a centrally planned system. Although this decentralization created some problems, it also gave local authorities strong incentives to grow and develop their economies. The success of the initial experiments created strong demonstration effects, which induced broad support for further reforms and opening of the economy. This created a virtuous cycle: as the reforms produced economic fruits, support for reforms became more widespread, allowing more reforms to be implemented.

China's experience shows that FDI contributes to GDP growth. The effect is likely to be strongest if foreign enterprises develop close links with domestic enterprises, so that the impact of FDI on productivity growth spreads beyond the firms receiving FDI.

FDI will continue to contribute to China's economic development. WTO accession should lead to a continuation of these contributions, as FDI can be expected to increase, particularly in the services sector, in activities such as finance, telecommunications, and wholesale and retail commerce. FDI will remain an important source of growth and will help offset potential output losses and create employment opportunities for workers whom state enterprise and banking reforms have made redundant. It is noteworthy that the Chinese authorities have invited foreign participation in the restructuring of state-owned enterprises and the resolution of the nonperforming loan problems in the banking sector. In sum, FDI can be expected to continue to play an important role in China's reform process for some time to come.

Some pitfalls in China's FDI experience also provide lessons for other countries. In particular:

- China remains burdened by an increasingly complex and biased tax incentive system. The system is heavily targeted at FFEs, favoring them over domestic enterprises. Indeed, two different enterprise income tax laws apply to FFEs and domestic enterprises. With the proliferation of OEZs and the widening of the range of eligible activities, China's system of enterprise income tax incentives has become increasingly complex and nontransparent, and it continues to impose revenue losses on the government. The problem has taken on greater salience with China's accession to the WTO, because some of China's fiscal incentives do not conform with the WTO principles of national treatment and prohibition of export and import replacement subsidies. China is in the process of amending various laws to meet its WTO commitments.

- Growing regional inequalities also remain a problem. By focusing on specific regions, China's FDI policy has contributed to the growing income disparity between coastal and inland provinces. The Chinese authorities are giving priority to reducing regional income disparities by developing the western and central regions of the country, among other things by attracting FDI to these regions through increased investment in infrastructure.

References

Chalk, Nigel A., 2001, "Tax Incentives in the Philippines: A Regional Perspective," IMF Working Paper 01/181 (Washington: International Monetary Fund).

Chen, C., 1996, "Regional Determinants of Foreign Direct Investment in Mainland China," *Journal of Economic Studies*, Vol. 23, pp. 18–30.

Cheng, L.K., and Y.K. Kwan, 2000, "What Are the Determinants of the Location of Foreign Direct Investment? The Chinese Experience," *Journal of International Economics*, Vol. 51, No. 2 (August), pp. 379–400.

Foreign Investment Administration, Ministry of Foreign Trade and Economic Cooperation, 1998, "Tax Exemption Policies on Importation of Equipment by Enterprises with Foreign Investment" (Beijing: Foreign Investment Administration).

Grub, P., and J. Lin, 1991, *Foreign Direct Investment in China* (New York: Quorum Books).

Harrold, Peter, and Rajiv B. Lall, 1993, "China, Reform and Development in 1992–93," World Bank Discussion Paper 215 (Washington: World Bank).

Head, K., and J. Ries, 1996, "Inter-City Competition for Foreign Direct Investment: Static and Dynamic Effects of China's Incentive Areas," *Journal of Urban Economics*, Vol. 40, No. 1, pp. 38–60 (July).

International Monetary Fund, 1997, "People's Republic of China—Selected Issues," IMF Staff Country Report 97/72 (Washington: World Bank).

Lardy, Nicholas, 1995, "The Role of Foreign Trade and Investment in China's Economic Transformation," *China Quarterly*, No. 144 (December), pp. 1065–82.

———, 2000, "Is China a 'Closed' Economy?" Statement for a Public Hearing of the United States Trade Deficit Review Commission, February 24, 2000.

Liu, X., Haiyan Song, Yingqu Wei, and Peter Romilly, 1997, "Country Characteristics and Foreign Direct Investment in China: A Panel Data Analysis," *Weltwirtschaftliches Archiv*, Vol. 133, No. 2, pp. 313–29.

Organization for Economic Cooperation and Development, 2000, "Main Determinants and Impacts of Foreign Direct Investment in China's Economy," Working Papers on International Investment 2000/4, December (Paris: Organization for Economic Cooperation and Development).

Wall, D., Beke Jiang, and Xiangshuo Yin, 1996, *China's Opening Door* (London: Royal Institute of International Affairs).

Wei, S., 1998, "Why Does China Attract So Little Foreign Direct Investment?" (unpublished; Cambridge, Massachusetts: Harvard University).

———, 2000, "How Taxing Is Corruption on International Investors?" *Review of Economics and Statistics*, Vol. 82, No. 1 (February), pp. 1–11.

Zhang, Kevin Honglin, 1999, "Foreign Direct Investment and Economic Growth: Evidence from Ten East Asian Economies," *Economia Internazionale*, Vol. 54 (November), pp. 517–35.

6

Foreign Direct Investment and Output Growth

HARM ZEBREGS

High rates of GDP growth have been associated with large inflows of foreign direct investment (FDI) to China, especially during the 1990s. This chapter examines how and to what extent FDI has contributed to China's growth performance.

The existence of a positive link between FDI and GDP growth in host countries has been widely documented in the literature (de Mello, 1997). Such a link has also been established in the case of China (Démurger, 2000; Mody and Wang, 1997; Wei, 1994; Zhang, 1999). In contrast with most other studies, however, the analysis in this chapter distinguishes between the direct and the indirect contributions of FDI to GDP. The direct contribution works through the formation of capital and leads to the augmentation of the total capital stock. The indirect contribution is the impact of FDI on total factor productivity (TFP) through the introduction of new technologies, managerial know-how, and other efficiency gains. In addition, this chapter examines whether the presence of foreign-funded enterprises (FFEs) produces spillovers to other sectors. According to the literature, these spillovers can be either positive or negative, depending on the nature of the linkages generated by FFEs (Rodríguez-Clare, 1996).[1]

---

[1]For example, FFEs that make intensive use of locally produced intermediate goods generate positive "backward" linkages when they raise the demand for intermediate goods in the host economy. By contrast, FFEs that displace local firms and import most of their intermediate goods might create negative backward linkages. FFEs can also create forward linkages when, for example, they bring new goods to the host economy that raise the productivity of domestic firms.

The results of the analysis indicate that FDI is a significant contributor to GDP and productivity growth in China. The contribution of FDI to annual GDP growth through capital deepening was on average 0.4 percentage point a year in the 1990s, and the contribution to long-run TFP growth was on average 2.5 percentage points a year over the same period. Hence the total contribution of FDI to GDP growth during the 1990s is estimated at about 3 percentage points a year. The positive link between FDI and GDP growth is found at both the national and the provincial level: provinces with larger inflows of FDI have tended to see both faster GDP growth and faster TFP growth. In addition, analysis of the output of FFEs suggests that their presence has generated positive spillover effects to other sectors in local economies.

The main policy conclusions are that FDI will continue to play an important role in sustaining growth in China, and that a more even distribution of FDI across provinces could help reduce income disparities. Additional FDI will not only add more high-productivity units to the capital stock, but also allow additional domestic enterprises to benefit from the presence of FFEs and raise their productivity. Because China's open-door policy initially focused on the coastal provinces, the inland provinces have had much less exposure to FDI and FFEs. FDI has been a catalyst of growth in the coastal provinces, and a policy aimed at attracting FDI to the inland provinces could help reduce the growing income disparity between these regions.

Background

China has gradually lowered barriers to FDI over the past three decades. As noted in Chapter 5, the open economic zones (OEZs) have played a central role in the opening of the economy to foreign investors, and, over time, economic links between the OEZs and the domestic economy have increased. The OEZs that were set up in the 1980s were located outside China's industrial centers, as the authorities sought to experiment with market-oriented reforms in limited localities and in the coastal provinces, which had natural advantages in terms of infrastructure and transport. In the early reform period, FDI was dominated by investors based in Hong Kong SAR and Taiwan Province of China, who sought to exploit relatively low-cost labor in the OEZs for export processing (Branstetter and Feenstra, 1999). As a result, links with domestic enterprises tended to be minimal. By contrast, in the 1990s, interaction between FFEs and domestic enterprises increased. As Naughton (1995) notes, the economic environment in the coastal areas was substantially changed by an emerging alliance between FFEs and township and village enterprises. In addition,

Figure 6.1. Real GDP and the Stock of FDI
(In logarithms)

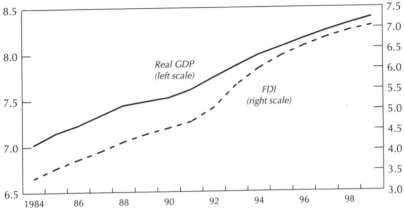

Source: Author's estimates.

FDI in China increasingly consisted of investments by European, Japanese, and U.S. multinationals seeking to supply the Chinese domestic market through local production capacity. These developments contributed to stronger links between FFEs and local economies and created channels for domestic firms to benefit from the presence of FFEs.

Contribution to Output Growth

Developments in the stock of FDI and in real GDP are closely linked in China (Figure 6.1). This chapter attempts to quantify the relation between these variables. A complicating factor in estimating this relation is that causality can run in both directions: FDI contributes to GDP through the transfer of resources, both tangible (physical capital) and intangible (new technologies, managerial know-how, and spillover effects), but at the same time FDI inflows can be motivated by the market size of the host economy.[2]

Zhang (1999) shows that long-run causality between the stock of FDI and GDP per capita runs in both directions in China. He also estimates

---

[2]Both directions of causality have received attention in the literature. Borensztein, De Gregorio, and Lee (1998) have shown, in a panel of 69 developing economies, that FDI inflows have contributed to GDP growth; Brainard (1997), Lecraw (1991), and Wheeler and Mody (1992) have shown the statistical significance of GDP growth in attracting FDI.

(using a Johansen cointegration test) that a permanent 1 percent increase in the stock of FDI raises real GDP by 0.6 percent in the long run, and that a 1 percent increase in real GDP raises the stock of FDI by 1.7 percent. (The estimated short-run elasticity of GDP with respect to FDI is 0.032.) Whereas these estimates measure the total impact of FDI on GDP, this chapter, as noted, attempts to quantify both the direct and the indirect effects of FDI on GDP.

Contribution to Capital Accumulation

FDI raises the rate of GDP growth by adding to the stock of capital. To assess the direct contribution of FDI to GDP growth, a simple growth accounting framework is employed with the following Cobb-Douglas production function:

$$Y = AL^{\alpha}K^{1-\alpha}, \tag{1}$$

where Y is real GDP, α is the share of labor compensation in GDP, A is TFP, L is labor, and $K = (K_d + K_f)$ is the total capital stock, including domestic and foreign capital (this implicitly assumes that domestic capital, K_d, and foreign capital, K_f, are perfect substitutes). At this stage it is assumed that the marginal products of domestic and foreign capital are the same, that is, that the derivatives of the production function with respect to K_d and K_f are identical. This assumption will be relaxed at the next stage when estimating the impact of FDI on TFP. Taking the derivatives of equation (1) with respect to A, L, K_d, and K_f, and rearranging terms, gives

$$\dot{Y} = \dot{A} + \alpha\dot{L} + (1-\alpha)\frac{dK_d + dK_f}{K},$$

where dK_d is net fixed-asset investment by domestic investors and dK_f is that by foreign investors. (A dot above a variable indicates a percentage change.) The direct impact of foreign investment on GDP growth is then given by $(1-\alpha)dK_f/K$. Estimates for α can be obtained directly from China's national accounts: these give an average labor share for 1990–99 of about 0.54, which implies a capital share parameter of 0.46. The capital stock has been constructed with data from the *Statistical Yearbook of China*.

When estimating the direct impact of FDI on GDP growth, the fact that not all FDI in the balance of payments contributes to fixed-asset investment should be taken into account. In some cases FDI inflows are used to finance the acquisition of a controlling share of the stock of a domestic company. Such a transaction is very similar to portfolio investment, that is, a transfer of claims on capital, not an augmentation of the capital stock. Hence FDI is not identical to dK_f. During 1990–99 FDI inflows were on average 1.7 percent of the total capital stock, and fixed-

Table 6.1. FDI and Growth of GDP by Province, 1990–97

Province	GDP Growth[1] (in Percent)	FDI as a Fraction of GDP (in Percent)	Direct Contribution of FDI to GDP Growth (in Percentage Points)
All China	10.88	4.63	0.69
Cities			
Beijing	11.13	6.49	0.87
Tianjin	12.15	11.69	1.55
Provinces with OEZs[2]			
Fujian	18.03	13.04	3.51
Zhejiang	16.99	2.66	0.73
Guangdong	16.62	14.01	4.11
Jiangsu	15.56	6.38	1.44
Shandong	15.27	3.62	0.86
Hainan	14.84	17.30	...
Guangxi	14.48	3.52	0.47
Hebei	14.14	1.65	0.29
Shanghai	12.97	9.28	1.99
Liaoning	9.81	4.11	0.79
Mean	14.87	7.56	1.58
Provinces without OEZs			
Anhui	13.90	1.46	0.23
Jiangxi	13.26	1.74	0.30
Hubei	12.97	1.86	0.31
Henan	12.72	1.13	0.14
Hunan	11.23	1.88	0.32
Jilin	11.08	2.12	0.32
Sichuan	10.92	2.79	0.41
Xinjiang	10.71	0.42	0.05
Tibet	10.42	0.00	...
Shanxi	10.27	0.74	0.09
Yunnan	10.09	0.53	0.10
Inner Mongolia	10.08	0.59	0.09
Gansu	9.75	0.69	0.08
Ningxia	9.42	0.53	0.04
Shaanxi	8.98	2.31	0.25
Guizhou	8.89	0.57	0.05
Heilongjiang	8.56	1.63	0.26
Qinghai	7.92	0.14	0.01
Mean	10.62	1.17	0.18

Sources: *China Statistical Yearbook* and author's estimates.
[1]Compounded at an annual rate.
[2]Open coastal cities or special economic zones.

asset investment by foreigners is estimated at 0.9 percent of the total capital stock, Thus the direct contribution of FDI to GDP growth was about 0.4 percentage point a year during that period.

The direct contribution of FDI to GDP growth has been greatest in provinces with OEZs, as they have attracted most foreign investment (Table 6.1). The direct contribution of FDI to GDP growth varies con-

Figure 6.2. TFP and the Stock of FDI
(In logarithms)

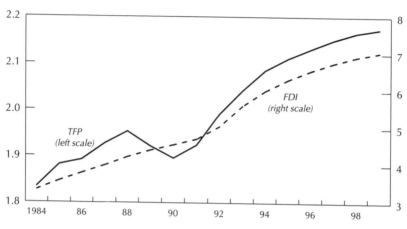

Source: Author's estimates.

siderably across provinces, from more than 4 percentage points a year in Guangdong to almost zero in the western provinces of Qinghai and Ningxia.[3] The open-door policy has clearly been effective in mobilizing resources for economic development, although the emphasis on coastal areas has also contributed to the widening income gap between coastal and inland provinces.

Contribution to TFP Growth

FDI and TFP have moved together over time (Figure 6.2). Again, a cursory look at the data suggests a positive relation between the stock of FDI and TFP, but in this case, too, causality can run both ways. FDI can, for example, contribute to TFP growth through the introduction of new technologies and managerial know-how, but it is also possible that FDI is attracted by high levels of know-how and technical expertise in the host economy, which make it easier for multinationals to introduce more-sophisticated production processes (Findlay, 1978; Borensztein and others, 1998). In this case FDI that does not contribute to fixed-asset investment is also included in the analysis, because technology transfers are not necessarily linked to such investment. New technolo-

---

[3]The provincial labor shares for the calculation of the direct contribution of FDI to GDP were obtained from the *China Statistical Yearbook*.

Table 6.2. Estimation Results from Single-Equation Regressions

	Regression Equation[1]			
Variable	(1)	(2)	(3)	(4)
Dependent variable	TFP	FDI	Change in TFP	Change in FDI
Sample period	1985–99	1984–99	1985–99	1985–99
Constant	1.3241	–4.9029	–0.0130	0.1851
	(0.0851)***	(1.3728)***	(0.0134)	(0.0320)**
Regression coefficient				
Trend	–0.0205	0.1645		
	(0.0077)**	(0.0185)***		
FDI	0.1649			
	(0.0289)***			
TFP		4.3330		
		(0.7595)***		
Change in FDI			0.1443	
			(0.0497)**	
Change in TFP				2.7227
				(0.0320)***
Summary statistics				
R^2	0.9771	0.9950	0.3928	0.3928
F-statistic	277.92	1,305	8.4086	8.4086

Source: Author's estimates.
[1]All equations are estimated by the ordinary least squares method; numbers in parentheses are standard errors.
***Indicates statistical significance at the 1 percent level.
**Indicates statistical significance at the 5 percent level.

gies or managerial know-how can also be introduced, for example after a foreign investor acquires a controlling share in the stock of a Chinese company and reorganizes the production process.

Empirical analysis suggests a significant positive relation between the stock of FDI and TFP. Table 6.2 reports the estimation results of several regressions designed to examine this relation. The following ordinary least squares regressions were run independently with the stock of FDI and TFP (in logarithms) both as the dependent and as the independent variable:

$$TFP_t = \theta_0 + \theta_1 FDI_t + \theta_2 trend + \mu_t,$$
$$FDI_t = \theta_3 + \theta_4 TFP_t + \theta_5 trend + v_t.$$

Augmented Dickey-Fuller tests were performed on the error terms in the two equations (μ_t and v_t) and were found to be stationary in both cases, which suggests a long-run relation between TFP and the stock of FDI. The same equations (without a trend) were also run in first differences and yielded comparable parameter estimates. The relation between FDI and TFP has also been examined in a vector autoregression (this was done in a Johansen cointegration framework). The results

Figure 6.3. Provincial FDI and TFP Growth[1]

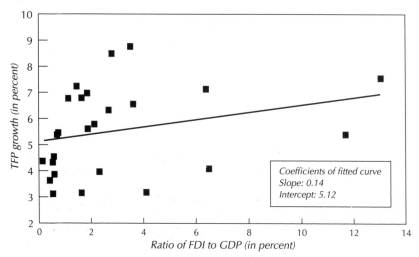

Source: Author's estimates.
[1] Each square represents a single province.

suggest a long-run elasticity between TFP and the stock of FDI of 0.09, and a short-run elasticity of 0.08. Furthermore, it is found that neither of the two variables is weakly exogenous, which indicates that causality runs both ways. On the basis of these findings, it is estimated that the indirect contribution of FDI to TFP growth was about 2.5 percentage points a year during the 1990s, a period during which the FDI stock is estimated to have increased by about 30 percent a year.

A positive relation between FDI and TFP growth is also identified at the provincial level in a cross section of provinces (Figure 6.3). Provinces with large inflows of FDI relative to their GDP have generally had higher growth rates of TFP.

Spillover Effects

FFEs tend to be the most dynamic and productive firms in the economy. Output of FFEs in the industrial sector expanded at four times the rate of other industrial enterprises during 1994–97, and their labor productivity was almost double that of state-owned enterprises.[4] Because

---

[4] The analysis of FFEs focuses on the period 1994–97, because that is the longest period for which consistent data for industrial output by FFEs and other enterprises are available.

FFEs in the industrial sector are also the main recipients of FDI in China, it is possible that provinces with large FDI inflows grow faster simply because the share of fast-growing FFEs in provincial GDP is larger. However, the positive contribution of the FFEs may extend beyond their own operations if other enterprises benefit from their presence. This could be the case if FFEs produce inputs for local enterprises or if they use local enterprises as their suppliers, thereby contributing to higher output and efficiency in enterprises that receive no FDI (Rodríguez-Clare, 1996). Such spillovers may have become progressively more important as the links between FFEs and domestic enterprises grew tighter in the 1990s.

Econometric analysis suggests the presence of positive spillovers from FFEs to the rest of the economy. To test for the presence of such spillovers, the following equation was estimated using panel data from 30 provinces with observations for 1995–97:[5]

$$x_{i,t} = \beta s_{i,t} + \gamma_{i,t} + dum97_t + \mu_{i,t}, \tag{2}$$

where $x_{i,t}$ is the growth rate of GDP excluding FFEs in province i in period t, $s_{i,t}$ is the share of value added of FFEs in GDP in province i in period t, β is a slope parameter, $\gamma_{i,t}$ is a province-specific intercept, and $\mu_{i,t}$ is the error term. A dummy variable, $dum97_t$, has been added to account for the onset of the Asian financial crisis in 1997. A fixed-effects panel estimation of equation (2), with $\gamma_{i,t} = \gamma_i$ for all i and t, provides supporting evidence of the hypothesis that FFEs generate positive spillover effects to the rest of the economy (Table 6.3).[6] The estimation results suggest that spillover effects from FFEs in China contributed 2.2 percentage points to annual GDP growth during 1995–97. Because there are many ways in which FFEs can contribute to increased output by other firms, the spillover effect is not directly comparable to the contribution of FDI to TFP growth calculated earlier in the chapter. The presence of FFEs may, for example, lead to more investment if their demand leads suppliers to increase capacity.

---

[5]The sample period is reduced by one year because of the calculation of the growth rate of provincial GDP excluding FFEs.

[6]A fixed-effects model was chosen because it allows for structural differences across provinces. For completeness, the table also gives the results of a pooled estimation, with $\gamma_{i,t} = \gamma$ for all i and t, and a random-effects estimation, with $\gamma_{i,t} = \gamma_i$ and $E(\gamma_i \mu_{i,t}) = 0$ for all i and t, of equation (2). The pooled estimation shows a small but negative spillover effect from FFEs to the rest of the economy, whereas the random-effects estimation fails to demonstrate the presence of any spillover effects.

Table 6.3. Results of Regressions of Growth in Non-FFE Output on FFE Share of GDP, Using Provincial Data

Variable[1]	Pooled Estimation		Random-Effects Estimation		Fixed-Effects Estimation	
	Coefficient	Standard error	Coefficient	Standard error	Coefficient	Standard error
Constant	0.1101	0.0003***	0.1104	0.0053***		
Share of FFEs in GDP	–0.0722	0.0268***	–0.0503	0.0619	0.3424	0.0613***
Dummy for 1997	–0.0084	0.0002***	–0.0100	0.0047**	–0.0110	0.0003***
Summary statistics						
Adjusted R^2	0.9980		0.4454		0.9977	
F-statistic	21,903		. . .		38,290	

Source: Author's estimates.
[1]The dependent variable is the growth rate of GDP excluding FFEs. Data are for 30 provinces over the period 1995–97 (balanced panel with 90 observations). The estimation method is generalized least squares with cross-sectional weights.
*** Indicates statistical significance at the 1 percent level.
** Indicates statistical significance at the 5 percent level.

Conclusions

FDI inflows have contributed significantly to China's impressive growth performance. Apart from being a significant source of fixed-asset investment, FDI has also enhanced TFP. Empirical results suggest that the impact on TFP accounted for about 2.5 percentage points of annual GDP growth in the 1990s. The contribution of FDI through fixed-asset investment is estimated at 0.4 percentage point a year. Hence the total contribution of FDI to GDP growth during the 1990s is estimated at about 3 percentage points a year.

FFEs, which are the main recipients of FDI, have generated significant positive spillovers to other firms in the economy. It is estimated that these spillovers added 2.2 percentage points to annual GDP growth in the 1990s. This suggests that the impact of FDI on productivity and output growth extends beyond the firms receiving FDI.

The empirical results also show that FDI has been attracted by the rapid expansion of China's economy. Both GDP and TFP are found to be significant determinants of FDI. The influx of FDI has been facilitated by external sector reforms that have gradually opened the door to foreign investors. China's accession to the World Trade Organization, which is expected to lead to more reforms and a reduction in barriers to foreign investment, is likely to trigger a further increase in FDI, particularly into the services sector.

Not all provinces appear to have benefited to the same extent from the presence of FDI. To date, the positive effects appear to be strongest in the coastal provinces. Hence a policy that attracts FDI and FFEs to the inland provinces could help those provinces catch up with the coastal provinces in terms of productivity and income.

FDI is expected to remain an important source of growth and can help to offset potential output losses resulting from state enterprise reform. In addition, promoting FFEs will generate positive spillovers to other sectors in the economy and result in a wider dispersion of new technologies and managerial know-how. Given the important role of FDI in private sector development, FDI can also help absorb workers that have become redundant in the state enterprise sector.

References

Borensztein, E., J. De Gregorio, and J-W. Lee, 1998, "How Does Foreign Direct Investment Affect Economic Growth?" *Journal of International Economics*, Vol. 45, No. 1 (June), pp. 115–35.

Brainard, S. Lael, 1997, "An Empirical Assessment of the Proximity-Concentration Trade-Off Between Multinational Sales and Trade," *American Economic Review*, Vol. 87, No. 4 (September), pp. 520–44.

Branstetter, Lee G., and Robert C. Feenstra, 1999, "Trade and Foreign Direct Investment in China: A Political Economy Approach" (unpublished; University of California, Davis).

de Mello, L., 1997, "Foreign Direct Investment in Developing Countries and Growth: A Selective Survey," *Journal of Development Studies*, Vol. 34, No. 1 (October), pp. 1–34.

Démurger, Sylvie, 2000, *Economic Opening and Growth in China* (Paris: Development Centre of the Organization for Economic Cooperation and Development).

Findlay, Ronald, 1978, "Relative Backwardness, Direct Foreign Investment and the Transfer of Technology: A Simple Dynamic Model," *Quarterly Journal of Economics*, Vol. 92, No. 1 (February), pp. 1–16.

Lecraw, Donald J., 1991, "Factors Influencing FDI by TNCs in Host Developing Countries: A Preliminary Report," in *Multinational Enterprises in Less Developed Countries*, ed. by P. Buckley and J. Clegg (Basingstoke, England: Macmillan).

Mody, Ashoka, and Fang-Yi Wang, 1997, "Explaining Industrial Growth in Coastal China: Economic Reforms . . . and What Else?" *World Bank Economic Review*, Vol. 11, No. 2 (May), pp. 293–325.

Naughton, Barry, 1995, *Growing Out of the Plan: Chinese Economic Reform, 1978–1993* (New York: Cambridge University Press).

Rodríguez-Clare, Andres, 1996, "Multinationals, Linkages, and Economic Development," *American Economic Review*, Vol. 86, No. 4 (September), pp. 852–73.

Wei, S., 1994, "The Open Door Policy and China's Rapid Growth: Evidence from City-Level Data," in *Growth Theories in Light of the East Asian Experience*, ed. by T. Ito and A.O. Krueger (Chicago: University of Chicago Press).

Wheeler, D., and A. Mody, 1992, "International Investment Location Decisions: The Case of U.S. Firms," *Journal of International Economics*, Vol. 33, No. 1–2 (August), pp. 57–76.

Zhang, Kevin Honglin, 1999, "Foreign Direct Investment and Economic Growth: Evidence from Ten East Asian Economies," *Economia Internazionale*, Vol. 54, No. 4 (November), pp. 517–35.

7

China and the Asian Crisis

PAUL GRUENWALD AND JAHANGIR AZIZ

China's economy performed well during the Asian financial crisis of 1997–99, especially when compared with other countries in the region. GDP growth remained high, the external current account in surplus, official foreign reserves at comfortable levels, and the exchange rate stable. Indeed, the stability of the renminbi was seen as an important factor in limiting the impact of the crisis on the region's economies.

This chapter discusses the factors behind China's successful passage through the Asian crisis. China's favorable performance is particularly remarkable given the presence of domestic vulnerabilities, such as a weak financial system and a poorly performing corporate sector, similar to those in the crisis-affected countries. The chapter concludes that low external vulnerability, especially due to ample official foreign reserves and low external debt, was among the main factors responsible for limiting the effects of the crisis on the domestic economy. The still-limited openness of the economy, including the capital account, also helped, even though the controls in place turned out to be porous during the crisis. Moreover, the Chinese authorities pursued timely countercyclical policies to address the growth slowdown and the associated social pressures. Importantly, the Asian crisis motivated the authorities to accelerate reforms in key areas of vulnerability, notably in the banking and state-owned enterprise (SOE) sectors.

Although the reforms undertaken have improved conditions, domestic vulnerabilities remain. The financial and corporate sectors still suffer from weak corporate governance, poor financial conditions, and inadequate regulatory oversight. Following China's accession to the

101

Figure 7.1. Growth in GDP
(In percent)

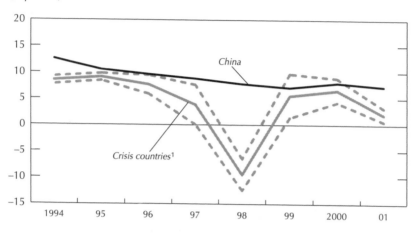

Source: IMF staff estimates.
[1]Dashed lines represent ± 1 standard error around the average for the crisis countries.

World Trade Organization, these sectors will face increased international competition, and the effectiveness of capital controls is likely to erode further over time. Left unchecked, the weaknesses in the banking and corporate sectors could eventually undermine fiscal sustainability, the external position, and growth. Thus, even though China successfully weathered the Asian crisis, tackling these weaknesses decisively remains key to safeguarding the economy from future crises.

Macroeconomic Performance

China passed through the Asian crisis relatively unscathed.[1] Output growth remained strong at an annual rate of 7–8 percent (Figure 7.1), although substantially below the double-digit rates recorded earlier in the decade, during a period of overheating. Indeed, the slowdown was due in part to the lagged effects of measures undertaken in the mid-1990s to cool the overheated economy. Reserves remained comfortable at over $150 billion, the external current account in surplus (Figure 7.2), and the exchange rate stable (Figure 7.3).

---

[1]India, too, weathered the crisis well. For an account see Callen, Reynolds, and Towe (2001, Chapter 2).

Figure 7.2. Current Account Balances
(In percent of GDP)

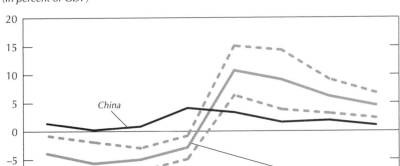

Source: IMF staff estimates.
[1]Dashed lines represent ± 1 standard error around the average for the crisis countries.

China was not entirely untouched by the Asian crisis, however.[2] Export growth dropped to near zero in 1998 (Figure 7.4), although import growth also fell sharply, partly reflecting the high import content of Chinese exports (estimated at about 60 percent), which dampened the impact on growth. Foreign direct investment (FDI) inflows stalled in 1998 and then declined in 1999. Capital flight, measured as unidentified capital outflows in the balance of payments, increased sharply in 1998.

How Did China Escape the Turmoil?

The interplay of several factors—macroeconomic, structural, and policy related—helps explain China's relatively favorable economic performance during the crisis. These factors combined to defend the economy against external shocks, contain domestic vulnerabilities, and support internal demand when exports slowed.

External Vulnerability

During the period leading up to the Asian crisis, China's external vulnerability indicators were generally favorable. International reserves

---

[2]In fact, some economists have argued that China was the "first domino" in the chain of events that led to the Asian crisis (Box 7.1).

Figure 7.3. Dollar Exchange Rates
(Index, 1994=100)

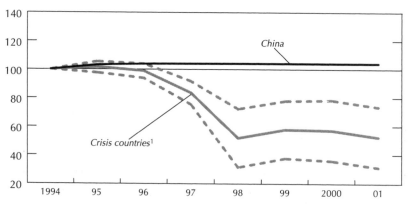

Source: IMF staff estimates.
[1]Dashed lines represent ± 1 standard error around the average for the crisis countries.

were large and rising, short-term external debt was low (Figure 7.5), and the current account was in surplus. Although the real effective exchange rate had been rising (that is, the currency had been strengthening in real terms; Figure 7.6), largely reflecting high domestic inflation, its rate of increase was slowing as macroeconomic policies aimed at cooling the overheated economy of the mid-1990s increasingly took effect. Similarly, the growth rate of real domestic credit was also slowing (Figure 7.7).

China's limited trade openness and capital controls further cushioned the economy against external shocks. Despite having increased rapidly through the 1980s and early 1990s, the ratio of exports plus imports to GDP was only around 25 percent in 1990–97, less than half of that in the crisis-affected economies (Figure 7.8). In addition, as already noted, the relatively high import content of exports limited the dependence of domestic output on external demand. Thus, notwithstanding the sharp decline in export growth (from an average annual rate of over 30 percent during 1990–97 to less than 5 percent in 1998–99), the impact on overall growth was relatively muted. The contribution of net exports to GDP growth shifted from 1¼ percentage points on average in 1990–97, when the overall growth rate was about 10¼ percent, to minus ¾ percentage point during 1998–99, when the overall growth rate dropped to 7½ percent.

Unlike in most of the countries affected by the crisis, China's capital account was relatively closed. China's system of capital controls has favored long-term FDI inflows. Portfolio investment was strictly segre-

Figure 7.4. Growth in Trade
(In percent)

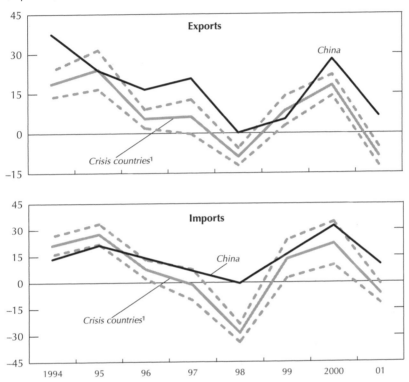

Source: IMF staff estimates.
[1]Dashed lines represent ± 1 standard error around the average for the crisis countries.

gated between residents and nonresidents, and these restrictions appear to have been at least partially effective given the divergent trends between shares in the same enterprise in the two different markets.[3] Likewise, restrictions on loans distinguished between domestic- and foreign-funded enterprises, with foreign currency borrowing by domestic enterprises (except for trade finance) subject to annual and multiyear borrowing plans requiring government approval.

---

[3]"A shares" were reserved for domestic investors and denominated in local currency whereas "B shares" were reserved for nonresident investors and denominated in foreign currency. The B-share market was relatively shallow and was more severely affected by the Asian crisis than the A-share market. In particular, valuations in the A-share market were significantly higher than in the B-share market. In early 2001 domestic investors were allowed to invest in B shares, and the gap between A- and B-share valuations narrowed.

Figure 7.5. Ratio of Short-Term Debt to Reserves
(In percent)

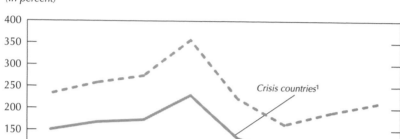

Source: IMF staff estimates.
[1]Dashed lines represent ± 1 standard error around the average for the crisis countries.

The capital controls limited the scope for speculative behavior during the crisis. Residents generally had no legal access to foreign exchange without an underlying current account transaction or amortization payment, nor could residents move freely between foreign and local currency. Access to the futures and forward markets was similarly limited; the only nondeliverable forward market is in Singapore and is thin and without direct links to the onshore market. As a result, investors could not take sizable positions against the renminbi. Thus, in contrast to the crisis-affected countries, where investors could shift out of local currency and reduce their country exposure, rapid exit strategies were largely unavailable in China.

The capital controls, however, did not provide complete immunity against capital outflows. Foreign banks reduced their exposure to China by over $30 billion (3 percent of GDP; figures based on Bank for International Settlements data) from the end of 1997 to the end of 1999. Unidentified capital outflows, which until the onset of the crisis had been around $15 billion a year, averaged $22 billion in 1997–98 before returning to precrisis levels in 1999–2000.

Domestic Vulnerability

In contrast to the relatively strong external position, China's banking and corporate sectors had significant weaknesses. China's reform process, which began in the late 1970s, is yet to be completed, and the

Figure 7.6. Real Exchange Rates
(Index, 1994=100)

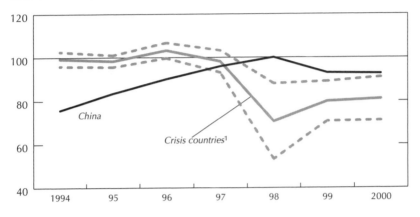

Source: IMF staff estimates.
[1]Dashed lines represent ± 1 standard error around the average for the crisis countries.

country remains in transition to a market-oriented economy. As discussed in Chapters 9 and 10, weak corporate governance of SOEs and state commercial banks (SCBs), inadequate regulation and supervision of the financial sector, and lack of transparency about firms' performance resulted in major inefficiencies and financial losses. The finan-

Figure 7.7. Growth in Real Domestic Credit
(In percent)

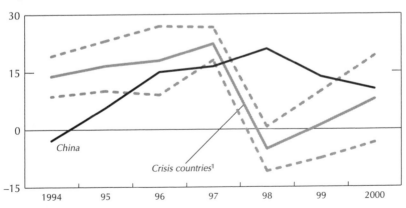

Source: IMF staff estimates.
[1]Dashed lines represent 1 standard error around the average for the crisis countries.

Figure 7.8. Ratio of Trade to GDP
(In percent)[1]

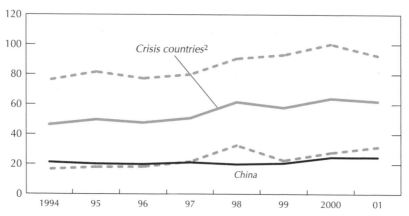

Source: IMF staff estimates.
[1]Trade is measured as exports plus imports.
[2]Dashed lines represent ±1 standard error around the average for the crisis countries.

cial position of the SOEs was, on average, considerably weaker than in the corporate sectors of the crisis-hit countries in Asia, with lower over-all profits and higher leverage (Table 7.1).

The weak financial position of the SOEs was closely linked with the health of the banking system. Losses of the SOEs were financed by the SCBs, resulting in high SOE bank leverage and poor bank asset quality. Private sector estimates at the time suggested that the recapitalizing cost of the SCBs could be on the order of 15–30 percent of GDP. The weak state of the corporate and banking sectors prompted several analysts, including Lardy (1998) and Goldstein (1998), to conjecture that China might also succumb to the crisis.

Table 7.1. Selected Financial Indicators in Six East Asian Countries, 1996
(In percent)

Indicator	Indonesia	Rep. of Korea	Malaysia	Philippines	Thailand	China
Nonperforming loans as a share of total loans (official)	8.8	0.8	3.9	3.5	7.7	20
Corporate sector debt-equity ratio	200	640	200	170	340	500
Corporate profits (return on assets)	4.7	0.4	6	4.7	1	0.1

Source: IMF staff estimates.

Box 7.1. Was China the First Domino?

Some economists have argued that although China did not succumb to the Asian crisis, the devaluation of the renminbi in 1994 made China the "first domino" in the chain of events that led to the crisis. Those who support this view (such as Makin, 1997) argue that China's 35 percent devaluation of the yuan against the dollar in January 1994 was preemptive, and the first in a number of events leading to the Asian crisis. Underlying this view is the supposition that China gained competitive advantage by virtue of its devaluation, and that its improved competitiveness and the subsequent rise in its export market share contributed to the pressure on and eventual devaluations of other Asian currencies, which precipitated the crisis.

However, a closer examination of the data casts doubt on the "first domino" theory. First, the 1994 move was not a devaluation in the traditional sense; rather, China's official exchange rate was unified with the swap market rate, which remained unchanged after the unification. Since the swap rate was estimated to apply to some 80 percent of China's external trade, the effective nominal devaluation of the renminbi was on the order of 7 percent rather than 35 percent. Second, given China's relatively high inflation at that time (24 percent in 1994), any nominal devaluation was quickly reversed in real terms. Indeed, the January 1994 devaluation is seen as a minor blip in the upward trend of the real effective exchange rate over 1993–98, when the currency *appreciated* in real terms by more than 60 percent. Finally, although China's exports did grow quickly following the devaluation of the official rate, the 1993–96 period was characterized by relatively stable export market shares across the Asian emerging markets, including China, the newly industrialized economies (Hong Kong SAR, Korea, Singapore, and Taiwan Province of China), and the major ASEAN economies. Thus, the assertion that China was the first domino appears to have little merit (see, for example, Fernald, Edison, and Loungani, 1999).

Supporting Growth and Accelerating Reform

The Chinese authorities responded to the Asian crisis by using countercyclical macroeconomic policies to support domestic demand, while accelerating reforms to address the domestic vulnerabilities. Like other countries in the region, China eased fiscal policy considerably during the Asian crisis. The fiscal deficit more than doubled, from 1.8 percent of GDP in 1997 to 4.0 percent in 1999 (Figure 7.9), largely reflecting increased public spending on infrastructure projects and social security. Low explicit public debt at the outset of the crisis and

Figure 7.9. Fiscal Balances
(In percent of GDP)

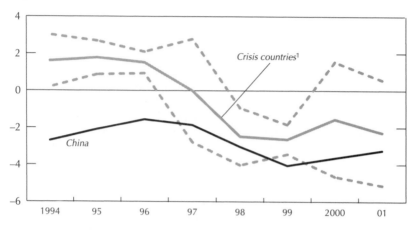

Source: IMF staff estimates.
[1]Dashed lines represent ± 1 standard error around the average for the crisis countries.

the absence of external financing needs provided room for this policy course.[4]

Whereas the crisis-affected economies initially had to tighten monetary policy and raise interest rates to stabilize their free-falling currencies, China did not. Thus, following the outbreak of the crisis, the People's Bank of China lowered domestic interest rates by about half between the end of 1997 and mid-1999 (Figure 7.10). Although the efficacy of these interest rate cuts in boosting activity has been limited given the weak monetary transmission mechanism, the interest rate cuts helped the SOEs, which were the main borrowers from the banking system, to reduce their debt service burden. The deposit base of the banking system held up well during the crisis, reflecting continued robust economic activity, the lack of investment alternatives, and the credibility of the implied government guarantee of the almost entirely state-owned banking system.

The Asian crisis pushed financial sector and SOE reforms to the top of the government's policy agenda (Chapters 9 and 10). In the financial sector the reforms aimed to gradually transform the SCBs into viable

---

[4]As explained in Chapter 8, broader measures of the public debt, including in particular the quasi-fiscal costs of nonperforming loans in the financial system, were much larger.

Figure 7.10. Nominal Interest Rates
(Index, 1994=100)

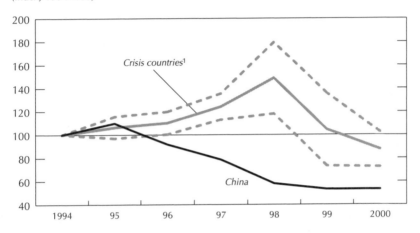

Source: IMF staff estimates.
[1]Dashed lines represent ± 1 standard error around the average for the crisis countries.

and competitive universal banks, consolidate and contain losses in the smaller financial institutions, and increase competition by allowing other (non-SCB) banks to assume a growing role in domestic financial intermediation. The reforms involved greater transparency regarding the financial condition of the financial system; stricter regulatory standards; less government interference in the system; recapitalization, balance sheet cleanup, and operational restructuring of the SCBs; the creation of asset management companies (AMCs) to deal with a sizable portion of the nonperforming loans of the SCBs and one policy bank (the China Development Bank); and the merger and closure of ailing small financial institutions.

The National Financial Sector Work Conference in November 1997 underscored the need for renewed efforts to reduce government interference in the financial system. Following this, the central bank was restructured in 1998 to give it greater independence on credit policy and supervisory decisions. That same year the government eliminated credit quotas for SCBs, conferring greater responsibility on them for their lending decisions. In 1999 interference in commercial lending was explicitly forbidden. In an effort to recapitalize the SCBs, the government injected capital equivalent to 3½ percent of GDP into these banks in 1998. During 1999–2000 the four SCBs and one policy bank transferred nonperforming loans equivalent to 17 percent of GDP to four newly established AMCs.

Closures and mergers were used extensively to consolidate smaller financial institutions. Insolvent rural credit funds were liquidated and solvent ones merged with rural credit cooperatives. The number of these cooperatives and of urban credit cooperatives was cut by several thousand in the last few years, mainly through mergers at the city and the provincial level. The reform of the trust and investment companies, including those with international exposure (many of which had run into financial difficulties), has proceeded along similar lines, involving a mix of mergers and closures.

In the SOE sector the authorities accelerated restructuring efforts despite the social pressures brought on by the slowing economy. In early 1998 the government announced a three-year program to revitalize China's medium-size and large SOEs. The program involved the broadening of earlier pilot reform initiatives (such as the adoption of "modern enterprise systems") to a national scale, combining them with new efforts to reorganize, upgrade, and improve enterprise management and governance, and strategic reorganization of key sectors designed to eliminate excess capacity and redundant labor. The social consequences of the accelerated reforms were to be dealt with by broadening the social safety net, including through reemployment programs.

References

Callen, Tim, Patricia Reynolds, and Christopher Towe, 2001, *India at the Crossroads: Sustaining Growth and Reducing Poverty* (Washington: International Monetary Fund).

Fernald, John, H. Edison, and P. Loungani, 1999, "Was China the First Domino? Assessing Links Between China and Other Asian Economies," *Journal of International Money and Finance*, Vol. 18, No. 4 (August), pp. 515–35.

Goldstein, Morris, 1998, *The Asian Financial Crisis: Causes, Cures, and Systematic Implications*, Policy Analyses in International Economics No. 55 (Washington: Institute for International Economics).

Lardy, Nicholas R., 1998, "China and the Asian Financial Contagion, 1998," *Foreign Affairs*, Vol. 77, No. 4 (July-August), pp. 1–12.

Makin, John H., 1997, "Two New Paradigms," *AEI Economic Outlook*, October (Washington: American Enterprise Institute).

8

Medium-Term Fiscal Issues

JAMES DANIEL, THOMAS RICHARDSON, RAJU SINGH,
AND GEORGE TSIBOURIS

At first glance, fiscal policy does not seem a pressing medium-term policy challenge for China. The measured debt stock is low, and the reported budget deficit is modest and easily financed. However, fiscal activity in China extends well beyond the state budget, and public finances will face a number of difficult challenges in the next few years. There is a sizable amount of quasi-fiscal debt in the form of nonrecoverable loans in the banking system, the legacy of central planning. Further, although efforts are being made to limit the flow of new nonperforming loans, through state-owned enterprise (SOE) and financial sector reforms, the possibility that part of ongoing bank funding will become nonperforming cannot be ruled out. The budget also faces heavy future expenditure demands for health and education, pension reform, and the government's ambitious infrastructure program.

As a result, a broader measure of China's public debt stock is larger than reported stock, and could grow further if corrective measures are not taken. Alternatively, if the budget deficit is reduced gradually over the next few years and the creation of new nonrecoverable loans is successfully contained, the debt stock should stabilize and then fall over the medium term.

The potential fiscal burden from the pension system is also large. Without reform, the existing, largely pay-as-you-go system cannot deal with either the long-term problem of a rapidly aging population or the short-term problem of providing pensions to the employees of SOEs. The World Bank's recommendations to address these problems include

Figure 8.1. State Budget
(In percent of GDP)

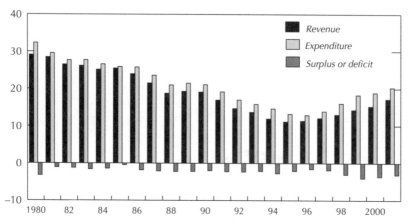

Sources: Ministry of Finance; and IMF staff estimates.

consolidating and unifying pension administration, fully funding individual accounts, and implementing parametric reforms such as raising the retirement age.

Meanwhile China's system of fiscal federalism needs to ensure greater equalization in public service delivery across provinces. The current transfer system relies heavily on regressive "revenue returned" transfers and not enough on progressive "subsidy" transfers and specific-purpose grants.

The Current State of Public Finances

Although China's official fiscal statistics show only a modest deficit and debt stock, on a broader definition both are larger. The official budget data should be adjusted for unrecorded budgetary spending, extrabudgetary account balances, and quasi-fiscal spending. The official debt data should be adjusted for unrecorded explicit debt and quasi-fiscal (contingent) liabilities.

According to the official data, the budget deficit has hovered at relatively modest levels over the last 20 years, with a major decline in both revenue and expenditure (Figure 8.1). Revenue collection fell from about 31 percent of GDP in 1979 to about 13 percent in 1995, before recovering to about 16 percent in 2000. The revenue decline after 1979 was in large part due to the separation of the financial accounts of the

Table 8.1. Official and IMF Measures of the Fiscal Deficit and the Debt Stock, 2001

Measure	Percent of GDP
Fiscal deficit	
State budget, official measure	2.6
State budget, IMF measure	3.2
Plus funds' balance	2.6
Plus funds' balance and policy bank net lending	3.6
Debt stock	
Explicit, official measure	15.6
Explicit, IMF measure	24.4

Sources: Ministry of Finance; and IMF staff estimates.

SOEs from the budgetary accounts, a move undertaken to improve the managerial and financial autonomy of the SOEs. A concomitant reduction in the financing of SOE investments out of the state budget resulted in a corresponding decline in expenditure. Since the mid-1990s, however, both revenue and expenditure have rebounded, and the budget deficit widened in response to the Asian crisis.

The official definition of the state budget has historically excluded three important items that should normally be included: central government on-lending to local governments of certain bond issues since 1998, external official borrowing by government agencies (such as loans from the World Bank), and interest payments (included since 2000). Also, subsidies to enterprises are recorded as negative revenue rather than expenditure. When these adjustments are made for 2001, the state budget is estimated to have had revenue of 17.2 percent of GDP, expenditure of 20.4 percent of GDP, and an overall deficit of 3.2 percent of GDP (Table 8.1). The primary deficit was 2.3 percent of GDP.

Revenue and expenditure related to extrabudgetary funds are sizable but probably broadly balanced. The off-budget funds and operations comprise three broad types of funds:[1] social funds, authorized extrabudgetary funds, and unauthorized extrabudgetary funds. Although no data are readily available from before 1994, aggregate revenue and expendi-

---

[1]Social funds include the Pension Fund, the Unemployment Fund, the Medical Fund, the Injury Fund, and the Maternity Fund. Authorized extrabudgetary funds are financed by properly legislated fees and surcharges and operate at the central, regional, and local government levels. Unauthorized extrabudgetary funds are not sanctioned by the State Council and therefore operate in contravention to the law. They are financed by a variety of taxes, surcharges, and fees.

ture of the social funds have hovered around 2–3 percent of GDP since then. Aggregate revenue of the extrabudgetary funds in 2000 was 7.8 percent of GDP, which exceeded aggregate expenditure by 0.6 percent of GDP. Unauthorized extrabudgetary funds are illegal; they probably do not enjoy significant access to bank borrowing and therefore would not be able to run substantial deficits.

In the past the government used the banking system extensively to finance SOEs. This mechanism served as a way of compensating for the decline in resources coming from the state budget and has been used particularly for investment projects and agricultural procurement. Lending to SOEs was done in the context of the annual credit plan, which until 1997 established gross lending targets for specific institutions and projects, and was provided by the state commercial banks and, more recently, by the policy banks created in 1994. According to the *Government Finance Statistics Manual*, lending for policy purposes should be incorporated into the fiscal accounts. There are several approaches to measuring the quasi-fiscal component of lending for public policy purposes:

- Develop an overall estimate of net lending, which refers to the outstanding stock of lending by banks at the end of each period in which government direction is involved.
- Attempt to isolate the grant component. The value of loans could be decomposed into two components: a pure loan component, which would represent the loan had it been undertaken on an exclusively commercial basis, and a grant component, which would represent the government's role as a promoter of public policy.
- Estimate the eventual impact of lending by banks on the government's net worth. This would correspond to policy lending and other lending by banks that is not being repaid by SOEs and would end up being reflected in the resulting cost of recapitalizing the banking system. This impact on government net worth would be particularly relevant for debt sustainability calculations.

Given data limitations, the first approach is the most practical, although the third is better suited for medium-term sustainability analysis. The second approach is not feasible for data reasons. The third approach is practical for estimating the existing debt stock, but estimating the flow deficit is more difficult, because it requires an assumption about the extent to which new loans are likely to become nonrecoverable. The first approach (directed lending) is also difficult to apply fully, because many loans made by state commercial banks to SOEs may be used either for commercial purposes or for purposes of public policy. However, a narrower definition can be used, namely, new lending by policy banks.[2] By definition, such lending is done for purposes of public policy and should be incorporated into the fiscal accounts. In 2001 the policy banks increased their stock of loans to the economy by 1.0 percent of GDP (and by 1.5 percent of GDP in 2000).

Including estimates of quasi-fiscal activity of the banking sector increases the broader fiscal deficit substantially. When only lending by policy banks is included (the first approach), the broader fiscal deficit was about 3.6 percent of GDP in 2001. If one includes an estimate of the potential cost to the government of all lending by the banking system in 2001 (the third approach), the broader fiscal deficit was probably still larger.

Explicit public debt is low by international standards. Central government debt is estimated to have reached 24.4 percent of GDP in 2001.[3] Of this, 20.1 percentage points was domestic debt and the rest public and publicly guaranteed external debt. This debt includes Y 270 billion (3.4 percent of 1998 GDP) in tradable treasury bonds issued to recapitalize the four state-owned commercial banks in 1998, although these bonds are excluded from official debt statistics.

Including contingent liabilities associated with bank loans, the total public debt stock at the end of 2001 was higher. Loan losses of the state-owned banks are not legally a liability of the government, but these are losses that the government may have to cover at some point in the future. Estimates of the stock of nonrecoverable loans are very difficult given data limitations, but it is likely that these loans will pose substantial demands on the public finances in the future.[4]

---

[2]As part of a long-term plan to convert specialized banks to commercial banks, three policy banks were created in 1994. These banks were designed as nonprofitmaking financial institutions for the purpose of providing financing for policy-oriented projects identified in the state development plan or to promote industrial policies for specific sectors. However, most existing policy loans were not transferred, nor have policy banks taken over sole responsibility for all policy lending. In particular, the large state banks have continued to be the principal source of working capital for SOEs. The formal credit plan was abandoned in 1998. Although informal governmental credit guidance likely persists (for example, by encouraging state commercial banks to lend to the government's priority projects), the state commercial banks are responsible for assessing the viability of projects and held accountable for their lending decisions.

[3]The central government is the only level of government legally authorized to borrow domestically or abroad. However, enterprises established by local governments may borrow.

[4]The authorities report that nonperforming loans of the state commercial banks amounted to 22 percent of GDP (31 percent of outstanding loans) at the end of 2001. In addition, Y 1.4 trillion (17 percent of 1999 GDP) of the nonperforming loans of the state commercial banks was transferred to asset management companies. Market estimates of nonperforming loans in China's state commercial banks are substantially higher.

The Medium-Term Fiscal Outlook

China's public debt stock will grow further if corrective measures are not taken. As noted above, although China's explicit debt stock is relatively modest, its implicit debt, which includes nonrecoverable bank loans (but not pension liabilities; see below), is substantial. Similarly, the broadly defined fiscal deficit is also large, taking into account new nonrecoverable loan growth and the cost of interest on the implicit debt stock.

The medium-term fiscal outlook is burdened by two main factors: further accumulation of nonperforming loans and greater budgetary expenditure pressures. Accelerated efforts are needed in banking reform to stem the flow of new nonperforming loans. Budgetary spending is likely to increase significantly to meet social and infrastructure policy objectives. Budgetary outlays on education and public health will need to be increased to raise expenditure per student, increase enrollment rates, and bolster public health programs (see World Bank, 1997). Large infrastructure programs are planned and are being executed in the areas of roads and communications, energy, agricultural improvements, and the environment. For example, the authorities' highway construction program is estimated to cost about $150 billion (12 percent of 2001 GDP) over the next 15 years, of which approximately 20 percent is expected to be funded by the state budget.

To ensure sustainable debt dynamics over the medium term, it will be necessary both to reduce the explicit budget deficit and to contain the flow of new nonrecoverable loans. The envisaged budgetary adjustment should come mostly from higher revenue, although it will also be necessary to reallocate expenditure further toward priority areas. Tax policy measures could include a reduction of tax preferences, unification of the corporate tax regime for domestic and foreign enterprises, extending the value-added tax to services,[5] and including the self-employed in the income tax net. Tax administration efforts should consolidate the reforms currently under way to enhance taxpayer compliance, increase the focus on arrears collection, and improve audit programs.

Strong growth alone will not solve China's public debt problem. Even with average real annual growth of 7–8 percent of GDP, timely reforms are needed to ensure fiscal sustainability. On the other hand, the analysis also shows that the public debt-to-GDP ratio can be con-

---

[5]Integrating the business tax into the value-added tax is also recommended on general efficiency grounds (for example, to reduce tax cascading). Capital goods should also be removed from the value-added tax base.

trolled with a modest, sustained fiscal adjustment effort and continued SOE and financial sector reforms.

Other Issues

In addition to facing the medium-term outlook described above, the government needs to reform its pension system and how it shares resources across provinces. Failure to address these problems will hamper the reform process and could have significant fiscal costs.

Pension System

China's pension system faces large contingent liabilities and hampers the SOE reform process.[6] Because of the aging of the population, the current pay-as-you-go system is heavily underfunded on an actuarial basis.[7] Because SOEs are still responsible for a substantial part of pension provision, the current system also makes it more difficult to tackle the problem of unprofitable firms and to increase labor mobility. The government has decided in principle to move toward a three-tier system as recommended by the World Bank, but it has yet to decide on a number of critical issues. These decisions, when made, should allow the reform to proceed, leading to greater unification of pension administration, funded individual accounts, and lower pension benefits.

The World Bank estimates the government's implicit pension debt at about 90 percent of GDP, with a financing gap of about 70 percent of GDP (Dorfman and Sin, 2001).[8] Although China's implicit debt is lower than in most OECD countries, this reflects mainly the fact that China's pension system only covers about 20 percent of the workforce, whereas pension systems in OECD countries cover about 90 percent.

---

[6]This section draws heavily on World Bank research, mainly by Mark Dorfman.

[7]The system currently has about 105 million contributors (about 12 percent of the working population) and 32 million beneficiaries. Although rates vary across localities, the average combined contribution rate is about 27 percent of wages, and the replacement rate is about 80 percent. The number of contributors is projected to increase modestly through 2010 and then decrease to 86 million by 2050. Conversely, the number of retirees is projected to increase markedly, to 95 million by 2050.

[8]Implicit pension debt is a measure of the present value of accrued benefits under the pension system if the system were terminated at a particular date (including benefits to be paid to current pensioners and pension rights that current workers have earned up to the termination date, which is assumed to be in 1998). The financing gap is measured by summing the net present value of the current balance (revenue less expenditure) throughout the projection period (75 years in the case of Dorfman and Sin).

The above estimates are highly sensitive to parameter changes, and reforms of the system could significantly reduce the financing gap. For example, Dorfman and Sin (2001) estimate that if the retirement age were gradually increased to 65 or if the individual account benefit followed a life annuity payout, the financing gap of the system would be reduced substantially. The gap could be narrowed to less than 10 percent of GDP through comprehensive reforms, including gradually increasing the retirement age to 65; paying out individual accounts using annuities calculated based on life expectancy at retirement; and indexing base and individual account pensions to consumer prices instead of wages.

Reforms in the pension system and the SOE sector are closely linked. The current system, which is mainly administered and paid by individual SOEs, impedes labor mobility, does not provide a level playing field for enterprises, and complicates SOE restructuring by failing to delink pension provision from enterprise management. Without a clear statement of an enterprise's legal obligations, it is difficult to value the enterprise, legally segregate the social and financial liabilities, and decide the hierarchy of claimants in bankruptcy proceedings.

In 1997 the government adopted a nationwide three-tier pension system, like that recommended by the World Bank. This system will comprise a public pension, mandatory individual pension accounts, and supplementary voluntary individual accounts.[9] So far the individual accounts are largely notional and are not funded; instead current contributions are being used to meet current pension payment needs. A pilot reform project for provincial pensions was initiated in 2001 in the northern province of Liaoning, which has a large concentration of SOEs. In June 2001 the government announced that, when joint-stock limited companies with state shares launch initial public offerings or issue additional shares, they must sell state shares up to 10 percent of the total funds to be raised, with the proceeds to be transferred to the national social security fund. The program was suspended in late 2001 following a sharp decline in share prices, which was partly attributed to the increased supply of SOE shares coming to the market under the program.

However, the problem of the implicit pension debt has not been fully addressed, nor has administration been unified. Although the envisaged sale of state shares will provide some funding, it will probably not be sufficient. Either the implicit pension debt will have to be reduced through

---

[9]Contributions would amount to about 24 percent of the wage, with employee contributions reaching 8 percent of their wage and employers contributing the rest. Although the system is still being finalized, the new scheme is likely to provide a pension with a replacement rate of 50–60 percent, with about 20 percentage points coming from a public pension provided by the budget and the rest from funded individual accounts.

parametric reforms,[10] or the debt will need to be financed by the government. Although the cash flow needs of the current system are not likely to be very large in the medium term, any transition to a funded system will likely require government financing. However, World Bank simulations suggest that the amount of government financing needed to fund the individual accounts would be modest if accompanied by the recommended parametric reforms.

Fiscal Federalism

China has partially succeeded in reforming its system of fiscal federalism, but more needs to be done to ensure greater equalization in service delivery across provinces. The design of intergovernmental fiscal relations is an important ingredient of a successful economic transition, and China's large and diverse population makes this issue especially important. Industrial location decisions under China's planned economy bore little relation to market signals, with the result that the transition process involves sharply uneven adjustment costs in different regions. Heavy industries were often located far from their markets, and these enterprises became unviable once they faced international and domestic competition and had to pay for transportation services at realistic prices. Furthermore, certain coastal provinces have been allowed to experiment with market-oriented reforms since 1978. Thus the social costs of transition are greater inland, whereas the engines of growth, and therefore of income, are located in the coastal provinces.

Intergovernmental relations over the last 20 years have evolved in two broad phases: decentralization before 1994 and recentralization since then. The fiscal revenue sharing system established in 1980 gave incentives for local government to reduce revenue transfers to the center. As a consequence of these and other factors (including the decline of the SOE sector), the central government's share of total revenue fell from 39 percent in 1985 to 22 percent in 1993. By the early 1990s the authorities considered central government revenue to be seriously inadequate, prompting the far-reaching fiscal system reform of 1994.

The 1994 reform significantly changed the revenue sharing rules and increased the importance of transfers. Under the new system, tax revenue assigned to the central government included 75 percent of the (newly introduced) value-added tax; excises and trade-related taxes

---

[10]In addition to the institutional reform (the three-tier system), the World Bank has recommended unifying and raising the retirement age, indexing pension payments to inflation (instead of indexing them to wages or raising them on an ad hoc basis), and linking the individual account pension to life expectancy at retirement.

(customs duties and excises and value-added taxes levied on imports); the enterprise income tax collected from central SOEs; turnover taxes on the railroads and the financial sector; and a securities stamp tax. At the same time, a national tax service was established to administer the new central and shared revenue system. Local governments were assigned the following revenue sources: 25 percent of the value-added tax; the business tax (apart from that collected from banks, railroads, and insurance companies); enterprise income taxes levied on local SOEs; the personal income tax; and a number of smaller taxes.[11]

The 1994 reform succeeded in increasing central government resources. Between 1995 and 2000 the state revenue-to-GDP ratio rose from 11.2 percent to 15.3 percent, and the central government's share of total revenue rose from 22 percent to 52 percent. Central government expenditure (excluding transfers to local governments) increased from 3.8 percent of GDP in 1993 to 6.2 percent in 2000.

Although the 1994 reform established a rules-based transfer system, it has not yet provided each province with sufficient resources to deliver a minimum standard of public services. The new system of transfers from central to local governments comprised four main parts:

- *Revenue returned.* This provides each province with 30 percent of the increase in value-added tax and excise tax collection in its province over the 1993 base. This is a regressive transfer (in the sense that richer provinces benefit most) but also the most important, accounting for 39 percent of total transfers in 2001 (2.3 percent of GDP). That share, however, has fallen from 72 percent in 1996.
- *Specific-purpose grants.* Hundreds of different earmarked grants are allocated on an ad hoc basis. They represent a large and, in recent years, growing share of total transfers, reaching 35 percent in 2001 (2.0 percent of GDP), up from 18 percent in 1996. These transfers are probably progressive in that they are targeted to projects in poorer provinces.
- *Subsidy transfers.* These are meant to ensure that each province has adequate resources. They are rules based and depend on variables such as provincial GDP and student-teacher ratios. These transfers have represented only a small but growing share of total transfers, rising from 6 percent in 1996 to 25 percent in 2001 (1.4 percent of GDP).
- *Fixed subsidies.* These transfers were designed to ensure that every province would have total nominal revenue no lower than in

---

[11]By law, local governments have very limited ability to set taxes. They can only modify the rates of a few minor taxes; all other decisions must be made by the central government. In practice, however, lower levels of government have used a variety of illegal taxes, fees, and surcharges.

1993. Specifically, the transfer would equal the province's 1993 base revenue minus the 25 percent share of value-added tax revenue and minus most other local revenue sources. As the 1993 level is fixed in nominal terms, this transfer is declining relative to other transfers and in 2001 amounted to 2 percent of total transfers (0.1 percent of GDP).

The focus of reforming the system of fiscal federalism should be on ensuring that each province has sufficient resources to deliver a minimum standard of public services. This means continuing to reduce the importance of revenue-returned transfers and greatly increasing the importance of subsidy and specific-purpose transfers to those provinces in need.

Conclusions

China's current fiscal position is much weaker than official data suggest, mainly because of the quasi-fiscal operations of the banking system. The already large public debt stock (including quasi-fiscal liabilities) will grow further if corrective measures are not taken. Alternatively, it could be reduced gradually—to a sustainable level—if the budget is tightened modestly every year and the flow of new nonperforming loans is significantly (but gradually) curbed.

Other medium-term fiscal issues, such as pension reform and fiscal federalism, also need to be addressed. The pension system's finances are unsustainable and its administration is fragmented. The system of intergovernmental transfers does not provide sufficient equalization in service delivery across provinces. Failure to address these issues not only will be costly but will also hamper economic reform.

The overall fiscal policy agenda is challenging. Revenue should be further increased. Expenditure, which will likely continue rising to meet pressing social needs, should be further prioritized. Quasi-fiscal spending through the banking system should be quickly reined in. Individual pension accounts should be fully funded, pension benefits should be made less generous, and pension administration should be further unified. The system of intergovernmental transfers should ensure greater equalization in public service delivery across provinces.

References

Dorfman, Mark, and Yvonne Sui, 2001, "China: Social Security Reform—Strategic Options" (Washington: World Bank).

World Bank, 1997, *China 2020—Development Challenges in the New Century* (Washington: World Bank).

9

State Enterprise Reforms

PAUL HEYTENS

Reform of state-owned enterprises (SOEs) has been among the most difficult and gradual of China's structural reforms. The financial performance of SOEs has been weak for much of the reform period, and the losses they have incurred have required heavy subsidization by the state. Early in the reform era this was effected through direct budgetary allocations, but thereafter it took the form of loans from the state commercial banks (SCBs), creating increasingly large contingent liabilities.

By the early 1990s it had become clear that fundamental restructuring of the SOEs—and, by extension, of the state-owned banks (see Chapter 10)—could no longer be delayed. Despite a broadening and acceleration of the process, the pace of reform remained conditioned by concerns over social stability and public support for reforms, as layoffs from SOEs added to regional income disparities and strained an inadequate social safety net. Some progress has nevertheless been made in hardening budget constraints, and enterprise profitability has improved following Premier Zhu Rongji's pledge in 1998 to revitalize medium-size and large SOEs. Although part of this improvement reflected one-time changes (such as the conversion of a sizable portion of nonperforming loans into equity), there have also been durable efficiency gains through layoffs, a reduced social welfare burden, and efforts to shed excess capacity in key sectors.

This progress notwithstanding, deep-rooted problems remain. Available balance sheet data suggest that some one-third of China's predominantly state-owned companies are unable to generate sufficient earnings to cover interest payments, and aggregate data indicate that

SOEs are less efficient and display considerably weaker financial profiles than enterprises under other forms of ownership (see Chapter 11). Moreover, enterprise management and operational efficiency have remained weak, outside governance remains limited, excess labor is still high, and exit channels for poorly performing SOEs remain limited.

The Reform Agenda

The overarching goal of China's reform process is to create a market economy with "socialist characteristics." In principle, this has meant an economy in which substantial public ownership of industry is retained, but where enterprises of all ownership types seek to maximize profits in response to market forces. As in other transition economies, the creation of a market economy in China has been seen less as an end in itself than as a necessary means to achieve growth and development in a manner consistent with the country's social and political objectives.

By the early 1990s the move toward a market economy was already well advanced. Most product prices, and to a lesser extent wages, were free to vary with market conditions. Competition was strong in many, if not all, industrial sectors. Overall, the economic behavior of enterprises had become more responsive to market forces as a result of increased competition in most consumer goods sectors, the rapid growth of the nonstate sector, and management reforms carried out in the SOEs in the 1980s. These reforms generally involved delegating greater authority to the enterprises and allowing them to retain a larger share of the profits they generated. However, some of the more difficult reform tasks remained to be accomplished, including the following: transforming the SOEs into modern commercial entities; restructuring and reorganizing the strategic or "pillar" economic sectors to achieve economies of scale in production; developing the financial, legal, and other institutions necessary for the functioning of a market economy; and completing the opening of the domestic economy to international markets.

The 1993 Reform Agenda

The basic parameters of China's current SOE reform program were set out during the Third Plenary Session of the 14th Communist Party Congress in November 1993. Although enterprise reforms had been undertaken during earlier periods, the approach and pilot policies adopted in 1993 were much broader and more sweeping than anything implemented previously. The central elements were

- The *introduction of corporate governance*, including incorporation under a new company law, the clear separation of ownership from management, and granting enterprises a list of "autonomous rights"[1]
- *Removal of social welfare functions*, such as hospitals, schools, and pension and unemployment liabilities, from enterprise balance sheets, as well as steps to reduce excess labor
- *Reduction of accumulated enterprise debts*
- Provision of *new financing* for technical updating, improvement, and expansion
- *Organizational and ownership restructuring* through sales, mergers, leasing, contracting, joint-stock participation, and, if necessary, liquidation and bankruptcy.

The guiding principle in applying these reforms was to "seize the large and release the small." The end result envisaged by the architects of these reforms was an economy in which larger enterprises in key economic sectors remained under state control, with the rest under other forms of ownership. Both state and nonstate enterprises were to have independent management and operate according to market principles, although it was expected that some sectors would benefit from natural oligopolies or barriers to nonstate entry. With few exceptions, the state sector was expected to be profitable and to attract resources on a competitive basis, with minimal recourse to budgetary subsidies.

The emphasis on large enterprises and key sectors constituted a substantial shift in SOE reform strategy. In contrast to earlier reform initiatives, which were aimed at improving the performance of the entire SOE sector, the current strategy has emphasized downsizing the overall scope of state activity while concentrating state resources and efforts on those areas that could feasibly stay under central control. For example, state ownership would be retained in sectors where there was a perceived social need for state management (such as natural monopolies), or where state intervention could exploit economies of scale (as in coal mining and steel), or where resource allocation represented a national development priority (as in electric power generation and telecommunications services).

For the first time, smaller enterprises as a group were explicitly encouraged to leave the state-owned fold. Responsibility for this process was essentially handed over to local governments. Small enterprises

---

[1]Fourteen such rights were specified, including the right to decide on production and pricing policies, the right to decide the size and composition of new investment, the right to decide on the hiring and firing of labor, and the right to retain profits and undertake foreign trade.

could be restructured in any way local governments saw fit, but no central financing or subsidies were to be provided in the process. This approach was based on the assessment that smaller enterprises accounted for a disproportionately large share of losses and indebtedness, which were best dealt with by moving them out of the hands of the state.

Pilot Programs

The State Council subsequently adopted a number of diverse pilot programs to carry out these reforms. The following are the most prominent:

- *Adoption of modern enterprise systems.* This comprehensive initiative initially involved 100 medium-size and large enterprises in 50 cities. The primary aim was to convert the enterprises into incorporated entities with modern corporate governance structures, clarified ownership rights, and strengthened management functions. This program also adopted many of the measures of the "pilot cities" project outlined just below.
- *Enterprise restructuring and recapitalization in pilot cities.* This program, managed by municipal governments in 111 (originally 18) cities and involving enterprises chosen by them, included specific measures to lower debt-to-assets ratios as well as a general framework for enterprise restructuring. The former included central and local tax credits and exemptions as well as accelerated annual depreciation deductions, all to be used for enterprise recapitalization. Restructuring measures included special procedures for mergers and bankruptcies of SOEs as well as divestiture of hospitals, schools, and other "nonproductive" social assets.
- *Revitalization of key enterprises.* The State Council selected 1,000 of the largest centrally administered SOEs, which were considered to form the core of the national economy. Of these, about 520 (the precise number has varied slightly over time) were chosen for central support, including the provision of new financing through "principal bank" agreements and the raising of equity capital. In addition, these enterprises were to receive broader operational autonomy, including autonomy with respect to financing modalities (such as issuance of corporate bonds) and direct foreign trading rights.
- *Formation of large enterprise groups.* One hundred and twenty (originally 57) key production enterprises were given the right to form large holding structures, which were meant to help achieve economies of scale in a number of industries and play an instrumental role in the restructuring and corporatization of related

enterprises. Other measures included privileges similar to those introduced in the pilot cities and the programs for the 1,000 core enterprises, with the addition of autonomy in trade, financing, and investment decisions and direct administration by the State Council.

In addition to these centrally directed programs, provincial governments were encouraged to develop their own pilot schemes and policies for strengthening larger SOEs under their ownership and control. Most of these initiatives have proceeded along the lines of their central counterparts. For example, provinces and municipalities identified nearly 2,600 additional enterprises to undergo "modern enterprise system" reforms and have formed thousands of regional and local enterprise groups.

Subsequent Modifications

The approach to SOE reform adopted following the 14th Party Congress was not all-encompassing. Like reforms in other areas, the process was an evolving set of pilot schemes with varying emphases and generally lacked an overarching vision of the future of the state sector or its role in the economy (following an old Chinese adage, the authorities were "crossing the river by feeling the stones"). This reflected in part the fact that the reform measures had generally arisen as a compromise between those who advocated a strong majority role for state ownership—but with reduced subsidies and greater incentives for efficiency—and those seeking to reduce the role of the state to a bare minimum. In addition, the reform strategy focused primarily on individual enterprises or enterprise groups, with policies and preferences determined according to size and scale, rather than the specific economic conditions in individual production sectors. There were no industry-specific reform blueprints.

By early 1997 the terms of the debate over the role of the state in the economy had begun to shift more decisively in favor of greater liberalization and nonstate participation. President Jiang Zemin, during the 15th Party Congress in September 1997, provided substantial clarification of the desired economic role of the state and the long-term goals of SOE reform. Most important, he clarified that the introduction of market mechanisms (such as stock markets and institutions of corporate governance such as shareholders' meetings) were consistent with a socialist market economy, and that the state did not have to dominate every sector or have majority ownership in every enterprise in order to maintain broad control of the economy. These clarifications opened the door for a further broadening of the scope of enterprise reform.

There was also a growing recognition, partly as a lesson from the Asian crisis, that the ongoing reforms were not deep enough or proceeding quickly enough to stem the declining performance of the SOEs, particularly the rising losses and resulting nonperforming loans in the banking system. SOE reforms were accelerated significantly following the ascension of Zhu Rongji to Premier in March 1998, who immediately embarked on a three-year program to revitalize China's medium-size and large SOEs. This was to be achieved by widening implementation of the pilot reform initiatives to a national scale and combining them with efforts to reorganize, upgrade, and improve enterprise management and governance, to change the way enterprises operate, and to carry out a strategic reorganization of key sectors. The social consequences of accelerated reforms were to be dealt with through complementary efforts to establish and secure adequate financing for a broad social safety net, including reemployment programs. The link between SOE problems and sector-specific conditions was also explicitly recognized, prompting the launch of industry-wide restructuring programs aimed at eliminating excess capacity and redundant labor, the main underlying causes of chronic losses.

The Progress of Reforms

The complexity and multidimensional character of China's SOE reforms make it very difficult to define clear indicators of progress or success. Enterprise reform in China has also been shaped by a number of special characteristics that need to be taken into account in drawing conclusions about the process. A key factor is the explicit policy choice to retain significant state ownership and control of industry. Another important characteristic is the perceived need by the Chinese authorities to proceed in a manner that minimizes social disruption and preserves public support for reforms.

Along with the achievement of Premier Zhu's three-year revitalization objective (see Box 9.1), important steps have been taken in virtually every reform area. However, progress has been uneven: considerable success has been achieved in small enterprise reform and labor downsizing; on the other hand, a number of critical governance issues in the larger enterprises are only now beginning to be addressed. Looking ahead, stronger reform and revitalization efforts in the larger SOEs have been identified as top priorities for economic policy in the 10th Five-Year Plan (2001–05). In assessing the progress that has been made, it is useful to break the reform process down into its main components: economic restructuring, reform of enterprise management and corporate governance, and ownership reform.

Box 9.1. Premier Zhu's SOE Revitalization Objective

During the March 1998 annual session of the National People's Congress, Premier Zhu Rongji announced an ambitious three-year program to revitalize medium-size and large SOEs. The program was aimed specifically at achieving the "two majorities," that is, to transform the majority of money-losing medium-size and large SOEs into profitable enterprises, and to have the majority of "core" SOEs adopt the modern enterprise system. The first objective was directed at the 6,599 medium-size and large SOEs (out of a total population of about 16,800) that were continuing to suffer losses at the end of 1997, whereas the second aimed primarily at the 100 central-level and 2,700 provincial-level pilot enterprises and the 520 "key" large SOEs.

At the opening of the March 2001 annual session, the premier announced that his revitalization objective had been "realized on the whole," citing the following indicators:

- Overall SOE performance had improved dramatically. Industrial SOEs had achieved profits of Y 239.2 billion in 2000, the highest level ever and 2.9 times their level of 1997.
- Most of the industrial sectors that had been recording large losses were now making profits. Of the 14 "key" industrial sectors targeted, 12 had become profitable by 2000, and the other two, the coal and defense industries, had reduced their losses considerably.
- State enterprises in all provinces, autonomous regions, and municipalities under the central government had also begun making profits in the aggregate. Of the 31 such entities, 12 had turned losses into profits and the other 19 had increased their profits in 2000.
- Most of the money-losing medium-size and large SOEs at the end of 1997 had been turned around. By the end of 2000, 4,799 of the 6,599 such enterprises had been removed from the list, either by becoming profitable, by merging with stronger enterprises, or by entering bankruptcy.
- Most core SOEs had also adopted the modern enterprise system. The vast majority of the targeted enterprises noted above had been incorporated under the company law and had adopted other aspects of the modern enterprise system by the end of 2000.

However, the improvement in SOEs' financial performance may not be as strong as the headline figures suggest. In particular, a sizable portion (estimated at some 75 percent) of the increase in profits in 2000 reflected outside factors, including higher oil prices and lower interest payments resulting from debt-equity swaps and other measures. In addition, more than a third of all industrial SOEs were still recording losses at the end of 2000, and the aggregate losses of ailing enterprises fell by a less impressive 27 percent in 2000.

Economic Restructuring

As enterprise restructuring gained momentum, it soon became constrained by the limited financial resources available to pay the costs. Principal among these has been the scarcity of fiscal resources, which are necessary to separate social welfare functions from enterprises, write off or restructure bank debts, and provide support for unemployed workers. Enterprise restructuring has therefore been reasonably well advanced in the wealthier coastal provinces, but much less so in the old industrial and mining areas of the less-affluent northeastern and interior provinces. A weak legal and institutional framework, in particular the lack of modern bankruptcy institutions, has also slowed the pace of enterprise restructuring. The World Bank recently identified a number of deficiencies in the current regime, including the lack of clear rules, like those in Chapter 11 of the U.S. bankruptcy code, for resolution of company bankruptcies, and insufficient protection of creditor rights.[2]

Mergers and Bankruptcy

The number of bankruptcies has increased but remains relatively small, and bankruptcy proceedings have yet to be applied widely to medium-size and large enterprises. The State Economic and Trade Commission (SETC) estimates that by mid-2001 only 2,300 enterprises, with assets totaling Y 290 billion (less than 4 percent of total assets of all medium-size and large SOEs), had exited the market since the special merger and bankruptcy procedures established under the pilot cities program were applied on a national scale in 1998. These figures are small in relation to the continued weak overall performance of SOEs and the large number of potential candidates for bankruptcy or other forms of fundamental restructuring. For example, nearly 45 percent of the 47,500 industrial SOEs continued to record some form of loss in early 2001.

In light of the financial and legal obstacles involved, formal bankruptcy has often not been the most practical alternative available to creditors and local governments. Many cash-strapped local governments have instead found it easier to idle production, send workers home on minimal monthly living wages (often paid for through continued bank lending), and keep accumulating interest arrears. The pilot

---

[2]World Bank (2000). China's bankruptcy regime is still based on the bankruptcy law promulgated in 1986. A new bankruptcy law that addresses many of these deficiencies was drafted several years ago but has not been promulgated, owing in part to concerns that it could accelerate enterprise closures beyond socially acceptable limits.

cities program provided a special central government charge-off fund for banks, which has been applied both to formal bankruptcies and to the write-down of overdue interest in merger cases, to help defray the costs of enterprise restructuring. However, the funds utilized under this mechanism have been quite meager—rising from Y 30 billion in 1997 to just over Y 80 billion in 2000—relative to the size of the remaining problem.[3]

The use of bankruptcy procedures has nevertheless become more widespread and socially acceptable in recent years. The World Bank has estimated the number of bankruptcies since the mid-1990s at about 20,000 nationwide, half of which have involved SOEs. Considerable experience has been gained and capacity built up in the courts and local administrations as a result of the widening application of bankruptcy procedures, which has also helped to create greater public understanding and acceptance of the process.

Exit of Surplus Labor

Labor redundancies are high in the SOEs. Official estimates by the Ministry of Labor and Social Security based on 1994–95 data suggest that the number of unneeded employees in the SOEs at that time was over 20 million, or more than one-fourth of the SOE workforce. Other estimates, taking account of subsequent increases in production capacity and competition as well as the need to close money-losing enterprises, have placed the number of labor redundancies at 30 million to 35 million at the end of 1997, or well over one-third of the 77-million-strong SOE workforce at that time.

Recent years have witnessed a significant acceleration in the number of layoffs. SOEs laid off a total of 16 million workers from 1998 through 2000,[4] thus eliminating roughly half of the estimated redundancies. Despite official concerns about the rising number of layoffs and the potential for social unrest, the declining financial performance of many SOEs and the increasing reluctance of banks to lend to them left local governments with no alternative but to allow workers to be laid off. Increased layoffs were also facilitated by stepped-up efforts to strengthen the social safety net for unemployed workers (Box 9.2). The proportion

---

[3]The total debt write-off under this program from 1997 to 2000 was just under Y 200 billion, or only 10 percent of the authorities' estimate of the remaining nonperforming loans in the four SCBs following the Y 1.4 trillion transfer of nonperforming loans to the asset management companies in 1999–2000.

[4]Labor ministry data indicate that about 9 million SOE workers were laid off from 1995 through 1997.

of redundant workers nevertheless remains high, at about one-third of the SOE labor force of 47 million as of the end of 2000.[5]

Reducing Indebtedness

Leverage among industrial SOEs has declined in recent years— liabilities-to-equity ratios among SOEs have fallen from about 200 per- cent in the mid-1990s to about 150 percent—but nevertheless remains high. The authorities have used a variety of channels to reduce SOE indebtedness. As noted above, debts have been written off in the con- text of the merger and bankruptcy program, as well as through a num- ber of other special programs. For example, old policy loans from the SCBs that had been transferred to the policy banks were converted to state equity shares in some SOEs. Nearly Y 38 billion of such debts were converted under this program in 1997, with another Y 50 billion tar- geted for conversion in 1998. Increased equity issuance on foreign and domestic stock markets has also helped to reduce SOE debt.[6]

In a more recent initiative, debts of about Y 310 billion from some 580 SOEs are in the process of being swapped for equity under the asset management company (AMC) initiative begun in mid-1999 (see Chapter 10), in order to reduce the debt burdens of large SOEs that have shown the potential to be financially viable. To qualify for debt- equity swaps, enterprises must be approved by the SETC and be con- sidered to have marketable products, advanced technology, and good management expertise. The AMCs will assume ownership stakes equivalent to the amount of equity they have in the enterprises. However, there are concerns that the AMCs have not been provided with sufficient powers to restructure SOE operations (for example, to reduce leverage ratios), thus limiting their capacity to improve enter- prise performance.

Reducing the Social Welfare Burden

Efforts to divest SOEs of their traditional social welfare burdens are aimed at making these enterprises more competitive with nonstate

---

[5]The SOE labor force has also been reduced by means other than layoffs, including through the conversion of small enterprises to other forms of ownership.

[6]As indicated in Chapter 11, liabilities-to-equity ratios among listed companies are about half those of the general SOE population. However, it has been common practice for SOEs to create a subsidiary firm for listing purposes, which receives productive assets by transfer, while leaving outstanding debts, redundant workers, pension obligations, and other obligations with the parent enterprise.

Box 9.2. The Social Safety Net for Laid-Off SOE Workers

Because layoffs of SOE workers were a new phenomenon when enterprise reforms were broadened in the mid-1990s, the social security system was partial and incomplete. A three-phase system was introduced to improve the social safety net for unemployed SOE workers (or *xiagang*[1]) to deal with the surge in layoffs:

- *Income support and reemployment of* xiagang. Reemployment centers were set up to aid the transition to new jobs. Laid-off workers became eligible for income support based on prevailing wages in their locality. The program was financed by local governments, local unemployment insurance funds, and the SOEs. The central government also increased transfers to the regions hardest hit by layoffs to help them meet their required contributions to the reemployment centers.

- *Unemployment insurance.* Xiagang who remain unable to find employment after three years have to sever their relation with their reemployment center and join the pool of registered unemployed; this implies, among other things, the loss of nonwage benefits provided by their former employer. Such workers are then eligible for unemployment insurance (which provides lower payments than the reemployment centers) for a

---

[1]*Xiagang* retain formal links to their state employers until reemployed and are not included among the registered unemployed.

---

enterprises, which do not carry such heavy burdens, and to improve labor mobility by delinking access to the social safety net from employment with an enterprise. These efforts have two main components: the transfer of "nonproductive" social services units, primarily in housing, medical services, and education, away from SOEs, and the disposal of (generally unfunded) pension and unemployment liabilities.

Progress to date in transferring these social assets off of SOE balance sheets is difficult to judge, given the lack of comprehensive time-series data available on such assets. The SETC reports that the transfer process has been very uneven: enterprises in many wealthier coastal provinces and cities have disposed of virtually all of their social welfare units, but in other areas (particularly in company towns in the SOE-laden interior and northeastern provinces) progress has been considerably slower. The National Bureau of Statistics estimates that SOEs' overheads came down only slightly from 9 percent of operating costs in the mid-1990s and remain about twice those of the collectives and foreign-funded enterprises, an indication that the social welfare burden is still very heavy. The authorities estimate that the divestiture process

period of two years. The unemployment insurance system is also financed by local governments, worker contributions, and enterprises. Because the funds are pooled locally, in some high-unemployment areas beneficiaries receive partial payments or none at all because of a lack of funds.

- *Minimum income program.* After eligibility for unemployment insurance expires, workers can collect a minimum living stipend under a program introduced in 1994 as part of a broad poverty alleviation initiative. These programs are locally financed, and in some cities stipends are very low or not paid at all because of local fiscal constraints.

Although the coverage of this social safety net has been far from complete, it has facilitated an acceleration of labor downsizing in the SOEs in recent years. By the end of 2000, some 21 million *xiagang* had entered the reemployment centers, and about 95 percent were reported to have received formal income support payments. Of these, 13 million have been reemployed elsewhere in the economy, and another 3.3 million have been moved to the general unemployment insurance scheme.

Beginning in 2001, no more reemployment centers are to be established in the pilot areas for national social security reform (currently only in Liaoning province), and newly laid off SOE workers will enter the general unemployment insurance scheme directly. Those workers currently in reemployment centers will remain there until their three years have elapsed, or until they are reemployed.

could take another 5–10 years to complete, given the financing constraints.

Central and local governments have also been actively reforming pension, medical, and unemployment insurance systems. The main emphasis has been on switching from unfunded (and poorly defined) benefits to partially or fully funded schemes, based on contributions from enterprises and employees as well as from various levels of government. Policies pertaining to unemployment insurance have already been discussed in Box 9.2. The authorities are also moving ahead with reforms of the medical insurance and pension systems. They intend to replace the current pay-as-you-go pension system with a three-tier model along the lines recommended by the World Bank,[7] and they initiated a pilot project in Liaoning province in 2001. They also began at about the same time to require that 10 percent of the proceeds of all new

---

[7]The first tier would be a social pension, the second a mandatory funded system with individual accounts, and the third a supplementary (also funded) tier.

share offerings by SOEs be used to fund the pension system.[8] However, parametric changes (such as raising the retirement age or lowering the replacement ratio, or both) will also be necessary to make the new pension scheme viable, in view of the size of the implicit pension debt (estimated by the World Bank at nearly 100 percent of GDP).

Reducing Excess Capacity

Excess capacity and production for inventory have long been identified as major contributors to SOE losses. Massive investment in excess productive capacity ("duplicated construction") during the early years of the reform period resulted in very low levels of capacity utilization by the mid-1990s. Although reliable time-series data for capacity utilization are not available (the last comprehensive data were compiled by the National Bureau of Statistics in 1995; see Table 9.1), anecdotal evidence suggests that additional capacity continued to come on line at least until late 1997, worsening an already very difficult market oversupply situation.

The high excess capacity prompted the State Council to initiate comprehensive restructuring programs in industries where oversupply and financial losses were most severe. Programs were started in the textile and coal industries in 1998; other industry-specific programs were launched in subsequent years (Box 9.3). Encouraging progress has been made in these programs: as noted in Box 9.1, SOEs in 12 of the 14 industrial sectors targeted for capacity reduction had become profitable in the aggregate by the end of 2000.

Recent surveys by the National Bureau of Statistics and the State Internal Trade Bureau (SITB) under the SETC nevertheless indicate that excess capacity remains very high in a broad range of sectors and product areas. For example, the SITB, in its biannual survey in early 2001, found that nearly 80 percent of 609 nonfood product categories were in excess supply. In addition, capacity utilization among the 5,000 principal industrial enterprises surveyed quarterly by the People's Bank of China was still only about 75 percent in mid-2001, although it had risen by about 15 percentage points since early 1998, when the capacity reduction programs were initiated and tighter controls imposed on enterprise capital investment.[9]

---

[8]This program was suspended in late 2001 following the sharp decline of share prices, which was attributed in part to the additional supply of shares coming to the market under the program.

[9]The SETC in early 1998 imposed a ban on new capital investment in the steel and chemical industries and announced that it would no longer approve bank loans to SOEs to fund the construction of new plants, except for "selected high technology or promising product renovation projects."

Table 9.1. Capacity Utilization by Industry, 1995[1]

Level of Utilization	Industries
Full	Natural gas, industrial timber, plywood, rubber, distilled spirits
90 percent or above	Paper pulp, crude oil, crude iron, fiberboard, electric fans
80–90 percent	Dyes and chemicals (acids, ammonia, alcohols, sodas, etc.), plate glass, railway locomotives and passenger carriages, magnetic tape, refined steel, cigarettes, paper, cement, coal, sawn timber, ceramic and glass products
70–80 percent	Copper, ferroalloys, plastics, large-scale integrated circuits, chemical fertilizers, radios, sewing machines, clocks
60–70 percent	Beer, railway freight cars, tractors, mining equipment, vacuum cleaners, steel products, cleansing agents
50–60 percent	Refrigerators, medicine, telephones, vegetable oil, tires, bicycles, motorcycles, cameras
40–50 percent	Video recorders, washing machines, automobiles, color televisions, engines, machine tools, paint
25–40 percent	Aluminum products, air conditioners, copy machines, pesticides, microwave ovens
Less than 25 percent	Electric power generators, mini- and microcomputers, film

Source: National Bureau of Statistics.
[1] Data are for enterprises at the township level and above with independent accounting systems.

Enterprise "Revitalization"

Another element of SOE restructuring has been the direct provision of economic resources and other financial preferences for key enterprises (including the 520 key SOEs and the 120 pilot large enterprise groups). The most important policy in this regard has been the adoption of the principal bank system, aimed at providing a steady flow of bank financing according to prearranged contracts and establishing centralized accounts at the bank to allow for greater monitoring of enterprises' financial performance. Other such preferences have included priority approval of and lending for investment projects, particularly those aimed at upgrading technological capabilities (the "technological renovation" program), and favorable consideration for stock market listings. The authorities in late 1999 began subsidizing interest payments on bank loans for technological renovation investment from the central budget in an attempt to accelerate the revitalization of key enterprises. A total of 880 projects involving Y 240 billion in investment outlays were initially identified for this subsidized financing.

Box 9.3. Restructuring Programs in Selected Industries

The Chinese authorities have introduced a series of industry-specific restructuring programs targeted mostly at basic industries such as textiles, coal, metallurgy, oil refining, sugar refining, electric power generation, cement, glass, caustic soda, and beer—industries where excess capacity and aggregate losses have been most severe. These programs have generally been aimed at reducing excess capacity and rationalizing the industrial structure through various measures, such as closing down small and inefficient firms, encouraging output restraints, restricting new investment, eliminating outdated equipment and obsolete products, and upgrading production technology. The following summaries of selected restructuring programs provide an indication of the scope of these efforts and their modalities.

Textiles

In April 1998 the State Council launched a three-year pilot program to restructure the chronically unprofitable textile industry. By targeting a reduction in obsolete production capacity by 10 million spindles (one-quarter of the capacity at the time) and laying off 1.2 million workers (one-third of total employment), the authorities aimed at returning the industry to modest profitability by the end of the three-year period. The focus of the program was broadened in 1999 to include mergers of efficient enterprises to achieve economies of scale, and bankruptcies of inefficient and technologically outmoded enterprises. More effective penetration of international markets, technological updating of the production base, and product innovation were also emphasized to arrest the decline in export performance. The program has been successful, and the sector returned to profitability in 1999, ending six consecutive years of losses. Sector performance improved further in 2000: aggregate profitability rose 41 percent, to Y 13.9 billion, and total exports rose 20 percent, to nearly $50 billion.

Other Industry-Level Restructuring

Industry-level restructuring has accelerated significantly in the wake of the November 1999 bilateral agreement with the United States on China's accession to the World Trade Organization (WTO). The current strategy is to grow "national champions"—firms with sufficient size, financial strength, and technological prowess in key industries to enable them to compete with global players following WTO accession. China is currently striving to cultivate 30–50 such companies and enterprise groups through overseas and domestic stock listings, mergers and acquisitions, enterprise alliances, and industry-wide reorganization. This

Coal

China's coal industry, the world's largest, had been plagued by excess capacity, bloated inventories, declining prices, and chronic losses for nearly a decade. The oversupply was attributed to the large number of small and technologically outmoded mines, which produced about half of national output. In November 1998 the State Council decided to begin overhauling China's coal industry by shutting down small mines to reduce total output and stockpiles, and to lay off 400,000 workers from large state-owned mines to reduce their overheads and improve profitability. The restructuring program also included outlays of Y 15 billion to implement 282 technological renovation projects, aimed at improving industry efficiency, and efforts to increase exports. By the end of 2000 more than 47,000 small mines had been shut, reducing annual output by more than 25 percent; coal exports in 2000, at $1.5 billion, were 50 percent above their 1998 level. Although the industry has yet to turn a profit, losses have been reduced significantly, from Y 5 billion to Y 3.3 billion in 2000 alone.

Sugar

The sugar refining industry was targeted for intensified restructuring efforts in early 1999. At that time more than 90 percent of state-owned sugar refiners were losing money, largely because of overcapacity, obsolete refining technologies, and inefficient operations. The program aimed to merge hundreds of small refiners with larger ones to achieve scale economies, upgrade refining technologies of key large producers, and close a number of heavily indebted refineries. In 2000, 140 such refineries were shut, reducing capacity from 10.5 million tons to 8.2 million, and Y 12.6 billion was used from the central debt write-off fund to offset debts owed to commercial banks. Nine saccharine plants have also been closed to increase domestic demand for natural sugar. The sugar industry achieved a modest profit of Y 500 million in 2000, the first in several years; profits were targeted to double to Y 1 billion in 2001.

strategy has been particularly apparent in telecommunications services,[10] but is being pursued in a number of other industries ranging from aviation to petroleum.

---

[10] The apparent strategy involves developing flagship companies in each industry segment by encouraging domestic competition and by large capital infusions through overseas stock listings. Recent restructuring in the telecommunications industry has divided the old monopoly service provider (China Telecom) into separate entities providing Internet, mobile voice and data, fixed line, and paging services, and two service providers (China Mobile and China Unicom) have listed on the stock exchanges in New York and Hong Kong SAR.

Reform of Corporate Governance

The traditional system of state-owned property management has proved problematic from a corporate governance perspective. In particular, it has no clear structure of ownership, with little separation between ownership and management functions. As a result, SOEs have encountered political interference in their decision making. Most major decisions have therefore typically been made in coordination with various government agencies rather than on the basis of market criteria. Thus production decisions have been coordinated with line ministries; capital construction and technical renovation investment have been approved by central and local planning agencies; tax payments and profit transfers have often been negotiated with the Ministry of Finance and the local tax bureaus; and employment decisions have generally been made in consultation with the labor ministry.

The authorities have sought to address these problems through adoption of the "modern enterprise system," which seeks to clarify and separate ownership and management functions, thus providing greater incentives to improve enterprise efficiency. Broadly speaking, the main elements have involved corporatization according to the 1994 company law and devolution of commercial decision-making authority from government agencies to the enterprises themselves. These elements have been supplemented in recent years by efforts to enhance financial transparency, more closely monitor enterprise performance, and improve the quality of enterprise management.

Incorporation Under the Company Law

Incorporation under the company law has now become fairly widespread among larger SOEs.[11] The process generally involves the creation of a board of directors and a board of supervisors. A key aim of the program has also been to clarify the ownership of state shares as well as to introduce outside supervision through incorporation with other investors, such as through the creation of limited-liability partnerships. Survey results suggest that 70–80 percent of medium-size and large SOEs had been incorporated by the end of 2000, including all of the 100 pilot enterprises and 430 of the 520 "key" SOEs selected by the State Council.

Although the two-tier board structure and other features of the modern enterprise system are potentially powerful mechanisms for improv-

---

[11]Most small SOEs are not large enough to meet the minimum capital requirements for formal incorporation under the company law. As discussed below, the preferred means of transforming the governance of small enterprises has been ownership transfer.

ing corporate governance, they have not functioned as effectively as envisaged. The supervisory boards in practice tend to have little power and independence to carry out their oversight function because they have largely been chosen by and are subject to the controlling share-holder (the state), and thus they have not effectively represented minority shareholders. Moreover, there has in practice been little accountability of senior management to directors who are genuinely independent. The roles of chairman of the board and general manager have often been combined, and boards have been dominated by direc-tors with managerial responsibilities within the firm.[12] The appoint-ment of the general manager and directors to the board has also largely been dominated by the controlling shareholder. As a result, the boards of directors have been neither independent from management nor accountable to minority shareholders (Lin, 2000).

Enterprise Autonomy

A major component of the authorities' efforts to increase enterprise autonomy has been the functional removal of government from enter-prise management and decision making. A major step forward in this regard was the reduction in the number of government ministries from 40 to 29 in August 1998. The primary rationale of the restructuring was to eliminate the last of the remaining industrial branch ministries—which formerly directly managed SOEs under their control, but are now only to guide enterprises indirectly by issuing sector development plans and regulations—and to remove the government from the microman-agement of enterprises. This restructuring left two new economic super-ministries—the Ministry of Information Industry (MII) and the SETC—which took over the management and supervision functions of the old industrial line ministries.

In the wake of the government restructuring, the majority of the for-mer industrial branch ministries were reduced to bureau status and placed under the jurisdiction of the SETC, effectively removing their direct enterprise management functions. To fill the vacuum, a Working Committee for Large Enterprises was created under the Central Party Committee to monitor performance of the large SOEs and, in coopera-tion with the Ministry of Personnel, to look after managerial and staffing issues. This has been complemented by the Supervisory Com-missioner System, a group of former senior government officials who—

---

[12]PetroChina, which was listed in 2000 in Hong Kong SAR and New York, became the first Chinese SOE to recruit "outside" members to its board of directors.

after receiving specialized training in auditing, accounting, and finance—have been closely supervising the operations of the 520 key large enterprises and assessing their financial performance, compliance with relevant legislation and sectoral development policies, and managerial performance.

Despite the significant reduction in the number of supervisory ministries and personnel, the government still retains considerable influence over the management of enterprises. In particular, the Ministry of Personnel continues to select all senior managers in large SOEs. In addition, the central government has maintained overriding control over all key aspects of strategic industries such as automobiles, energy, steel, and telecommunications. The streamlining of responsibilities for information technologies in the MII highlights the ways in which the government restructuring has strengthened central control over a key sector.

Another form of enterprise autonomy is the granting of economic decision-making powers, as codified in the 14 "enterprise rights" outlined above. Some of these, for example profit retention, price setting, and self-determination of production levels and the product mix, have been introduced almost completely. In addition, foreign trading rights have been granted much more widely in recent years, including to nonstate enterprises, and this has significantly eroded the competitive advantage of the state foreign trade companies. However, the scope for independent action is much more limited in some other areas, such as making investment decisions, choosing enterprise managers, and firing workers.

Enhancing Financial Transparency

In late 1998 the Ministry of Finance introduced new accounting standards based on modern principles, and disclosure requirements and supervision of enterprise performance have been strengthened considerably since then, particularly for listed companies. In particular, the securities law promulgated in late 1998 has set out stringent disclosure standards, which has prompted a sharp rise in the number of listed companies reporting losses.[13] Disclosure requirements for listed companies were tightened further, and companies will now have to begin reporting detailed financial data on a quarterly basis and provide a public explanation if their earnings' forecasts are off by more than 10 percent.

Despite the introduction of more stringent accounting and disclosure standards and stepped-up supervision of SOEs' financial activities in

---

[13]For example, about 90 listed companies issued profit warnings in the first half of 1999, shortly after the law was passed, in comparison with only 10 in all of 1998.

recent years, fraud remains widespread. For example, the Auditor General's Office found financial irregularities worth Y 100 billion in the 1,290 SOEs audited during 2000. In addition, several spectacular share price manipulation scandals involving the spread of false financial information were uncovered in 2000. More generally, as described in Chapter 11, significant data problems still complicate the analysis of enterprises' financial conditions.

Improving Enterprise Management

Considerably more attention has been paid in recent years to improving the quality of SOE managers. To this end, in early 1998 the SETC began a "management training project." Managers are now required to participate in a comprehensive training program focused on developing competent, technocratic managers capable of leading enterprises in a competitive market economy. The authorities are also experimenting with headhunters and auctions for management professionals in an attempt to lure the best managerial talent into SOE management positions, and since 1998 hiring preference has been given to managers educated after the Cultural Revolution of the late 1960s. Systems have been developed to more closely link compensation and promotion with performance, including experimentation with stock option schemes. The personnel ministry has also drafted new regulations for the supervision of SOE managers with a view to establishing more flexible personnel management practices in line with the modern enterprise system.

Ownership Reform

"Releasing" Small SOEs

Ownership reform of small SOEs has been one of the most active components of SOE reform. Small enterprises and the local governments that own them were given broad freedom of choice in choosing channels of ownership change, including outright sale, merger, leasing, contracting, joint-stock participation, and, if necessary, liquidation and bankruptcy proceedings. The primary requirement has been that the fiscal costs of such transactions be minimal, which has generally required that new owners assume responsibility for any debts as well as that redundant labor be redeployed.

Efforts to diversify ownership of small enterprises accelerated significantly in the wake of President Jiang's speech at the 15th Party Congress in September 1997. Viewing themselves as having received the central government's blessing to transform their small SOEs, city and provincial officials responded with enthusiasm. Hitherto slowly reforming provinces dramatically picked up the pace of ownership transfer, while provinces that were already quite far down the road of enterprise divestiture extended the process from industrial to nonindustrial, and from smaller to larger, enterprises. Indeed, in early 1998 there was a flood of announcements of small enterprise sales and auctions in various localities; some local authorities even traveled abroad to offer their enterprises for sale.

The SETC estimates that 41,500 of the 63,500 small SOEs in the state's hands at the end of 1996 had been transformed to other forms of ownership (or been bankrupted), with another 10,000 enterprises leased out to the private sector, by the end of 2000. Of the total transformed, roughly one-third merged in some manner with another enterprise, 20 percent were converted to joint-stock companies, about 10 percent sold outright to private investors, and another 10 percent bankrupted. The authorities will continue to transform the ownership of the enterprises that remain under state control, but no timetable has been set for the completion of this process.

Listing Large SOEs

The stock market has assumed a greater role in China's enterprise reform process since the 15th Party Congress. Issuance of shares on domestic and foreign stock markets has been the mainstay of efforts both to diversify ownership in large enterprises and to strengthen their balance sheets, and the number of listed firms has increased significantly. Funds raised both on the domestic market and overseas set all-time highs in 2000, at Y 160 billion and $21 billion, respectively. The latter figure included several high-profile share issues by very large SOEs, including China's two largest petroleum companies and two largest mobile phone service providers. At the end of 2001 there were 1,160 firms listed on the Shanghai and Shenzhen exchanges, with a total market capitalization of Y 4.4 trillion (45.4 percent of GDP), up sharply from about 750 firms and Y 2 trillion (about 25 percent of GDP) at the end of 1997.

Despite the surge in listings and in funds raised, the domestic stock market has done little to improve the financial performance or corporate governance of the companies listed there. The domestic market has functioned primarily as a funding vehicle for poorly performing SOEs since its inception in late 1990. Indeed, as the analysis in Chapter 11 illustrates, China's domestically listed companies are financially very weak, in part because of a poorly developed regulatory framework for the securities markets and a selection mechanism that until early 2001 placed listing decisions in the hands of local governments. Given the lack of a credible delisting threat, the domestic stock market has largely failed to impose greater discipline on listed companies. Nor have the benefits of listing, in terms of reducing debt-equity ratios, been as significant as they should have been, as many listed companies have had to provide financial assistance to smaller and weaker enterprises in exchange for being allowed to list.

Future Reform Priorities

The remaining agenda for SOE reform is a challenging one, which the authorities expect will take up to a decade to complete.[14] In particular, the authorities understand that the realization of Premier Zhu's three-year revitalization objective is just an interim achievement, and that the underlying operational efficiency of SOEs has not fundamentally improved. During the March 2001 session of the National People's Congress, the new SETC Minister Li Rongrong summarized the current situation with the SOEs as follows:

> The SOEs still encounter a number of in-depth issues and problems in their reform and development, and those problems have not been fundamentally solved. The overall profitability of the SOEs remains weak and the foundations for difficulty relief remain soft. The channels for enterprises to exit from the market are far from operating smoothly, and the operating mechanisms of enterprises have not been fundamentally altered. The management and technical production levels of enterprises are not high enough, and major safety accidents occur every now and then. The remaining tasks to consolidate and enlarge the achievements from the reform and difficulty relief of the SOEs, and to further boost the reform and development of the same, are quite heavy.[15]

The reform of SOEs will therefore remain at the center of the authorities' economic policy agenda during the tenth Five-Year Development Plan. In this context the following ongoing reforms have been given priority:

- *The establishment of modern enterprise systems.* This will involve deepening the implementation of the shareholding system (with independent boards of directors and supervisors); introducing a

---

[14]The communiqué of the September 1999 Fourth Plenary Session of the 15th Central Committee of the Communist Party, which primarily focused on SOE reform, cast the reform process over a 10-year time frame.

[15]State Council press release transcribing Li's press conference during the March 2001 National People's Congress.

more diversified ownership structure (particularly by listing on the stock market and bringing in more strategic investors, including foreigners); further separating government functions from enterprise management; and further improving incentive and internal control mechanisms.

- *The creation of internationally competitive large enterprises and groups.* This seeks to build on the progress that has been made in the telecommunications services and petroleum industries in establishing enterprises that will be able to succeed with greater foreign competition following WTO accession.
- *The technological upgrading of the state sector.* The technological renovation program, which since late 1999 has included subsidized loans to finance new capital investment for key enterprises, will be continued. State support for the development of high-technology industries (information technology, bioengineering, and new materials) will also be deepened, including through the formation of state-financed venture capital funds.
- *The exit of poorly performing enterprises.* Mechanisms will be gradually standardized to facilitate the orderly and prompt exit of weak enterprises from the market. In the meantime, relatively large numbers of enterprises will continue to exit the market through the various ongoing sector-specific restructuring programs (for example, those in steel, sugar, oil refining, and coal).
- *The "revitalization" of small SOEs.* With roughly two-thirds of small SOEs already transformed, the emphasis will shift to providing greater support services to those small enterprises that remain in the state sector. This includes broadening access to the credit guarantee schemes and enterprise support centers established by the SETC for small and medium-size enterprises of all ownership types.

The authorities also have high hopes for the AMCs and view the start of their operations as an important change in the environment for SOEs. The authorities expect that the AMCs' efforts at asset resolution will impose additional financial discipline on the SOEs, and that debt-equity swaps will be a catalyst for SOE restructuring. The AMCs have begun work on classifying their SOEs into three groups: companies that are viable following debt restructuring or debt-equity swaps; companies that might be viable with operational and financial restructuring, particularly if strategic (foreign) partners are found; and companies that are not viable and need to be liquidated. They also understand the importance of moving ahead quickly to resolve bad assets, and they have started bringing in foreign investors to participate in the process of disposing of nonperforming loans.

Concluding Observations

The discussion in this chapter suggests that significant progress has been made in a wide range of areas essential to the ultimate success of the SOE reform effort. Durable efficiency gains have been achieved in recent years through layoffs, a reduced social welfare burden, and efforts to shed excess capacity in key sectors. These gains have boosted profits and reduced the scope of losses in the SOE sector. The authorities' current enterprise reform agenda, if fully and effectively implemented, offers good prospects of continued efficiency gains and improvement in SOE performance in the coming years.

However, the reforms thus far have generally only alleviated the effects of past problems and distortions, and they have been noticeably less successful in improving corporate governance and in imposing external financial discipline on enterprises. The financial weaknesses that are still evident in China's SOE sector and the large nonperforming loans problem that remains in the banking system highlight the difficulties in achieving a fundamental improvement in enterprise behavior. Although important structures and mechanisms for better governance are being put in place, key constraints on their effective functioning remain. These include

- *Lack of a well-developed credit culture.* The development of a credit culture is a fundamental requirement if financial intermediaries are to exercise effective discipline over SOEs. As noted in the next chapter, full commercialization of SCBs' lending decisions is an essential prerequisite in this regard.
- *Poor transparency of enterprise operations.* Limited information and lack of transparency of enterprise operations hamper effective surveillance by financial intermediaries and markets and increase the comparative advantage of enterprise insiders to pursue their own interests.
- *Limited enterprise exit channels.* The lack of well-developed exit channels has resulted in poor enterprise behavior going largely unpunished. A new bankruptcy law that adequately protects creditors' rights, and more decisive efforts to delist poorly performing enterprises from the stock market, would be important steps toward developing an effective "stick" with which to improve enterprise performance and strengthen market discipline.
- *Weak protection of minority shareholders' rights.* Enterprise management is generally not accountable to minority shareholders. Allowing the AMCs effective exercise of their ownership rights and bringing in more outside directors to enterprise boards would be important steps forward in this regard. International experience

and the corporate governance literature suggest that the role of boards of directors can be strengthened substantially by appointing sufficient numbers of independent, outside directors.

- *Privatization.* Ultimately, effective corporate governance will require outside shareholder control by owners focused on profit maximization. For many enterprises, including the large ones, this will have to involve a more complete break from control by the government, which inevitably tends to have a much broader, including political, objective function.

References

Lin, Cyril, 2000, "Corporate Governance in China," paper presented at the OECD/DRC Conference on Corporate Governance of SOEs in China, Beijing, January.

World Bank, 2000, "Bankruptcy of State Enterprises in China—A Case and Agenda for Reforming the Insolvency System" (unpublished; Washington: World Bank).

10

Financial System Soundness and Reform

CEM KARACADAG

The past two decades have witnessed great strides in China's financial system transformation. The authorities replaced the monobank system—typical of centrally planned economies—with a multilayered system and placed a central bank at the helm.[1] In 1994, they created policy banks to take over policy lending duties from the state banks. A commercial bank law, enacted in 1995, laid the foundation for commercially oriented banking. The authorities intensified reform efforts in the wake of the Asian financial crisis and established asset management companies (AMCs), recapitalized banks, and restructured trust and investment corporations and small and medium-sized financial institutions. They strengthened prudential regulations through the introduction of a new loan classification and provisioning standards that approach international best practices. State-owned banks have taken steps to strengthen corporate governance, increase transparency, consolidate branch networks, and downsize staff. Also, stock, bond, and money markets are being developed. Finally, with its entry into the World Trade Organization (WTO), China has committed itself to allowing full market access to foreign banks by 2006.

Nevertheless, a substantial unfinished reform agenda remains. The extensive institutional reforms notwithstanding, the quality of financial intermediation needs to be improved by strengthening the incentives faced by banks, improving corporate governance, and upgrading financial

---

[1]Under the monobank system, the People's Bank of China combined the roles of central and commercial banks and was subject to strict cash and credit plans set in accordance with the production plans drawn up by the State Planning Commission. Banks were part of the administrative hierarchy, whose primary goal was to ensure that national production plans were achieved (Wong and Wong, 2000).

market infrastructure. Virtually all banks are still state owned and enjoy the implicit guarantee of the government. The legal framework needs further development to provide effective recourse for creditors to pursue bad debtors among the state-owned enterprises (SOEs) and foreclose on collateral. The prudential framework needs to be improved to achieve international best practices in surveillance and enforcement. The stock and bond markets also need development to provide the competition and market discipline needed to steer banks toward greater efficiency and soundness. The tax system still overtaxes banks. Banks' ability to extend loans on commercial terms remains constrained by the need to fund SOEs and government projects.[2]

The financial system thus has become saddled with nonperforming loans, which have emerged as one of the most important of China's reform challenges.[3] The large size of the Chinese financial system by emerging market standards (with total assets equivalent to nearly twice GDP in 2001) underscores the acute fiscal challenge and the potential drag on growth that continued financial system inefficiencies will pose over the next decade.

The interdependence of legal, regulatory, fiscal, state enterprise, and financial sector reforms has limited the speed with which reforms can be pursued in any one area. The scarcity of skilled bank and corporate managers presents enormous challenges to instilling profit-maximizing behavior in creditors and borrowers alike in any transition economy, even under the best of circumstances. The vast size of China's economy and population, surpassing those of all of the transition economies in Central Asia and Europe combined, magnifies the challenge.

Looking ahead, the central policy challenge in the financial sector is to balance the intertemporal economic, financial, and social costs of reform. Experience in other countries suggests that the longer decisive action on financial sector reforms is delayed, the higher the economic and financial costs will be. China's medium-term fiscal constraints, coupled with the country's accession to the World Trade Organization, provide an outer bound on the time frame in which financial sector soundness needs to be achieved. The next 5–10 years are thus critical. Policymakers in China have reiterated their determination to deepen financial sector reforms to meet the challenges ahead, particularly by dealing decisively with the nonperforming loan problem.

---

[2]As discussed in Chapter 11, SOEs continue to employ over half the industrial workforce and still provide essential social welfare services to workers, including health, education, and housing.

[3]See the section on "Financial System Soundness" below and Chapter 8.

Figure 10.1. Banking System Credit to the Private Sector and GDP per Capita in Developing Economies, 2000

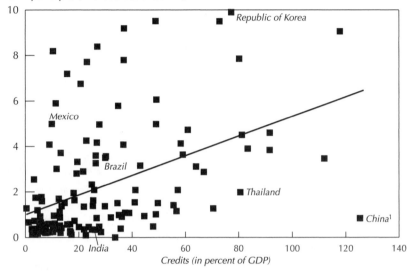

GDP per capita (in thousands of dollars)

Source: IMF, *International Financial Statistics*, various issues.
¹Includes credits to SOEs.

Size and Structure of the Financial System

This section presents an overview of the size and structure of China's financial sector.

Size

China's financial system is among the largest in the world. By the end of 2001 the combined assets of the country's commercial and policy banks, credit cooperatives, and finance companies stood at nearly 200 percent of GDP, a ratio comparable to that in many G-10 countries and substantially higher than in most emerging market economies. Among its peers in terms of income per capita, China is a distinct outlier. Despite an income per capita in 2000 of only $839, bank credit to nongovernment entities was equivalent to 125 percent of GDP, a ratio that exceeded that of all other countries with incomes per capita up to $10,000 (Figure 10.1).[4]

---

[4]If nonbank financial institutions' credits to the private sector are included, the financial sectors of the Republic of Korea and Malaysia (with incomes per capita of $9,900 and $3,880, respectively) surpass that of China on this measure.

The size of the banking sector reflects China's high saving rate, depositor confidence in the system, and the lack of other investment vehicles. At 35 percent of GDP, China's saving rate is second only to Singapore's. Confidence stems from the public's faith in the state guarantee of deposits held in the banking system, which in turn rests on state ownership of banks and the government's creditworthiness. Despite their steady growth in recent years, the stock and bond markets are still small relative to banking assets, leaving deposits as the main financial instrument for savers.[5]

China's large financial sector provides a basis for financial intermediation with the potential to play a key role in supporting long-term economic growth.[6] However, the inefficiency of intermediation has thus far deprived creditworthy entrepreneurs and corporate borrowers of a critical source of investment financing, and therefore, it has yet to realize its full potential to contribute to economic growth (see Chapters 4 and 8).

Structure

The current structure of the financial system reflects the significant institutional changes made over the last decade to create a modern and commercially oriented system.[7] The sector comprises state commercial and policy banks, joint-stock and city commercial banks, urban and rural credit cooperatives, and trust and investment corporations, whose origins, relative size, and systemic importance are summarized below.

State commercial banks (SCBs) remain the backbone of the financial system, accounting for two-thirds of system assets at the end of 2001 (Table 10.1). The four SCBs—the Agricultural Bank of China, the Bank of China, the China Construction Bank, and the Industrial and Commercial Bank of China—are among the world's largest banks, with total assets in the range of $300 billion to $500 billion (Table 10.2). They are vertically integrated throughout their extensive branch networks (with a total of 120,000 branches at the end of 2000), with over 1.4 million employees. The SCBs have been the primary source of

---

[5]At the end of 2000, total bonds outstanding, including those issued by the government, banks, and enterprises, equaled 24.5 percent of GDP. Stock market capitalization, including the Shanghai and Shenzhen stock exchanges, stood at 45 percent of GDP at the end of 2001, but most shares are owned by the state, and only about one-third are tradable.

[6]As noted in Chapter 4, the literature on the relationship between finance and economic growth has amply demonstrated the strong correlation between the depth of financial intermediation and growth.

[7]This section draws on OECD (2002).

Table 10.1. Financial System Assets by Type of Institution
(In percent of total except as noted otherwise)[1]

Institution	1998	1999	2000	2001	2001 as Percent of GDP
State commercial banks	69.3	69.2	66.7	64.7	127.1
Other commercial banks[2]	8.9	9.1	10.4	12.0	23.5
Urban credit cooperatives	4.6	4.5	4.9	5.0	9.8
Rural credit cooperatives	8.4	8.4	8.9	9.3	18.2
Finance companies	1.0	1.0	1.2	1.4	2.8
Specific deposit institutions	7.8	7.8	8.0	7.7	15.1

Source: People's Bank of China.
[1]Data are as of the end of the year.
[2]Includes TICs and two of the three policy banks (China Development Bank and the Export-Import Bank of China).

financing for large SOEs, which also account for the bulk of their non-performing loans.

The four SCBs were originally established in the mid-1980s, each to serve a different economic sector and to extend loans for policy objectives. In 1994 they were reestablished as commercial banks and officially absolved of their policy lending responsibilities. Since then they have expanded beyond their original sectors and have increasingly come into competition with one another (Wong and Wong, 2000). They also have been a prime focus of reform efforts in recent years.

Joint-stock commercial banks (JSCBs) and *city commercial banks (CCBs)* accounted for 10 percent of financial system assets at the end of 2001. Unlike the SCBs, the JSCBs have diverse ownership structures, with SOEs and local governments as their main shareholders.[8] Also unlike the SCBs, the JSCBs finance smaller SOEs and nonstate firms, including small and medium-size enterprises, and maintain much smaller branch networks, typically confined to the region where they originated or to the fast-growing coastal provinces.[9] CCBs have been created by the merger of urban credit cooperatives into commercial banks since the mid-1990s. CCBs also have diverse ownership structures: their equity is held by urban enterprises and local governments, and they lend to small and medium-size enterprises, collectives, and local residents in their municipalities.

---

[8]China Minsheng Bank, with total assets of Y 48.6 billion ($6 billion) in 2000, is the one exception: the majority of its shares are held by nonstate entities. It is the only privately owned Chinese bank.

[9]The Bank of Communications and CITIC Industrial Bank, China's fifth- and sixth-largest banks, with assets of Y 628 billion ($76 billion) and Y 235 billion ($28 billion), respectively, in 2000, are the two largest JSCBs.

Table 10.2. Assets and World Ranking of State Commercial Banks

Bank	Assets (Billions of Dollars)	Rank Among World's Largest Banks
Industrial & Commercial Bank of China	483.0	15
Bank of China	382.7	23
China Construction Bank	305.9	30
Agricultural Bank of China	262.6	37

Source: *The Banker,* July 2001.

China's *policy banks* were created in 1994 to assume the policy lending roles previously performed by the SCBs. The three policy banks— the Agricultural Development Bank, the China Development Bank, and the Export-Import Bank of China accounted for around 10 percent of system assets at the end of 2001. Unlike the SCBs and other commercial banks, policy banks fund themselves through central bank loans, government deposits, and the issuance of government-guaranteed bonds held by commercial banks. Policy banks primarily extend long-term loans for infrastructure projects, including those financed by central government public investment bonds, and they finance development in the poorer western and central regions. The creation of the policy banks, however, has not put an end to noncommercial lending by the SCBs.

Rural and urban credit cooperatives (RCCs and UCCs) were established in the 1980s to diversify the financial system, provide small-scale banking services, and finance small, collectively and individually owned enterprises. RCCs, in particular, have become a key vehicle for channeling credit to farmers. The lending operations of RCCs, normally financed by deposits, have been funded increasingly by central bank loans, which accounted for 18 percent of their new loans in 2001. With assets equivalent to 14 percent of the financial system total in 2001, credit cooperatives have assumed systemic importance.

Trust and investment corporations (TICs) were also created in the 1980s to support the development of the nonstate sector and to provide financing outside the credit quotas imposed on commercial banks. TICs soon moved increasingly into the banking business, a trend the authorities have sought to curtail in recent years.

International trust and investment corporations (ITICs) were established by many provinces and cities in order to mobilize foreign funds (through the issuance of bonds) to finance local companies and infrastructure projects. Major financial weaknesses, including the bankruptcy of the Guangdong International Trust and Investment Corporation (GITIC) in 1998, involving a default on its debts to foreign creditors, have prompted the consolidation of TICs and ITICs since 1998. The subsector as a whole accounted for only 3 percent of financial system assets.[10]

The Regulatory Framework

This section describes the legal, regulatory, and prudential framework of the financial system.

The Legal Framework

The laws pertaining to monetary policy and banking were improved with the enactment in 1995 of laws governing the People's Bank of China (PBC) and the commercial banks. Before then the framework consisted largely of a loose amalgamation of provisional regulations. The PBC law assigns the three key responsibilities of a central bank—monetary stability, banking supervision, and oversight of the payments system—to the PBC. The law also placed the PBC under the direct control of the State Council and prohibited intervention in its operations by local governments and other administrative bodies at the central level.

However, the PBC did not enjoy full independence: local governments interfered in the operations of its provincial branches. This prompted the reorganization of the PBC along regional lines in 1998 to reduce such interference. Moreover, the PBC does not have full power to conduct monetary policy or to close insolvent financial institutions. Major monetary policy and supervisory decisions must be approved by the State Council. The PBC is empowered to set supervisory standards, but the Ministry of Finance is responsible for rules on provisioning and loan write-offs.

Similarly, banks have not enjoyed the autonomy accorded by law to conduct their operations on a fully commercial basis. The commercial bank law provides a framework for transforming the SCBs into commercial entities, including by granting them operational autonomy and making them responsible for their financial performance, and the authorities are in the process of implementing the law (see Reform Strategy, below).

Important gaps in the legal framework also remain. Although several important laws have been passed in recent years (including laws on negotiable bills, insurance, auditing, securities, guarantees, contracts,

---

[10]The China International Trust and Investment Corporation (CITIC) dominates the subsector, accounting for over half the assets of all TICs, although the bulk of its consolidated assets derives from its fully owned banking subsidiary, CITIC Industrial Bank.

and trust operations), other essential laws have yet to be adopted. A revised bankruptcy law that would strengthen the position of creditors is still to be passed. Moreover, even though several laws give creditors a senior claim on the proceeds from liquidation of bankrupt borrowers, a State Council regulation accords priority to fulfilling the social welfare obligations of workers in liquidated firms (Lardy, 2000).

The banking environment is also distorted by existing tax laws. The effective tax burden is excessive, undermining incentives to maximize profits. Banks are subject to a "business tax" of 6 percent and a corporate income tax of 33 percent.[11] Business taxes are levied against gross income (including accrued interest on nonperforming loans), which results in the taxation even of institutions that lose money. At current levels of profitability, the effective tax burden approaches 70–80 percent.

Prudential Regulation

Prudential regulations have been gradually strengthened in recent years. Nevertheless, much more remains to be done to bring them up to standards practiced in more modern financial systems and to enforce them effectively.

Since 1998, important steps have been taken to tighten prudential regulation, especially with respect to loan classification. Until the end of 2001, the loan classification system was far behind those in industrial countries and advanced emerging market economies (Table 10.3). Effective January 1, 2002, the authorities have adopted the five-category system widely used in other emerging market economies, according to which the entire balance of the loan is classified as nonperforming, and interest accrual suspended, once interest or principal is more than 90 days past due.

Provisioning rules have also been substantially improved. Until early 2001 the maximum allowable provision, on a cumulative basis, was 1 percent of outstanding loans. As a result, banks were not permitted to make provisions commensurate with the credit risks on their loan books. Effective January 2002, the authorities introduced a new provisioning regulation designed to complement the new loan classification system, and which is comparable to practices in more advanced emerging market economies. The regulation requires general provisions of 1 percent of total loans to cover potential losses on normal loans, and specific provisions of 2, 25, 50, and 100 percent of the loan amount for

---

[11]The business tax rate is scheduled to decline to 5 percent in 2003 but remains excessive even at that level.

Table 10.3. Selected Prudential Regulations

Category	Regulations in Effect
Loan classification	*As of January 2002* • Loans are classified in five categories: normal, special mention, substandard, doubtful, and loss, where the latter three categories are considered as nonperforming. • A loan is classified as nonperforming once principal or interest is past due more than 90 days. Once a loan is classified, the entire balance of the loan is classified as nonperforming. • Unpaid interest is suspended after it is in arrears for more than three months. • However classification of a loan as loss is still subject to several preconditions related to the borrower (bankruptcy, decease, natural calamity, or deregistration), according to the Ministry of Finance regulation on provisioning, adopted in 2001. *Effective until December 2001* • Loans were classified in four categories: normal, overdue, idle, and loss, where the latter three categories were considered as nonperforming. • A loan was classified as overdue after principal payment(s) were in arrears by more than 1 day, and idle after 12 months. Only the scheduled but unpaid portion of principal, not the entire balance, was classified. • Unpaid interest was suspended after it was in arrears for more than six months. • Overdue, idle, and loss loans could not exceed 8, 5, and 2 percent of loans, respectively.
Loan concentration	• Lending to a single borrower may not exceed 10 percent of capital. • A bank's 10 largest exposures combined may not exceed 50 percent of its net capital.
Provisioning and write-offs	• Until 2001 banks could maintain loan-loss reserves (stock) up to 1 percent of outstanding loans. • Effective January 2002, banks are required to allocate general provisions of 1 percent of total loans and specific provisions in the following amounts: 2 percent of special-mention loans, 20–30 percent of substandard loans, 40–60 percent of doubtful loans, and 100 percent of loss loans. Banks are expected to fully comply with these requirements by the end of 2005. • Classifying a loan as loss for provisioning purposes and loan write-offs require approval of the Ministry of Finance.
Capital adequacy	• Definitions of capital and weighted risks are generally consistent with the Basel capital accord, with the important exception of the treatment of large SOEs. • Risk weights assigned to large SOEs range between 50 and 70 percent, in contrast to the 100 percent risk weight stipulated in the Basel accord. • Minimum ratios of total capital and core capital to risk-weighted assets are 8 percent and 4 percent, respectively.

Table 10.3 *(concluded)*

Category	Regulations in Effect
Liquidity	• Banks are required to maintain reserves equal to 6 percent of local currency deposits and 2 percent of foreign currency deposits.
	• Loan-to-deposit ratio is to be kept under 75 percent for renminbi loans and deposits.
	• Interbank debts are to be kept under 4 percent of deposits.
Foreign exchange risk	• Foreign currency liquid asset-liability ratio must be no less than 60 percent.
	• Loan-to-deposit ratio may not exceed 85 percent for foreign currency loans and deposits.
	• Bank overseas borrowing may not exceed 60 percent of net capital.
	• Open positions may not exceed 30 percent of paid-in foreign currency capital.
	• Overnight open positions may not exceed 5 percent of paid-in foreign currency capital.

Sources: People's Bank of China, State Administration for Foreign Exchange, and Fitch IBCA, Duff & Phelps (2001).

special-mention, substandard, doubtful, and loss loans, respectively. The specific provisions are not tax deductible. The PBC expects banks to fully comply with the new requirements by the end of 2005, but sanctions for noncompliance remain undetermined.

The minimum capital adequacy requirement is broadly consistent with the Basel capital accord, with the important exception of the treatment of large SOEs. Whereas the Basel accord stipulates a 100 percent risk weight for SOEs, the Chinese regulation assigns risk weights ranging from 50 to 70 percent for large SOEs. Given the heavy exposure of banks to large SOEs, their risk-weighted assets may be higher than reported. In addition, because of insufficient loan-loss provisioning, reported capital and capital-adequacy ratios do not reflect the true capital strength of banks.

The prudential regulation of foreign exchange risk management is an area of increasing importance, given the growth in cross-border transactions that is likely to result from China's entry into the WTO and its growing integration with the world economy. The surge in foreign currency deposits in recent years (from $77 billion in 1997 to $135 billion in 2001), moreover, has already given rise to additional credit, liquidity, and exchange rate risks, which require careful management. Prudential regulation and supervision thus need to ensure that banks safeguard the liquidity and credit quality of their foreign currency assets to avoid their foreign currency liabilities becoming a contingent liability of the government and a potential claim on central bank foreign reserves. Foreign exchange risk management will assume even greater importance as the exchange rate regime becomes more flexible over time.

Regulations for managing foreign exchange risk need to be strengthened (Table 10.3). For example, the minimum liquidity ratio does not provide adequate protection against foreign currency liquidity risks, because short-term foreign currency loans are included among eligible liquid assets even though such loans may not be easy to liquidate in practice. In addition, not all existing prudential regulations appear to be enforced. For example, total foreign currency loans exceeded foreign currency deposits in 1998, indicating that some banks were noncompliant with the 85 percent cap on the loan-to-deposit ratio. Moreover, because bank capital is overstated as a result of underprovisioning, the 30 percent cap on open positions is not an effective limit on foreign exchange risk. Finally, most regulations on foreign exchange risk are administered by the State Administration for Foreign Exchange from an "exchange regulation" perspective, rather than by the PBC from a supervisory perspective.

Financial System Soundness and Efficiency

This section assesses the financial condition of the financial sector, with an emphasis on its contribution to economic growth and on the size of the nonperforming loan problem.

Systemic Soundness and Potential Losses

A notable achievement since 1998 has been the increasing transparency of the supervisory authorities and of commercial banks in disclosing financial information. Disclosure on nonperforming loans in particular has enabled more accurate assessments of potential systemic losses and set the stage for a more intense reform effort to meet the financial sector's challenges (see Financial Sector Reform, below). The SCBs and policy banks have begun publishing annual reports and financial statements that are closer to international banking and accounting standards.

The financial system suffers from substantial weaknesses, largely reflecting the legacy of policy lending. Even after the transfer to AMCs of nonperforming loans equivalent to 14 percent of total loans in 1999–2000, the reported nonperforming loans of SCBs averaged over 30 percent of total loans at the end of 2001. However, reported nonperforming loans may be subject to revisions,[12] owing to the inherent difficulty in examining loan files in numerous branches, limited central oversight of branch operations, and differences in accounting practices among branches.[13]

JSCBs are younger than SCBs and thus carry less of the burden of past quasi-fiscal lending. Reported nonperforming loans of selected JSCBs indicate that their asset quality is stronger than that of the SCBs, but their nonperforming ratios are still high compared with other emerging market economies in Asia. For example, the Bank of Communications, the largest JSCB, reported a nonperforming loan ratio in 2000 of 18 percent, and several smaller banks reported ratios in the range of 9–39 percent in 1999 and 4–29 percent in 2000 (Table 10.4). The rapid growth of JSCBs, with credit expansion averaging 30 percent annually during 1998–2001 ("other commercial banks" in Figure 10.2), entails risks that a portion may become nonperforming in the future unless credit evaluation and monitoring improve significantly.

Although information on credit cooperatives is very limited, they are probably the weakest subsector of the financial system. RCCs' nonperforming loans reportedly reached 38 percent of total loans in 1996 and have since risen further (Lardy, 2000). Another sign of the RCCs' troubled financial condition is that their consolidated balance sheet showed negative equity and a largely negative "other items net" in 1999.[14] The health of UCCs is similarly poor, as evidenced by their liquidity problems, which prompted the central bank to merge UCCs into CCBs. Lack of information on the TICs and ITICs also rules out a quantitative assessment of their asset quality. However, the collapse of numerous TICs in recent years, starting with the high-profile case of the GITIC, suggests that this subsector has also been weak.

---

[12]For example, the PBC's own estimates of nonperforming loans have been subject to upward revisions in recent years. In 1998 the PBC estimated the SCBs' nonperforming loans to be 25 percent of their total loans. After the transfer of many nonperforming loans to AMCs in 1999–2000, the PBC once again released an estimate of 25 percent for the SCBs, based on the old classification system, implying a substantial increase in the estimated ratio from 1998. Following the introduction of a new loan classification system effective January 2002, the four SCBs revised their nonperforming loan ratios upward, to a combined average of 30 percent of total loans at the end of 2001.

[13]Information on asset quality for the remainder of the financial system outside the SCBs is more sketchy and subject to even greater margins of error (again mostly on the downside). Nonetheless, this chapter attempts an overall systemic assessment based on a range of qualitative factors.

[14]See Table 8 (p. 216) in the *Almanac of China's Finance and Banking* (English edition), 2000.

Table 10.4. Reported Nonperforming Loans at SCBs and Selected Other Financial Institutions

(In percent of total)[1]

Bank	1999	2000	2001
State commercial banks[2]			
Agricultural Bank of China	. . .	35[3]	42
Bank of China	39	27	28
China Construction Bank[4]	. . .	21	23
Industrial and Commercial Bank of China	. . .	34	30
All SCBs (weighted average)	. . .	30	30
Selected JSCBs and development banks			
Bank of Communications	22	18	. . .
China Merchants Bank	10	10	8
China Everbright Bank	39	29	21
China Minsheng Bank	9	4	. . .
CITIC Industrial Bank	17	15	. . .
Guangdong Development Bank	23	. . .	. . .
Shanghai Pudong Development Bank	9	11	. . .
Shenzhen Development Bank	25	23	. . .

Sources: Fitch IBCA, Duff & Phelps; Wong and Wong (2000); and institution annual reports.
[1]Data are as of the end of the year.
[2]Data for 2000 and 2001 are reported according to the new, five-category loan classification system, except where noted otherwise.
[3]Reported according to the old, four-category system.
[4]Includes Y 50 billion for 2001 and Y 17 billion for 2000 in debt-equity swaps from previously nonperforming exposures.

The potential losses of the financial system are thus substantial, and the bulk of those losses ultimately may have to be borne by the government, given the banks' already weak capital positions, negligible loan-loss reserves,[15] and poor profitability. Worldwide experience has shown that banks and supervisors often underestimate nonperforming loans and that asset quality can deteriorate quickly under adverse economic conditions. The analysis in Chapter 11 of the sensitivity of enterprise performance to modest interest rate and demand shocks confirms the potential for a further deterioration of borrowers' creditworthiness under economic adversity.

Bank profitability has been very low. Among the SCBs, the Agricultural Bank of China registered losses in recent years (but then turned a small profit in 2000), and the remaining three have reported barely positive earnings; the SCBs as a group reported a return on assets of 0.2 percent in 2001. Even these levels of earnings are overstated given the lack of provisioning and, until recently, the accrual of interest on loans in

---

[15]Provisions averaged only 1.3 percent of loans in 1999.

Figure 10.2. Change in Credit Growth from Previous Year
(In percent)

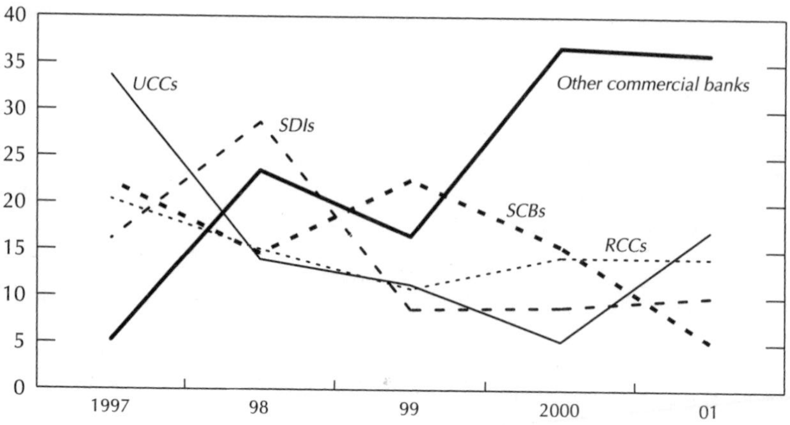

Sources: People's Bank of China; and IMF staff estimates.

arrears for six months. The low profitability of the SCBs also reflects their lack of business diversification, minimal sources of noninterest income, and still-high operating costs related to their large workforces and branch networks, despite the cutbacks of recent years.[16] Available data also illustrate the tax burden imposed on financial institutions. For example, the SCBs paid taxes in excess of net income in 1999.

In contrast to the SCBs, the JSCBs appear to be more profitable, with a return on assets of 0.4 percent in 2001. This stronger profitability stems from their stronger asset quality (a larger share of loans to the nonstate sector), lower overhead costs, and fast-growth strategies. However, the JSCBs' earnings are also inflated by shortfalls in provisions, and their rapid-growth strategies may backfire in the form of loan losses in the future.

Despite weak asset quality and low profitability, systemic liquidity is high. Reserves (cash and deposits with the central bank) account for 12 percent of system deposits, nearly double the required level of 6 percent. This ample liquidity reflects continued strong deposit growth—which averaged 16 percent annually during 1997–2001—driven by China's high saving rate and the lack of investment alternatives.

---

[16]Despite their financial costs, the four SCBs' extensive branch networks—even at potentially smaller levels—carry considerable franchise value, which should support their ability to compete with foreign banks as well as their future restructuring and privatization.

Figure 10.3. Lending by the People's Bank of China to the Financial System
(In percent of deposits)

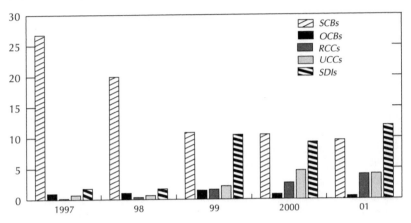

Source: People's Bank of China.

Although high in the aggregate, liquidity is spread unevenly across the financial system, and the interbank market is neither developed nor integrated enough to bridge the liquid segments of the system with the illiquid segments. The SCBs are highly liquid, but pockets of illiquidity appear to exist among the credit cooperatives. At the end of 2000, the SCBs held reserves in excess of 8 percent of their total assets, and another 19 percent of their balance sheet was invested in government securities, in part reflecting the SCBs' growing risk aversion and shift toward assets with lower credit risk. Signs of illiquidity among the rural credit cooperatives are visible in the PBC's lending patterns to them: its loans to cooperatives have doubled each year since 1998, albeit from a low base (Figure 10.3).

Governance

State ownership of the financial system and of major borrowers reduces incentives for good corporate governance.[17] With the sole exception of China Minsheng Bank, a medium-sized JSCB, the financial system is entirely state owned. This is in sharp contrast to the nonfinancial part

---

[17]Evidence from the JSCBs suggests that the more concentrated public sector ownership is (that is, the more a bank is owned by a single local government rather than by multiple state enterprises in different provinces), the more likely is the bank to experience interference in its operations (Wong and Wong, 2000).

of the economy, where nonstate enterprises account for more than half of gross annual output. The asymmetry in ownership structures between the financial and the nonfinancial sectors limits the economy's growth potential because of the financial system's inability to adequately select and support nonstate firms. Banks have little incentive to exert market discipline over borrowers, particularly the large SOEs, given the government's implicit guarantee. That guarantee, in turn, creates moral hazard on the part of both lenders and borrowers and slows the development of a "risk culture" in which lenders are able to assess and price credit risks, and of a "credit culture" in which borrowers assume responsibility for repaying their debts.

Mirroring the state ownership of banks, the bulk of bank lending has gone to SOEs rather than to the faster-growing nonstate sector. Although a precise measure of the composition of lending by borrower is unavailable, the stock of "direct" loans to the nonstate sector was only 5–6 percent of total lending in 2001, and under 50 percent even when "indirect" loans are included, according to a PBC survey (PBC, 2000).[18] A 1999 survey conducted by the International Finance Corporation of 600 private Chinese enterprises also revealed that private firms primarily relied on self-financing and that 80 percent cited lack of access to outside financing as a major constraint (Gregory and Tenev, 2001). In the same vein, the contribution of financial intermediation to growth appears to have been marginal: Chapter 4 finds, based on provincial lending and growth patterns, that bank lending to the state sector has made no discernable contribution to economic growth, and that lending to the private sector has had only a small impact.

Inadequate competition in the banking industry has contributed to the inefficiency of financial intermediation, especially on the part of the SCBs (Wong and Wong, 2000). In particular, a number of administrative rules discriminate against JSCBs' ability to compete with the SCBs. The central bank imposes quotas on the number of new branches that each JSCB may establish, and enterprises usually have to open deposit accounts with banks from which they borrow, a rule that works in favor of the SCBs. Moreover, government administrative and nonprofit units are required to open their accounts for revenue collection and extra-budgetary funds with SCBs, and central bank lending appears to favor SCBs, which receive a much larger share of central bank financing than do the JSCBs in relation to their own resources. (However, this could be attributable to past policy loans of the SCBs funded by the PBC; see

---

[18]Indirect loans include those made to SOEs, which in turn relend some of those funds to nonstate firms with which they conduct business (OECD, 2002).

Figure 10.3). Although these distortions are detrimental to competition, JSCBs have still experienced rapid growth in recent years. The absence of reliable financial information on enterprises is an impediment to credit risk assessment. Corporate fixed assets, inventories, receivables, and earnings are often overvalued, whereas leverage is understated (see Chapter 11). Having developed in a difficult environment that until recently favored state enterprises, private firms tend to be opaque (Gregory and Tenev, 2001). Channeling a larger share of credit to creditworthy private enterprises thus hinges on fostering greater adherence to formal accounting rules.

The rapid pace of credit growth throughout the 1990s has been a major contributor to the weaknesses of the financial system today. Credit growth was particularly fast from 1991 through 1997, averaging 26 percent a year. Bank lending financed massive investments in real estate and property, excess capacity building, and inventory accumulation (Lardy, 2000). Although the rate of expansion in overall credit has decelerated by half since 1998, the surge of new credits in certain financial subsectors, particularly the JSCBs, risks new problem loans emerging in the future.

Financial Sector Reform

This section reviews the progress made in financial sector reforms to date and discusses elements of a comprehensive reform program for the future.

Reform Strategy

The Asian financial crisis of 1997 pushed financial sector reform to the top of the government's reform agenda. The reforms aimed to gradually transform the SCBs into viable and competitive universal banks; to contain losses in and consolidate the credit cooperatives and the TICs and ITICs, which remain the weakest links in the financial system; and to increase competition by allowing commercial banks other than the SCBs to assume an increasingly important role in domestic financial intermediation. The reforms have involved greater transparency with regard to the condition of the financial system; stricter regulatory standards; reduction in government interference in the system; recapitalization, balance sheet clean-up, and operational restructuring of SCBs; the creation of AMCs; the merger and closure of ailing credit cooperatives, TICs, and ITICs; and opening to foreign competition pursuant to China's WTO commitments.

Recognition and public acknowledgment of the extent of the financial sector's weaknesses have been a catalyst for deeper reforms. The government has announced more-credible statistics on banking soundness, particularly with respect to asset quality. Official recognition of bad loans has been complemented by a willingness on the SCBs' part to disclose more comprehensive and accurate financial information, and there has been some movement toward international accounting standards with the aid of external audits of main branches.

Progress on transparency has been brought about in part by *improvements in prudential regulation*, particularly with respect to loan classification and provisioning. The recent adoption of the five-category risk-based loan classification system and corresponding provisioning requirements represents a critical step in improving the accuracy and credibility of bank financial statements. They are also prerequisites to building risk and credit cultures in the financial system.

The renewed effort to *reduce government interference* in the financial system began with the National Financial Sector Work Conference in November 1997, where a consensus was reached on allowing the financial sector to operate commercially. This was followed by the restructuring of the central bank in 1998. PBC branches in each of China's provinces were replaced by nine regional branches, which enjoy greater independence on credit policy and supervisory decisions. That same year the government eliminated credit quotas on the SCBs, conferring greater responsibility on them for their lending decisions. In 1999 the PBC, provincial governors, and Communist Party secretaries held another Financial Sector Work Conference, which explicitly forbade government interference in commercial lending.

The *rehabilitation of balance sheets* has involved recapitalization and the removal of nonperforming loans. The government injected Y 270 billion (equivalent to 3½ percent of GDP) in equity into the SCBs in 1998. During 1999–2000 the four SCBs and one policy bank (the China Development Bank) transferred, at book value, Y 1.4 trillion in nonperforming loans (14 percent of their total loans and the equivalent of 17 percent of 1999 GDP) to four newly established AMCs.[19] The AMCs provide a basis for asset resolution, and notable progress has been made in asset valuation and disposal, aided by the use of foreign expertise. Thirteen percent of AMC assets had been

---

[19]The transfer removed the following from the banks' books: those loans with no prospect of recovery as of September 1999; nonperforming loans made before the end of 1995 and loans that as of the end of 1998 were classified as "idle" (that is, over a year past due); loans extended before 1995, which will be converted into equity; and interest receivable on the transferred loans (provided it was recorded on the balance sheet).

sold by the end of 2001, including some sales to foreign investors, with an average cumulative cash recovery rate of 21 percent (Box 10.1).

SCB reforms have focused on cutting costs and strengthening bank governance, internal controls, and credit risk management. The four SCBs cut staff by nearly 130,000, and branches and savings outlets by some 40,000, between 1997 and 2000. Each SCB is establishing boards of supervisors and boards of directors to monitor and oversee their operations. Credit departments are developing internal risk rating systems, and credit analysis and approval functions have been separated, with approval authority centralized at headquarters and subjected to credit committee review. Moreover, the composition of new loans has shifted in favor of lower-risk housing and consumer loans, and among corporate loans to more creditworthy clients in the coastal regions. Nevertheless, much remains to be done to ensure sustained improvements in risk management and internal controls. In particular, skills in pricing and managing credit risks are scarce, and training of staff in risk management skills will take time, given the size of the SCBs. More-sophisticated information systems also need to be put in place. The PBC has set a goal of reducing the SCBs' combined nonperforming loans ratio to 15 percent by 2005 (from 30 percent at the end of 2001), implying a 4-percentage-point reduction per year in the nonperforming loans ratio of each SCB.

In the long term, the authorities plan to list the SCBs on the stock exchanges in order to diversify their ownership, in a manner akin to JSCBs. Three JSCBs have already listed on the domestic bourses, most recently China Minsheng Bank in October 2000, and two others have announced plans to be listed during 2002, with more to follow.[20]

Closures and mergers have been the principal means used to *consolidate the credit cooperatives and the TICs and ITICs.* Insolvent rural credit funds were liquidated, and solvent ones were merged with RCCs. The number of RCCs has been cut by several thousand in recent years. Restructuring plans for the RCCs involved the consolidation by merger at the city and the provincial level and a strengthening of supervision. However, the RCCs' nonperforming loans problem remains to be addressed. A key factor influencing restructuring has been the desire to avoid disrupting the flow of credit to farmers at a time when raising rural incomes has become a prime policy objective. The reform of UCCs is

---

[20]The Bank of China also recently listed its Hong Kong SAR subsidiaries on the Hong Kong Stock Exchange.

Box 10.1. Operations of the Asset Management Companies

In 1999 the government established four AMCs—one for each SCB—each of which assumed problem loans from its SCB counterpart. (Huarong AMC also assumed problem loans from the China Development Bank.) Nonperforming loans with a face value of Y 1.4 trillion, the equivalent of 14 percent of total loans and 17 percent of 1999 GDP, were transferred at book value. In exchange, the AMCs recorded a debt to the SCBs of about Y 820 billion, with a 10-year maturity and an annual interest rate of 2.25 percent, and were released from corresponding PBC refinance credits (about Y 570 million), which are now PBC claims against the AMCs. Nearly one-fourth of the loans transferred—an estimated Y 300–350 billion—is being swapped for equity in SOEs, which will be held by the AMCs in the form of an ownership stake to facilitate the restructuring of selected SOEs. The AMCs will assume ownership stakes in some 580 SOEs. (See Chapter 9 for a more detailed description of the debt-equity swap program.)

The AMCs were created as independent financial institutions with the primary goal of maximizing recoveries from nonperforming loans through various asset resolution techniques. In light of the diversity and large number of debtors under their management, the AMCs have increasingly used foreign expertise to manage and dispose of the loans, including through auctions to foreign investors. Thus far the AMCs have sold only 13 percent of total assets assumed. Cash recovery rates have ranged between 7 and 31 percent among the four AMCs, with an average cumulative cash recovery rate of 21 percent as of the end of 2001 (Table 10.5). These recovery

---

proceeding along similar lines; closures are also part of the process.[21] As with the UCCs, the consolidation of the TICs and ITICs involves a mix of mergers and closures, through which their number will be cut to 60 from 239.[22]

China's *accession to the WTO* will open the financial system to greater foreign competition, which will serve as an important source of market

---

[21]In 2000 the number of UCCs was reduced by 1,296, to about 1,650, through conversion into city commercial banks (90 former UCCs), outright closure (56), acquisition by SCBs (114), and conversion into RCCs (1,036).

[22]Since the GITIC closure, the authorities have emphasized negotiated settlements with foreign creditors in the 20 or so remaining TICs. The PBC has also held firm on its "no bailout" policy, leaving local governments to take charge of the restructuring and assume responsibility for the foreign debts of their TICs. Also noteworthy is the PBC's issuance of a new regulation aimed at tightening supervision and control over the TICs by placing them firmly under PBC supervision; barring them from raising foreign debt,

rates are likely to decline as the AMCs dispose of assets of increasingly poor quality.

Despite the progress made in asset disposal, the AMCs face important hurdles and deficiencies in governance, the removal of which will be important in maximizing the value of assets they hold:

- *Shortage of staff and skilled expertise.* AMCs are understaffed and lack the skilled expertise to assess the value of their nonperforming loans and to manage the companies in which they have ownership stakes. For example, at one AMC a workforce of 1,300 (including clerical staff) manages the debts of 70,000 borrowers.
- *Legal impediments.* AMCs lack the power, even when they are majority shareholders, to replace SOE management and restructure their companies. They are also unable to sell their shares for a period of three years, or at a discount at any time. Moreover, legal uncertainties remain over the transferability of ownership, the tax treatment of potential capital gains, and foreigners' ability to repatriate their investments in AMC assets.
- *Governance.* The financial operations and policies of the AMCs diverge widely: some have not serviced their debts to the SCBs and the PBC, while others have made payments in full. The lack of transparency and consistency in AMCs' financial operations may undermine incentives to maximize recoveries and make it difficult to gauge their performance and hold management accountable.

discipline. Foreign banks will be allowed to conduct domestic currency business with Chinese firms in 2003, and with retail customers in 2006. Although foreign banks' market share in these sectors is likely to remain modest, their entry should still have a positive impact on domestic banks by intensifying competition and introducing knowledge and new technology.

The Future Reform Agenda

The achievements to date notwithstanding, there is a broad consensus on the need to deepen and accelerate reforms. Building on recent and planned reforms, the future reform agenda should include the following items.

---

issuing bonds, and taking deposits; and confining the scope of their business to provision of trust services for investment funds.

Table 10.5. Operations and Recoveries of Asset Management Companies, December 31, 2001

(In billions of yuan except where noted otherwise)

Item	Cinda AMC	Huarong AMC	Orient AMC	Great Wall AMC	Total
Book value of assets assumed	373.0	407.7	267.4	345.8	1,393.9
Recoveries at face value	61.2	31.1	23.4	61.0	176.7
Cumulative recoveries	27.3	15.8	11.0	12.9	67.0
Cash	17.3	9.6	5.7	4.4	37.0
Noncash	10.0	6.2	5.3	8.5	30.0
Assets disposed of (in percent)	16.4	7.6	8.8	17.6	12.7
Cash recovery rate (in percent)	28.3	30.9	24.4	7.2	20.9
Total recovery rate (in percent)	44.6	50.8	47.0	21.1	37.9

Sources: AMC data, news reports, and IMF staff estimates.

Formulation and Public Announcement of a Comprehensive Reform Strategy

The plan could include, among other things, a statement of the authorities' reform objectives and the legal, regulatory, prudential, and institutional measures planned over the next 3–5 years to achieve those objectives. The strategy should also include a long-term vision for the financial sector, which could envisage creating a financial system that is more diversified and specialized—reflecting China's geographic and socioeconomic diversity—than the current one, which is dominated by vertically integrated SCBs.

Transfer of Ownership to the Private Sector

Transferring management control and ownership to the private sector could proceed along the following lines: comprehensive diagnosis of the asset quality and solvency of financial institutions; identification of viable and nonviable parts of financial institutions and the separation and spin-off of good assets under wholly owned subsidiaries of the parent; and the listing or sale to strategic investors of solvent institutions and subsidiaries.

Stricter Accounting, Internal Reporting, and Disclosure Standards

Accounting rules and practices should be strengthened by moving toward international standards and by requiring more independent audits of banks and nonbank firms. These steps should be accompanied by more frequent publication of detailed financial information to enable the exercise of market discipline.

Gradual Liberalization of Interest Rates

Deposit and lending rates remain largely fixed,[23] inhibiting banks' pricing of credit risks. More market-based interest rates would allow banks to allocate resources more efficiently. Interest liberalization could proceed in stages, starting with a gradual widening of the existing band around lending rates.

Reduction of the Tax Burden

Consideration could be given to phasing out the business tax altogether, while holding banks more accountable for their financial performance.

Accelerated Operational Reforms

Weak banks not in compliance with prudential requirements should be subject to time-bound operational restructuring agreements, including specific financial performance and prudential compliance targets against which management is held accountable. When banks' business plans and performance fail to meet the specified criteria and targets, management should be improved and possibly replaced. Operational reforms should emphasize the strengthening of risk management practices relating to credit, market, and liquidity risks. Risk management skills will also have to be strengthened in parallel with the growing market and foreign currency risks that more-flexible interest and exchange rates will engender.

Strict Regulatory and Prudential Enforcement

With prudential regulations having been considerably strengthened in recent years, strict enforcement of rules is critical to securing their intended benefits, including the exit of nonviable institutions and the development of risk and credit cultures in the economy.

Improvement of the Framework for Asset Resolution

Although the AMCs provide a basis for efficient asset resolution, important impediments remain. Legal uncertainties about loan collat-

---

[23]Since October 1999, banks are allowed to set renminbi lending rates within a range from 30 percent above to 10 percent below the official lending rate for small and medium-size enterprises, and 10 percent above or below that rate for SOEs in urban areas; since January 1998 the corresponding range for small and medium-size enterprises in rural areas is from 50 percent above to 10 percent below the official rate.

eral, foreclosure, and creditor rights deter potential investors in distressed assets, and AMCs possess little power to restructure and improve the performance of ailing enterprises in which they hold substantial shares. The diversity and magnitude of distressed assets also highlight the need for AMCs to acquire skills, train staff, and maximize the use of foreign expertise in asset valuation and recovery. More generally, a good framework for resolving distressed corporate debts is critical to the development of a sound corporate sector as well as a sound banking sector.

References

Fitch IBCA, Duff & Phelps, 2001, "Chinese Bank Prudential Regulations," September (London: Fitch IBCA, Duff & Phelps).

Gregory, Neil, and Stoyan Tenev, 2001, "The Financing of Private Enterprise in China," *Finance & Development*, Vol. 38, No. 1 (March), pp. 14–17.

Lardy, Nicholas, 2000, "When Will China's Financial System Meet China's Needs?" paper presented at the Conference on Policy Reform in China, Stanford, California, November 18–20, 1999, revised February 2000.

Organization for Economic Cooperation and Development, 2002, "Challenges to China's Banking Industry," in *China in the World Economy*, March (Paris: Organization for Economic Cooperation and Development).

People's Bank of China, 2000, *Annual Report* (Beijing: People's Bank of China).

Wong, Richard Y.C., and Sonia M.L.Wong, 2000, "Competition in China's Banking Industry," October (Hong Kong SAR: Hong Kong Centre for Economic Research).

11

The Finances of China's Enterprise Sector

PAUL HEYTENS AND CEM KARACADAG

Solving the closely related problems of the state enterprise and financial sectors and of China's medium-term fiscal sustainability represents the central economic challenge facing China. The weak performance of the state-owned enterprises (SOEs) has burdened the state commercial banks (SCBs) with a large amount of nonperforming loans, creating contingent liabilities that could threaten medium-term fiscal sustainability. Although the authorities have made progress in improving the governance and performance of the SOEs and the SCBs, the remaining agenda is formidable, and the financial costs of reforms are high but difficult to quantify. The difficulty of quantifying the costs of reform is exemplified by the substantial and still-continuing revisions made to measures of asset quality in the financial system.[1]

---

[1] As noted in Chapter 10, in 1998 the PBC estimated the SCBs' nonperforming loans to be 25 percent of their total loans. After the transfer of many nonperforming loans to AMCs in 1999–2000, the PBC once again released an estimate of 25 percent for the SCBs, based on the old classification system, implying a substantial increase in the estimated ratio from 1998. Following the introduction of a new loan classification system effective January 2002, the four SCBs revised their nonperforming loan ratios upward, to a combined average of 30 percent of total loans at the end of 2001. Until the end of 2001, loans were classified only after principal (not interest) payments were past due, and only the portion of principal past due (according to the original payment schedule) was classified as nonperforming, not the entire loan, and not any unpaid interest. Similarly, provisions were capped at 1 percent of total loans, and most Chinese banks maintained loan-loss reserves of only 1–2 percent of total loans. The authorities recently adopted a new loan classification and provisioning standard, (see Chapter 10).

This chapter examines the systemic risks arising from China's state banks and state enterprises and their policy implications from the perspective of enterprise balance sheets. It examines the leverage, efficiency, and debt repayment capacity of China's enterprise sector. The risk profile of enterprises, in turn, holds a mirror to the financial system's soundness, given that until recently most credit has been lent to enterprises.

The analysis uses aggregate financial data published by the National Bureau of Statistics and two firm-level data sets on China's listed companies (see Appendix I). The aggregate data describe China's enterprise sector (both state and nonstate enterprises), whereas the firm-level data allow an examination of the finances of listed enterprises (most of which remain under majority state ownership and control).[2] The cash coverage of interest expense forms the bridge between the enterprise sector analysis and the assessment of financial sector asset quality. This measure has provided useful insights into financial sector vulnerabilities elsewhere in the region (Ramos and others, 1998, 2000) but has not been applied to China before now.

Overview of SOE and Financial Sector Reform

The restructuring of SOEs and of the financial sector has been the most difficult of China's structural reforms. The financial performance of the SOEs has historically been weak, reflecting both macroeconomic and industry-specific factors, including poor management, overstaffing, heavy indebtedness, outdated products and technologies, an excessive social welfare burden, and high tax rates. SOE losses have required heavy subsidization by the state; before the start of reform in the late 1970s this was provided by direct budgetary allocations, but thereafter it took the form of loans from the SCBs. By the mid-1990s reform of the SOEs and the SCBs could no longer be delayed. Even so, the pace of reform remained conditioned by concerns about social stability, as layoffs from the SOEs added to regional income disparities and strained an inadequate social safety net.

The focus of recent SOE reform has been to privatize small enterprises and to commercialize large ones under the principle of "seize the large and release the small." Some progress has been made on harden-

---

[2]The aggregate data span 1994–2000, and the two firm-level data sets span from 1998 to mid-2000, and 1995–98, respectively. Although the rise in SOE profitability, particularly in 2000, is reflected in the aggregate data and analysis, the firm-level statistics do not fully capture the recent improvement in enterprise sector performance.

ing budget constraints, and enterprise profitability has improved follow-ing the authorities' initiative in 1998 to revitalize medium-size and large SOEs. Better earnings mainly reflect outside factors such as higher oil prices and interest savings from debt-equity swaps, but durable effi-ciency gains have been secured through layoffs, a reduced social welfare burden, and reductions in excess capacity.[3]

Financial sector reforms have focused on commercializing SCBs' lending operations. The reforms were initiated by establishing policy banks to relieve the four large SCBs of their policy lending, while tak-ing steps to commercialize the SCBs and hold them accountable for their own operations and financial results. After the onset of the Asian crisis a range of new reforms were introduced, which included limiting local government interference in bank lending decisions, abolishing the credit plan, recapitalizing the SCBs through a Y 270 billion bond issue in 1998, and transferring Y 1.4 trillion in nonperforming loans to four asset management companies (AMCs) during 1999–2000. Internal SCB reforms have included the revamping of loan approval and analy-sis procedures, the introduction of more incentive-based compensation systems, branch rationalization, and staff reductions.

These efforts, however, have so far not succeeded in ending non-commercial lending to SOEs or in overcoming their operational ineffi-ciencies. Enterprise management is still weak, outside governance minimal, excess labor high, and exit channels for poorly performing SOEs limited. Bank loans satisfy the working capital and investment needs of SOEs, many of which accumulate inventories unlikely to be sold and receivables with little prospect of payment. Cash-short enter-prises then accumulate tax liabilities and are kept afloat by debt rollovers and new loans from banks, whose capacity to assess and price credit risk remains limited. Even if lenders intended to distinguish good risks from bad ones, corporate accounting practices distort financial statements to a degree that makes it difficult to screen and monitor borrowers.[4]

---

[3]According to official statistics, the aggregate profits of large and medium-size SOEs surged by 135 percent in 2000, to Y 240 billion. Available data through September 2001 suggest that the upward trend in SOE profitability had leveled off.

[4]Firms overstate profits and assets. All goods produced are valued at market prices, regardless of whether they are sold or paid for. Unsold goods accumulate as inventories, while sales of goods that are not paid for accumulate as receivables. Both are then val-ued at market prices and classified as current assets. Furthermore, both inventories and receivables are credited as revenues in the income statement and included in profits, even though neither generates cash. Appendix I details the statistical adjustments made to correct for the data anomalies.

Enterprise Sector Analysis

This section examines two types of data on Chinese enterprises: an aggregate data set for all industrial enterprises, including SOEs, published in the annual *China Statistical Yearbook*, and data on individual listed enterprises, most of which are state owned. The available data confirm the weak financial condition of the enterprise sector. They also suggest that enterprise finances are vulnerable to considerable downside risk from even a moderate weakening of their business environment. Deficiencies in the quality of corporate financial data, however, warrant some caution in interpreting these conclusions.

The financial condition of enterprises, particularly SOEs, has important implications for the soundness of the banking system, given that SOEs are the predominant users of bank credit. SOEs accounted for over half of outstanding credit in 2000; two-thirds of these loans were of less than one year's maturity.[5] Although loans to consumers (currently around 3–4 percent of total loans) have been growing rapidly in recent years, credit to enterprises will continue to represent a large share of bank assets. The financial system's risk exposure to the enterprise sector should decline over time, however, as a growing share of new credits are granted to private enterprises, and as banks lend on an increasingly commercial basis.

Aggregate-Level Analysis

Although the share of SOEs in China's industrial sector has been declining, it is still sizable. The share of state enterprise output and employment has been on a declining trend since 1994 (Table 11.1).[6] Nevertheless, SOEs continue to generate over 50 percent of industrial value added and employ more than half the industrial workforce. Also noteworthy is the steady rise in the value added of foreign-funded enterprises, which doubled between 1994 and 2000, in contrast to that of collective-owned firms, which fell by more than half.[7]

---

[5]The credit stock, at 125 percent of GDP at the end of 2000, is high by emerging market standards, reflecting China's high saving rate.

[6]The jump in SOEs' share of industrial value added in 1998 (as well as in their share of industrial fixed assets; see Table 11.2) resulted in part from a broadening of the classification to include enterprises in which the state has a controlling share. In addition, it may reflect the impact of increased fiscal spending—which was largely channeled through SOEs—to support growth following the Asian financial crisis.

[7]Shareholding companies doubled their share of industrial value added in both 1999 and 2000, but the increase stems in part from the reclassification of collectives and SOEs as shareholding companies.

Table 11.1. Output, Employment, and Value Added of Industrial Enterprises by Ownership Type

(In percent of total)

Type of Ownership	1994	1995	1996	1997	1998	1999	2000
Output							
State owned[1]	37.8	34.6	34.0	30.2	26.5	26.3	...
Collective owned	38.2	37.3	36.9	36.4	36.1	32.9	...
Individual owned	10.2	13.1	14.5	17.1	16.1	16.9	...
Shareholding	4.3	3.1	3.1	4.2	7.3	9.1	...
Foreign funded[2]	9.6	11.9	11.4	12.1	14.0	14.8	...
Employment							
State owned[1]	66.4	66.5	66.3	65.0	57.2	54.5	51.1
Collective owned	24.4	22.7	22.2	21.4	16.9	15.2	13.7
Other	9.2	10.7	11.5	13.6	25.9	30.3	35.2
Value added							
State owned[1]	54.5	54.5	49.4	47.3	58.3	55.7	51.9
Collective owned	28.4	25.4	29.2	27.1	17.4	14.6	11.6
Shareholding	5.8	5.1	5.4	7.4	3.0	7.4	13.5
Foreign funded[2]	11.3	15.0	16.1	18.2	21.3	22.3	23.0

Source: *China Statistical Yearbook,* various issues.
[1]For 1998–2000, includes enterprises in which the state held a controlling share.
[2]Includes enterprises owned by investors in Hong Kong SAR, Macao SAR, and Taiwan Province of China.

SOEs control the bulk of productive assets in the industrial sector. They held two-thirds of the net fixed assets of all industrial enterprises in 2000 (Table 11.2).[8] By contrast, collective enterprises' share of fixed assets fell by two-thirds between 1994 and 2000, with shareholding and foreign companies increasing their shares modestly. The decline in the share of collectives is attributable to falling growth in and investment by township and village enterprises (which are classified as collectives), and because many collectives were actually private and were reclassified as such in 1998. A noteworthy trend is the rising share of fixed assets in the total assets of all enterprises, particularly SOEs. The share of net fixed assets in SOEs' total assets stood at 44 percent in 2000, up from less than 36 percent in 1994.

However, the efficiency of investment in the SOE sector is relatively low (Figure 11.1). The ratio of value added to fixed assets for SOEs was 37 percent in 2000, compared with 56 percent for shareholding companies, 61 percent for foreign companies, and 94 percent for collectively

---

[8]The increase in SOEs' share of fixed assets may also reflect (in addition to the broadening of classification just noted) a pickup in "technological renovation" investment following the authorities' plan, adopted in 1998, to rehabilitate large SOEs.

Table 11.2. Net Fixed Assets of Industrial Enterprises by Ownership Type
(In percent)

Type of Ownership	1994	1995	1996	1997	1998	1999	2000
As a share of total fixed assets of industrial enterprises							
State owned[1]	65.7	64.4	64.9	62.4	71.3	68.1	65.4
Collective owned	16.9	15.8	14.9	13.9	8.6	7.2	5.8
Shareholding	5.2	4.7	4.9	6.7	1.5	6.6	11.4
Foreign funded	7.2	6.6	7.8	9.2	9.3	9.4	9.3
Hong Kong and Macao SARs, and Taiwan Province of China	5.1	8.4	7.6	7.8	9.3	8.8	8.1
As a share of total assets of indicated ownership type							
State owned[1]	35.5	36.8	42.0	41.5	42.6	42.2	43.9
Collective owned	29.5	29.9	32.3	33.0	33.9	33.9	33.9
Shareholding	26.0	28.8	30.3	32.2	34.3	35.7	43.2
Foreign funded	36.6	31.1	33.0	35.3	37.9	38.6	37.9
Hong Kong and Macao SARs, and Taiwan Province of China	32.3	36.6	37.7	39.0	40.2	40.1	38.4
All enterprises	33.6	34.7	38.4	38.5	40.8	40.5	42.0

Source: *China Statistical Yearbook,* various issues.
[1]For 1998–2000, includes enterprises in which the state held a controlling share.

owned firms. Although the efficiency of all groups fell during 1994–2000, the relative drop in this ratio was sharpest for SOEs, at 35 percent.

Leverage among industrial enterprises remains high, despite the downward trend in recent years (Table 11.3). The liabilities-to-equity ratio for all enterprises stood at 144 percent in 2000—down from 200 percent in 1994. Enterprise leverage is on a par with levels prevailing in Brazil, Indonesia, and Thailand in the run-up to their financial crises and much higher than in the Czech Republic, Hungary, and Poland, where the median debt-equity ratios of listed companies stood at 43, 14, and 45 percent, respectively, in 1998–99.[9]

Interest coverage has strengthened, mirroring the decline in leverage, but remains low.[10] Chinese enterprises' interest coverage averaged 3.6 times in 2000 (that is, operating profits were 3.6 times interest expense), which is low by international standards (Table 11.4).[11] SOEs had the

---

[9]Cross-country leverage indicators are obtained from a database constructed from corporate financial indicators in the Worldscope database.

[10]Interest coverage (the ratio of operating profits to interest expense) is computed by estimating interest expenses, which in turn are calculated by multiplying reported total liabilities by the prevailing interest rate on short-term loans.

[11]In the run-up to the Asian crisis, median interest coverage ratios for the domestically listed companies of the crisis countries ranged between 2 and 3 in 1996 (Claessens, Djankov, and Lang, 1998).

Figure 11.1. Ratio of Value Added to Fixed Assets of Industrial Enterprises
(In percent)

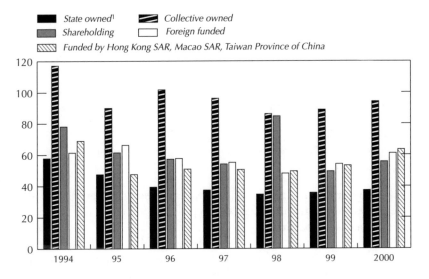

Source: *China Statistical Yearbook,* various issues.
[1]For 1998–2000, includes enterprises with a controlling share by the state.

lowest coverage at 2.9 times, and shareholding companies the highest at 5.7 times. By contrast, interest coverage ranged between 10 and 20 times for listed companies in Hong Kong SAR and Singapore, and between 5 and 10 for listed companies in Germany, Japan, and the United States (Pomerleano, 1998). Listed companies in the Czech Republic, Hungary, and Poland also had strong interest coverage of 6–11 times in 1999.

Profitability was weakest among industrial enterprises during 1994–2000 (Table 11.5). Foreign-funded enterprises were the most profitable, with an operating profits-to-assets ratio of 17 percent, almost double that of SOEs.

Firm-Level Analysis

Firm-level data allow a more in-depth analysis of China's enterprise sector than has been available in the literature until now. Two sets of firm-level data are analyzed: data for a subset of listed enterprises (from the Worldscope database), and a data set of virtually all listed enterprises, pursuant to the disclosure requirements of the China Securities Regulatory Commission (CSRC). Indicators of enterprise financial risk are generated for each company.

Table 11.3. Ratio of Total Liabilities to Equity of Industrial Enterprises by Ownership Type
(In percent)

Type of Ownership	1994	1995	1996	1997	1998	1999	2000
State owned[1]	211	192	186	184	176	160	155
Collective owned	234	243	249	234	209	192	188
Shareholding	117	122	130	131	191	109	97
Foreign funded	167	120	131	129	129	125	127
Hong Kong and Macao SARs, and Taiwan Province of China	161	164	174	164	148	140	136
All enterprises	200	186	184	177	171	152	144

Source: *China Statistical Yearbook,* various issues.
[1]For 1998–2000, includes enterprises in which the state held a controlling share.

To summarize what follows, firm-level analysis suggests that Chinese enterprises are financially weak and exposed to adverse macroeconomic developments. In particular:

- *China's corporate sector is largely unprofitable and illiquid.* Several enterprises in the firm-level data sets—accounting for 20–30 percent of the total debt of all firms in the sample—are unable to generate enough cash flow to pay interest on their debts.

- *The corporate sector is susceptible to even modest interest rate and demand shocks.* Sensitivity analysis suggests that a moderate rise in interest rates or drop in sales could cause 40–60 percent of the debts of all firms to become unserviceable, underscoring the financial fragility of the sector.

- *The interest coverage analysis corroborates the high level of nonperforming loans in the banking system.* With implied nonperforming loans in the 20–30 percent range, the analysis suggests that the figure reported by the four large SCBs of nearly 30 percent is a

Table 11.4. Ratio of Operating Profits to Interest Expense of Industrial Enterprises by Ownership Type
(In percent)

Type of Ownership	1994	1995	1996	1997	1998	1999	2000
State owned[1]	1.7	1.6	1.5	1.6	1.9	2.4	2.9
Collective owned	2.3	2.1	2.3	2.7	3.4	5.5	4.3
Shareholding	2.4	2.2	2.0	2.3	3.9	3.6	5.7
Foreign funded	2.3	2.3	2.3	2.7	3.3	4.6	5.1
Hong Kong and Macao SARs, and Taiwan Province of China	1.9	1.7	1.7	2.0	2.7	3.4	3.9
All enterprises	1.9	1.8	1.8	2.0	2.3	3.0	3.6

Source: *China Statistical Yearbook,* various issues; and IMF staff estimates.
[1]For 1998–2000, includes enterprises in which the state held a controlling share.

Table 11.5. Operating Margins of Industrial Enterprises by Ownership Type

(In percent of assets)[1]

Type of Ownership	1994	1995	1996	1997	1998	1999	2000
State owned[2]	12.7	11.4	10.5	9.4	8.6	8.7	10.4
Collective owned	17.3	16.8	17.0	16.7	16.1	21.7	16.7
Shareholding	14.5	13.5	11.9	11.6	17.8	11.4	16.8
Foreign funded	15.5	14.1	13.5	13.6	13.0	15.2	17.2
Hong Kong and Macao SARs, and Taiwan Province of China	13.0	11.4	11.3	11.2	11.2	11.9	13.4
All enterprises	13.9	12.7	12.1	11.3	10.3	11.0	12.5

Sources: *China Statistical Yearbook,* various issues; and IMF staff estimates.
[1]Operating margin equals sales minus cost of goods sold.
[2]For 1998–2000, includes enterprises in which the state held a controlling share.

lower bound (since the interest coverage analysis does not include amortization).

The results of the firm-level analysis are broadly consistent with those for the aggregate enterprise sector. The financial parameters and results derived from the two samples of listed enterprises are compatible with and, where directly comparable (that is, with respect to leverage, profitability, and interest coverage), similar to the aggregate-level figures discussed earlier.[12]

Asset Structure and Leverage

The large share of receivables and inventories in total assets indicates that SOEs have been producing goods that few want to buy or can pay for, and that their assets are overvalued. Fixed assets account for the largest share of total assets (32–36 percent), followed by receivables (16–27 percent) and inventories (12–15 percent; Table 11.6). Fixed assets' share in total assets is broadly comparable to equivalent figures reported in the aggregate data (42 percent; Table 11.2). Receivables are higher for all listed companies, at 22–27 percent, than for the Worldscope subset, at 16–18 percent, whereas inventories represent near-equal shares for both groups. The difference in receivables may be attributable to the relative strength of companies represented in the Worldscope data set, which appear to have higher rates of cash collection per unit of sales.

---

[12]The sample of listed companies accounts for 16 percent of total assets of all medium-size and large industrial enterprises. Assets of companies in the sample totaled Y 1,915 billion at the end of 1999, compared with Y 8,047 billion for all medium-size and large SOEs reported in the *China Statistical Yearbook.* However, the two figures are not directly comparable because listed companies include firms in the utilities and transportation sectors, which are excluded from the aggregate industrial enterprise data.

Table 11.6. Inventories, Receivables, and Fixed Assets of Listed Companies
(In percent of total assets)

Sample and Item	1995	1996	1997	1998	1999	2000[1]
Worldscope database						
Inventories	15.2	13.1	11.9	11.7	. . .	. . .
Net receivables	15.5	17.7	18.3	16.5	. . .	. . .
Fixed assets	32.9	35.5	34.0	33.2	. . .	. . .
CSRC financial disclosures						
Inventories	. . .	. . .	. . .	12.3	12.1	11.6
Net receivables	. . .	. . .	. . .	21.8	26.8	26.0
Fixed assets	. . .	. . .	. . .	33.2	32.9	31.5

Sources: Worldscope, company disclosures, and IMF staff estimates.
Note: CSRC, China Securities Regulatory Commission.
[1]Data are for the first half of the year.

The leverage of listed companies appears to be relatively low, but this may be misleading because of the overvaluation of inventories, receivables, and fixed assets. For both data sets the leverage of listed companies is under 100 percent (Table 11.7), well below the 144 percent reported in the aggregate figures (Table 11.3). This may reflect the fact that listed companies in the sample have access to more-diverse sources of financing (including equity) than the enterprise population as a whole. In addition, several studies have shown that SOEs overvalue their assets (Lardy, 1998; Steinfeld, 1998). Various adjustments have been made to assets and equity to illustrate the potential impact of asset overvaluation on measures of leverage and solvency.[13]

The leverage indicators increase significantly, and several companies become insolvent, when equity is adjusted for the possible overvaluation of assets (Table 11.7). The deduction from equity of 75 percent of the value of inventories results in nearly one-fifth of all domestically listed companies becoming insolvent and in a more than doubling of liabilities-to-equity ratios. A 75 percent reduction in the value of fixed assets pushes more than a third of all domestically listed companies into insolvency and results in a three- to fivefold increase in their liabilities-to-equity ratios.

---

[13]Several illustrative scenarios have been calculated. First, the balance of receivables and payables is deducted from equity in all adjusted leverage ratios (liabilities-to-equity ratios I-VII in Table 11.7). Second, three progressively larger reductions in value—25, 50, and 75 percent—are applied to inventories and fixed assets, which are then deducted from equity. The reductions are applied to inventories (liabilities-to-equity ratios II-IV) and fixed assets (liabilities-to-equity ratios V-VII) separately, not simultaneously.

Table 11.7. Leverage of Listed Companies Under Illustrative Scenarios

(In percent)

Sample and Indicator	1995	1996	1997	1998	1999	2000
Worldscope database[1]						
Liabilities-to-equity[2]	87.6	87.0	80.5	84.7	. . .	. . .
Liabilities-to-equity I	78.9	78.4	69.7	76.8	. . .	. . .
Liabilities-to-equity II	83.4	83.8	78.1	85.0	. . .	. . .
Liabilities-to-equity III	93.4	90.3	84.6	93.0	. . .	. . .
Liabilities-to-equity IV	109.0	96.4	94.8	100.7	. . .	. . .
Liabilities-to-equity V	101.7	96.6	86.2	104.0	. . .	. . .
Liabilities-to-equity VI	126.4	123.9	116.8	140.7	. . .	. . .
Liabilities-to-equity VII	193.1	174.0	175.3	261.9	. . .	. . .
Insolvent companies in						
Worldscape database						
Negative equity I[3]	0.6	1.0	1.0	3.0	. . .	. . .
Negative equity II	5.5	1.0	1.8	4.4	. . .	. . .
Negative equity III	6.6	3.5	4.2	5.4	. . .	. . .
Negative equity IV	11.9	8.8	6.2	9.2	. . .	. . .
Negative equity V	0.6	7.8	7.2	10.0	. . .	. . .
Negative equity VI	2.4	12.6	13.8	16.6	. . .	. . .
Negative equity VII	12.0	15.0	22.0	25.0	. . .	. . .
CSRC financial disclosures[1]						
Liabilities-to-equity	. . .	. . .	. . .	72.0	74.9	76.0
Liabilities-to-equity I	. . .	. . .	. . .	94.0	114.9	115.9
Liabilities-to-equity II	. . .	. . .	. . .	102.7	129.5	132.9
Liabilities-to-equity III	. . .	. . .	. . .	114.3	146.8	147.2
Liabilities-to-equity IV	. . .	. . .	. . .	127.2	170.7	166.0
Liabilities-to-equity V	. . .	. . .	. . .	117.0	152.6	154.4
Liabilities-to-equity VI	. . .	. . .	. . .	156.7	232.4	227.0
Liabilities-to-equity VII	. . .	. . .	. . .	226.0	463.5	406.9
Insolvent companies among						
CSRC financial disclosures						
Negative equity I[3]	. . .	. . .	. . .	3.0	7.1	6.9
Negative equity II	. . .	. . .	. . .	3.3	8.5	10.9
Negative equity III	. . .	. . .	. . .	5.7	11.4	14.0
Negative equity IV	. . .	. . .	. . .	10.1	15.1	18.1
Negative equity V	. . .	. . .	. . .	10.2	24.0	23.8
Negative equity VI	. . .	. . .	. . .	13.7	32.1	30.2
Negative equity VII	. . .	. . .	. . .	33.8	45.8	43.2

Sources: Worldscope database, company disclosures, and IMF staff estimates.

[1]Data for liabilities-to-equity ratios are medians of the firms in the sample.

[2]No adjustment made to reported numbers in this line. For the remaining leverage indicators I–VII, the balance of receivables minus payables is deducted from reported equity. In addition, except for I, equity is adjusted by a reduction in the value of inventories (II, 25 percent; III, 50 percent; IV, 75 percent) *or* of fixed assets (V, 25 percent; VI, 50 percent; VII, 75 percent).

[3]As a share of sample total assets.

Leverage indicators for the Worldscope subset deteriorate under these scenarios to a similar degree, although the number of companies that become insolvent is considerably smaller (mirroring the smaller number of insolvent enterprises in the baseline scenario). The impli-

Table 11.8. Profitability of Listed Companies
(In percent)[1]

Sample and Profitability Measure	1995	1996	1997	1998	1999	2000[2]
Worldscope database						
Return on assets	5.4	4.8	3.5	1.6	. . .	. . .
Return on equity	10.3	10.0	7.2	4.0	. . .	. . .
Operating margin I[3]	11.8	9.3	8.8	6.5	. . .	. . .
Operating margin II[4]	28.8	28.3	28.7	26.9	. . .	. . .
CSRC financial disclosures						
Return on assets	. . .	. . .	. . .	5.6	5.0	4.0
Return on equity	. . .	. . .	. . .	10.1	9.1	7.0
Operating margin I	. . .	. . .	. . .	3.7	6.2	4.7
Operating margin II	. . .	. . .	. . .	33.9	35.4	35.3

Sources: Worldscope database, company disclosures, and IMF staff estimates.
[1]Data are medians of the firms in the sample.
[2]Data are for the first half of the year.
[3]Sales minus total operating costs.
[4]Sales minus cost of goods sold.

cation for locally listed companies as a whole is that overvaluation of assets may account for a substantial portion of reported enterprise equity.

Profitability and Liquidity

The profitability of listed companies fell during the periods examined and is now weak. The median return on equity was 7 percent in the first half of 2000 (on an annualized basis) for all domestically listed companies and ranged from 4 to 7 percent during 1997–98 for the subset of listed companies covered by Worldscope. Further, although the operating margin relative to the total cost of sales (operating margin II in Table 11.8) is high, margins based on a broader measure of net operating income that incorporates total operating costs (operating margin I) are considerably lower, reflecting the still-high social welfare burden borne by Chinese enterprises.

The liquidity position of listed companies is also weak. Long-term debt accounts for only 6–8 percent of the total debt of domestically listed companies (Table 11.9). For the set of firms covered by World-scope, the share is higher (15–19 percent) but still relatively small. The dominant share of short-term debt puts current liabilities well above liquid assets. Current assets, which include illiquid and overvalued inventories and receivables, cover less than a third of current liabilities. The degree of mismatch would widen further if current assets were adjusted

Table 11.9. Liquidity of Listed Companies
(In percent)[1]

Sample and Liquidity Measure	1995	1996	1997	1998	1999	2000[2]
Worldscope database						
Long-term debt to total debt	19.0	18.4	17.0	14.6	. . .	. . .
Current assets to current liabilities	32.7	31.7	33.0	29.6	. . .	. . .
CSRC financial disclosures						
Long-term debt to total debt	. . .	. . .	. . .	7.4	6.0	7.9
Current assets to current liabilities	. . .	. . .	. . .	24.2	28.5	27.9

Sources: Worldscope database, company disclosures, and IMF staff estimates.
[1]Data are medians of the firms in the sample.
[2]Data are for the first half of the year.

downward for the overvaluation of inventories and receivables or for their illiquid portion.

Interest Coverage and Implied Nonperforming Loans

The cash coverage of interest expense is an indicator of the quality of bank loan portfolios. It measures the capacity of enterprises to service their debt, thus linking enterprise financial performance to the quality of assets in the financial system. Experience in other countries has shown that this indicator often provides greater insights into the asset quality of financial institutions than do conventional banking indicators, because of weak accounting and classification standards, which can result in the understatement of problem loans.[14] Of course, the information content of the cash coverage indicator itself hinges on the accuracy of enterprise financial statements.

In the case of China, the reported cash flow data likely overstate profits. In particular, reported earnings include accrued income from receivables. As explained in Appendix I, several adjustments are made to earnings before interest, taxes, depreciation, and amortization (EBITDA) and to interest expenses in order to provide a better measure of the interest coverage ratio. With these adjustments, the EBITDA-to-interest expense ratio is calculated for each firm. Those enterprises whose interest coverage ratio is below 100 percent are assumed to be in default on their debts, and the entire balance of their outstanding debt is treated as a "nonperforming loan." The nonperforming loans of all

---

[14]See Ramos and others (1998, 2000) for an analysis of the Republic of Korea, Malaysia, Thailand, and Taiwan Province of China, among others.

companies are then tallied to yield an "implied nonperforming loan ratio" for the sample of enterprises as a whole.

The nonperforming loans of companies with negative EBITDA are considered to be "structural." The intuition behind segregating this sub-set from total implied nonperforming loans is that "structural" nonper-forming loans belong to firms whose debt servicing capacity will not be improved by interest rate cuts or debt restructuring. As money losers they presumably have serious operational deficiencies that cannot be rectified by financial restructuring alone (Ramos and others, 2000).

Based on interest coverage, the implied nonperforming loan ratios broadly range between 20 and 30 percent (Table 11.10). This result cor-roborates the problem of large nonperforming loans in the banking sys-tem. With interest coverage of 2–3 times for the Worldscope sample, and 2–4 times for all domestically listed companies, average enterprise interest coverage is weak. The interest coverage measure, however, pro-vides only a upper bound on debt servicing capacity, since it does not include amortization. The short-term duration of claims on enterprises probably means that actual levels of nonperforming loans are much higher.

Enterprise interest coverage is quite sensitive to adverse changes in interest rates and demand. Two scenario analyses are carried out on the interest coverage ratios to assess the extent to which implied nonper-forming loans rise in the face of adverse financial and economic devel-opments. The first scenario is a 2-percentage-point rise in interest rates for all firms. The second is a 10 percent fall in sales revenue, which translates into a 3 percent decline in earnings, given operating margins of around 30 percent of sales in the two samples. The combined impact of the two stress scenarios is also reported. Under the higher-interest-rate scenario, implied nonperforming loan ratios rise by 3–7 percentage points. Lower sales have a greater impact: implied nonperforming loans for the Worldscope sample more than double in three out of the four years analyzed; they rise by 6–7 percentage points in the larger sample of domestically listed companies. The combined effect of the two shocks raises implied nonperforming loan ratios to 44–57 percent and 31–45 percent, respectively, for the two samples (Table 11.10).

A substantial proportion of implied nonperforming loans are struc-tural. For the Worldscope sample, in 1996–98, about a quarter to half of implied nonperforming loans are structural; for all listed companies, some half to two-thirds are structural during 1998–2000 (Table 11.10). The share of structural nonperforming loans in the total approaches 80 percent in both samples under the severest scenarios applied to them (EBITDA-to-interest expense III for Worldscope and EBITDA-to-interest expense IV for CSRC financial disclosures).

Table 11.10. Interest Coverage and Implied Nonperforming Loans of Listed Companies

(In percent)

Sample and Item	1995	1996	1997	1998	1999	2000[1]
Worldscope database						
Implied interest rate	6.0	5.6	8.5	7.9	. . .	. . .
Adjusted interest rate	11.0	10.5	9.0	7.9	. . .	. . .
Interest rate plus 2% shock	13.0	12.5	11.0	9.9	. . .	. . .
EBITDA to interest expense	306.9	215.9	235.4	220.2	. . .	. . .
Implied NPL ratio	11.0	38.1	19.0	17.0	. . .	. . .
Structural NPL ratio	0.0	8.5	10.6	13.2	. . .	. . .
EBITDA to interest expense I[2]	259.7	181.4	195.5	185.9	. . .	. . .
Implied NPL ratio	14.3	44.9	19.3	21.5	. . .	. . .
Structural NPL ratio	0.0	8.5	10.6	13.2	. . .	. . .
EBITDA to interest expense II[3]	−4.6	78.0	38.7	−66.0	. . .	. . .
Implied NPL ratio	43.7	44.2	49.0	56.5	. . .	. . .
Structural NPL ratio	36.9	20.9	40.4	52.6	. . .	. . .
EBITDA to interest expense III[4]	−3.9	65.6	31.8	−51.4	. . .	. . .
Implied NPL ratio	44.4	49.0	49.0	56.5	. . .	. . .
Structural NPL ratio	36.9	20.9	40.4	52.6	. . .	. . .
CSRC financial disclosures						
Implied interest rate	. . .	. . .	. . .	7.3	5.9	5.4
Adjusted interest rate	. . .	. . .	. . .	7.3	6.0	5.4
Interest rate plus 2% shock	. . .	. . .	. . .	9.3	8.0	7.4
EBITDA to interest expense	. . .	. . .	. . .	260.4	409.7	418.6
Implied NPL ratio	. . .	. . .	. . .	30.3	21.2	32.0
Structural NPL ratio	. . .	. . .	. . .	16.1	12.1	22.9
EBITDA to interest expense I[2]	. . .	. . .	. . .	211.8	323.7	253.2
Implied NPL ratio	. . .	. . .	. . .	32.6	24.4	37.1
Structural NPL ratio	. . .	. . .	. . .	16.1	12.1	22.9
EBITDA to interest expense II[3]	. . .	. . .	. . .	179.6	313.9	303.5
Implied NPL ratio	. . .	. . .	. . .	36.3	28.1	38.6
Structural NPL ratio	. . .	. . .	. . .	21.5	15.9	28.0
EBITDA to interest expense III[4]	. . .	. . .	. . .	147.2	243.1	188.6
Implied NPL ratio	. . .	. . .	. . .	42.3	31.2	44.5
Structural NPL ratio	. . .	. . .	. . .	21.5	15.9	28.0
EBITDA to interest expense IV[5]	. . .	. . .	. . .	. . .	244.1	221.1
Implied NPL ratio	. . .	. . .	. . .	. . .	40.7	39.8
Structural NPL ratio	. . .	. . .	. . .	. . .	35.2	33.7

Sources: Worldscope database, company disclosures, and IMF staff estimates.

Note: NPL, nonperforming loans.

[1]Data are for the first half of the year.

[2]Interest expense incorporates a 2-percentage-point interest rate shock.

[3]Earnings incorporate a 10 percent negative shock to sales.

[4]Ratio incorporates both a 2-percentage-point interest rate shock and a 10 percent negative shock to sales.

[5]Earnings incorporate full repayment of annual buildup in short-term nonbank liabilities.

Conclusions

The empirical results indicate that the financial condition of China's enterprise and financial sectors is weak:

- Across a range of indicators, SOEs are less efficient and display poorer financial profiles than do enterprises under other forms of ownership. They are more leveraged, less profitable, and less liquid, and they possess a disproportionate share of fixed assets relative to their output and value added.
- The enterprise sector has seen a buildup of leverage to finance the acquisition of fixed assets.
- The study points to a large problem of nonperforming loans in the banking system, underscoring the urgency of stemming the flow of new bad loans. To the extent that banks continue to finance unworthy borrowers, they run the risk of amassing a growing stock of liabilities that are unmatched by performing assets, presenting a potentially large future fiscal liability and drag on growth.
- The analysis also suggests that the financial position of the enterprise and financial sectors could deteriorate further under modest economic and financial stress.

These conclusions highlight the need for decisive action to strengthen SOEs and financial institutions and have the following policy implications:

- The weak performance of SOEs and the contingent fiscal costs underscore the importance of accelerating planned SOE and financial sector reforms. In striking a balance between the pace of reforms and social stability, it is vital to avoid escalating quasi-fiscal losses that threaten medium-term fiscal sustainability.
- The persistence of money-losing enterprises points to the need to harden enterprise budget constraints, improve enterprise governance, and accelerate the exit of nonviable SOEs.
- Enterprise accounting and reporting practices need to be strengthened so that lenders can accurately assess the true financial condition and risk profile of borrowers.
- The large stock of problem loans highlights the importance of strengthening bank governance, the prudential regulation and supervision of banks, and the capacity to resolve distressed debts.
- Particular focus is needed on improving and monitoring the quality of new bank lending. Ongoing efforts to improve the risk management and operations of banks are yielding results, with recent reports suggesting that SCBs are reducing their stock of nonperforming loans.[15]

---

[15]The government has targeted a 4 percent annual reduction in SCBs' stock of nonperforming loans over the next five years. Official data suggest that the SCBs are on track to meet this goal in 2002.

Table 11.11. Sources of Financial Data on Chinese Firms

Data Set	Coverage (No. of Companies)	Years	Selection Criteria
Aggregate data	465,239 in 1994 162,885 in 2000	1994–2000	Industrial enterprises with annual sales of over Y 5 million
Worldscope database	118 in 1998	1995–98	Companies with higher market capitalization and investor interest given priority
CSRC disclosures	883 in 1998 1,055 in 2000	1998–2000	All companies listed on the Shanghai and Shenzhen stock exchanges

Sources: *China Statistical Yearbook,* various issues; Worldscope; company disclosures.

Appendix I: Data Sources

As noted in the text, this study draws upon one aggregate and two firm-level data sets in the analysis of China's enterprise sector. The aggregate data set comes from annual editions of the *China Statistical Yearbook* and covers all state and nonstate industrial enterprises with annual sales of over Y 5 million ($0.6 million; Table 11.11). The data are disaggregated in various ways—by ownership, provincial location, type of industry (heavy or light), and sector—and covered 162,885 enterprises in 2000.

The first firm-level data set comes from the Worldscope database, which covers 22,000 listed companies in 53 countries (Primark Corporation, 2000).[16]

Financial data are gathered from company reports and adjusted to conform with the evolving principles of the International Accounting Standards Committee. The overwhelming majority of these companies are industrial companies, with a few in the transportation and utilities sectors. The selection criteria for inclusion in the database give priority to firms with higher market capitalization, which command greater investor interest and whose financial statements are relatively more reliable. The companies chosen are therefore likely to represent top-tier firms with above-average management and financial performance among listed Chinese companies. For example, the 1998 sample of Chinese companies includes 118 listed companies, 29 of which are listed on the Hong Kong Stock Exchange, and the remainder on the Shanghai and Shenzhen bourses.

---

[16]Worldscope has data for only 37 companies in 1999, most of which are listed in Hong Kong SAR. Figures for 1999 are thus biased. The analysis, therefore, is based on the 1995–98 period results for the Worldscope sample.

The second firm-level sample is a much larger data set of virtually all companies listed on the Shanghai and Shenzhen stock exchanges—there are 1,055 such companies in the sample for the first half of 2000. The database includes detailed balance sheet and income statement items made public pursuant to the disclosure requirements of the CSRC and spans the period from 1998 through the first half of 2000. The average firm in this data set underperforms its counterpart in the Worldscope database but is likely to enjoy better management and stronger finances than unlisted SOEs because of the disclosure and enterprise governance standards imposed by the CSRC.

A number of adjustments have been made to the firm-level data in order to correct for deficiencies in Chinese enterprise accounting and reporting practices, which distort the true financial condition and risk profile of enterprises. These distortions and the adjustments made to the firm-level data are summarized below:

- *Overvalued inventories.* Reductions are made to inventory stock values in order to obtain more accurate measures of assets, equity, and leverage. Where possible, adjustments are also made in earnings figures that are known to include revenue from the buildup of inventories.

- *Overvalued receivables.* Most firms have accumulated sizable amounts of both receivables and payables on their balance sheets. Given that most receivables are unlikely to be collected and most payables unlikely to be paid, payables are subtracted from receivables to yield net receivables. The stock of net receivables is then deducted from assets and capital, resulting in higher leverage ratios. Earnings (EBITDA) are also adjusted by the annual change in net receivables when calculating the interest coverage ratio.

- *Overvalued fixed assets.* As with inventories, reductions are applied to reported fixed assets, which are not sufficiently depreciated over time, in order to obtain more realistic measures of assets, equity, and leverage.

- *Understated interest expenses.* The extent of understatement is estimated by deriving the implied interest rates from reported total debt and interest expenses: reported interest expense is divided by reported debt. If the implied interest rate is lower than the prevailing fixed interest rate on short-term loans, interest expenses are adjusted upward by an amount reflecting the difference between them. This results in lower interest coverage ratios and higher implied nonperforming loans.

References

Claessens, Stijn, Simeon Djankov, and Larry Lang, 1998, "East Asian Corporates: Growth, Financing and Risks over the Last Decade," Policy Research Working Paper 2021 (Washington: World Bank).

Lardy, Nicholas R., 1998, *China's Unfinished Economic Revolution* (Washington: Brookings Institution Press).

Pomerleano, Michael, 1998, "The East Asia Crisis and Corporate Finances—The Untold Micro Story" (unpublished working paper; Washington: World Bank).

Primark Corporation, 2000, *Worldscope: Data Definitions* (Waltham, Massachusetts: Primark).

Ramos, Roy, and others, 1998, "Asian Bank NPLs: How High, How Structural? Tying NPL Estimates to the Real Sector," September (New York: Goldman Sachs).

———, 2000, "Asian Bank NPLs, III," December (New York: Goldman Sachs).

Steinfeld, Edward S., 1998, *Forging Reform in China: The Fate of State-Owned Industry* (Cambridge, England: Cambridge University Press).

12

The Impact of WTO Accession

THOMAS DORSEY, DAVID ROBINSON, YONGZHENG YANG,
AND HARM ZEBREGS

After 14 years of negotiations, China acceded to the World Trade
Organization (WTO) on December 11, 2001. A key step in negoti-
ation of the final agreement, the U.S.-China bilateral agreement, was
reached on November 15, 1999, and is generally regarded as the core of
the final agreement. Because this document was made public at the time
the agreement was reached, whereas other bilateral agreements have not
been, there has been greater opportunity to assess its impact, and some of
the material referenced below is based on this bilateral agreement. More
recently, an official summary by the WTO of the entire agreement has
been released, and the first outside assessments of the entire agreement are
now becoming available (WTO, 2001). Some additional information is
available on the bilateral agreements with the European Union and with
other countries, even though the texts of these agreements have not been
made public. The summary of the key features of the agreement below is
based on the WTO summary and, to a lesser extent, the U.S.-China bilateral agreement (Boxes 12.1 and 12.2 provide additional detail):

- China will reduce tariffs on nonagricultural products (which
  account for 95 percent of its imports) to 8.9 percent by 2005, and
  tariffs on agricultural products to 15 percent by January 2004;[1]

---

[1]There is some uncertainty about the tariff reductions implied by WTO accession,
because the average base rate of existing applied tariffs is not known with certainty, nor
is it clear whether the new tariff levels are simple or weighted averages. For the purposes
of this note, the following World Bank estimates of weighted-average tariffs in 1998 are
used: 20 percent for agricultural products and 18½ percent for manufactures (corresponding simple averages are estimated to be 18 percent and 17½ percent).

eliminate quotas and nontariff restrictions on industrial products by 2005; introduce a new tariff rate quota system in agriculture; and provide full trading and distribution rights to foreign firms.

- China will significantly expand market access in the services sector, among other things by eliminating geographic and other restrictions in most key industries by 2005; increasing foreign ownership limits in telecommunications to 50 percent by 2002; opening import-export, wholesale, and retail trade to foreign enterprises; opening the life insurance and securities businesses to foreign investment (for life insurance, allowing ownership of up to 50 percent on accession, and for securities, to 49 percent by 2003); and giving full national treatment to foreign banks (by 2005).

- WTO members maintaining textile quotas under the WTO Agreement on Textiles and Clothing—including the United States, the European Union, and Canada—will eliminate quotas on China's textile imports by January 1, 2005. This will put China on a par with the founding members of the WTO, but this opening is subject to special safeguard provisions through 2008. The United States has granted China permanent normal trade relations status, which was approved on December 27, 2001.

- China will eliminate trade-related investment measures (such as minimum levels of domestic content of output, and minimum export requirements) and will not enforce any such requirements in existing contracts or agreements from the date of accession.

The European Union concluded its bilateral agreement on WTO accession with China on May 19, 2000. It has released a brief summary of the contents insofar as they affect EU exporters and investors. On trade in goods, the agreement provides for additional tariff reductions for products of particular interest to European exporters (alcoholic beverages, textiles, leather products, ceramics, glass, and machinery and appliances), liberalization of fertilizer import quotas and the silk export monopoly, and reductions in tariffs applied under agricultural tariff rate quotas for important European agricultural export products such as rape oil, pasta, butter, and olives. On trade in services, the agreement provides for acceleration of mobile telephone service liberalization by two years after accession, effective management control by foreign partners in 50–50 life insurance joint ventures, and other measures liberalizing trade in banking and insurance beyond the provisions of the U.S. bilateral agreement.

In addition to the United States and the European Union, some 35 other WTO members conducted bilateral negotiations with China, with results also reflected in the final agreement. As is standard prac-

Box 12.1. Main Elements of China's WTO Accession Agreement

Agriculture

China will:

- Reduce average tariffs for agricultural products from 20 percent to 15 percent
- Establish a tariff rate quota system for bulk commodities (including wheat, cotton, and rice), with quotas increasing over time, and subject to tariffs between 1 and 3 percent, and eliminate export subsidies on cotton and rice and limit subsidies on production to 8.5 percent of the value of farm output
- Give foreign exporters the right to sell and distribute imported goods directly to consumers on the mainland, without going through state trading enterprises or other specified middlemen.

Industrial goods

China will:

- Reduce average tariffs from 18½ percent in 1998 to 8.9 percent, mostly by 2004 but in no case later than 2010, with particularly large cuts for automobiles, high-technology products, wood, and paper
- Eliminate quotas and nontariff restrictions within five years (and most in 2002–03); in the interim, base-level quotas will grow at 15 percent annually
- Give foreign companies full trading and distribution rights for imported goods.

Services

China will:

- In telecommunications, join the Basic Telecommunications Agreement, phase out all geographic restrictions on services in five years, and permit 49 percent foreign ownership in all telecommunications services within three years of accession

tice with WTO accession negotiations (and had been standard practice in negotiations on accession to the General Agreement on Tariffs and Trade), this was followed by multilateral negotiations on China's accession protocol to tie the bilateral agreements together and resolve some overarching issues. These multilateral negotiations also had to be completed before accession, and the process of modifying China's laws and regulations to be consistent with China's WTO obligations is well under way.

This chapter discusses the potential impact of WTO accession on China, on the assumption that the U.S.-China agreement approximates

- In insurance, phase out geographic and service restrictions over two to five years, permit 50 percent foreign ownership in life insurance and 51 percent ownership in nonlife insurance on accession (the latter rising to 100 percent in two years), and, for reinsurance and large-scale commercial risks, ensure completely open markets within five years of accession
- In banking, allow foreign banks to conduct local currency business with Chinese enterprises after two years, and retail business after five years, and allow nonbank companies to offer automobile financing on accession
- In the securities business, allow foreign firms to hold minority stakes in securities funds, with maximum shares rising from 33 percent initially to 49 percent after three years
- In distribution and sales, allow foreign companies with existing domestic investments to undertake wholesale business with a Chinese partner on accession, allow foreign-invested retail business in a limited set of major cities on accession with all quantitative and geographic restrictions removed by January 2003, and allow foreign firms full access to import and export rights three years after accession
- In other services, allow foreign firms with foreign majority control to provide a broad range of professional services, including accountancy, taxation, and management consultancy; allow foreign movie companies to form joint ventures for distribution of video and sound recordings; and allow 100 percent foreign ownership of hotels in three years.

Other WTO members will:
- Eliminate import quotas on China's textile and clothing exports maintained under the WTO Agreement on Textiles and Clothing by the end of 2004, subject to special safeguard provisions through 2008
- Maintain current antidumping methodology (treating China as a non-market economy) for 15 years after accession.

the final terms of accession. Given the limited detail presently available, the analysis seeks only to review the impact in broad terms, focusing on the main channels through which China will be affected, the potential risks, and the policy implications.

Background

Over the past two decades, the opening of the external sector has been a key element of China's economic reforms. The exchange rate regime

---

Box 12.2. Financial Sector Components of China's WTO Accession Agreement

Banking Sector

Currently, foreign banks are not permitted to do local currency business with Chinese clients (although a few can engage in local currency business with their foreign clients), and China imposes severe geographic restrictions on the establishment of foreign banks. China has made commitments to full market access in five years for foreign banks, as follows:

- Foreign banks will be able to conduct local currency business with Chinese enterprises starting two years after accession.
- Foreign banks will be able to conduct local currency business with Chinese individuals starting five years after accession.
- Foreign banks will have the same rights as Chinese banks (that is, national treatment) within designated geographic areas within five years.
- Both geographic and customer restrictions will be removed in five years.

Nonbank Financial Institutions

China has made commitments for nonbank foreign financial institutions to be able to provide automobile financing upon China's accession. This, in combination with commitments regarding importation, distribution, sale, financing, and maintenance and repair of automobiles, will help open up this key sector to foreign competition.

Securities Business

China will permit minority foreign-owned joint ventures to engage in fund management on the same terms as Chinese firms. As the scope of business

---

has been unified, a national foreign exchange trading regime established, and the trade and foreign investment system substantially liberalized.

Since the mid-1980s an essentially dualistic system has emerged:

- The regime for export processing, which covers goods produced entirely for export and is dominated by foreign invested enterprises (FIEs), is very liberal; imports of inputs and investment goods are duty free, and most enterprises can engage directly in foreign trade.
- The system for other ("ordinary") trade, however, remains quite restrictive. Tariff rates are relatively high and widely dispersed, and there are substantial exemptions and numerous and frequently overlapping nontariff barriers, including restrictions on trading rights and distribution (which must be undertaken by Chinese firms).
- Foreign direct investment in the export-oriented manufacturing sector has been substantially liberalized (as is reflected in the rapid growth of processing trade), but significant constraints remain on

expands for securities firms, Chinese and foreign joint venture companies will benefit equally. Minority joint ventures will be allowed to underwrite domestic securities issues and underwrite and trade in foreign currency-denominated debt and equity securities.

Insurance Business

Currently, foreign companies may operate only in Shanghai and Guangzhou. Under the agreement:

- *Geographic limitations.* China will permit foreign property and casualty firms to insure large-scale risks nationwide immediately upon accession and will eliminate all geographic limitations in three years.

- *Scope.* China will expand the scope of activities for foreign insurers to include group, health, and pension lines of insurance, which represent about 85 percent of total premiums, phased in over five years.

- *Prudential criteria.* China agrees to award licenses solely on the basis of prudential criteria, with no economic needs test or quantitative limits on the number of licenses issued.

- *Investment.* China agrees to allow 50 percent ownership for life insurance. Life insurers may now choose their own joint venture partners. For non-life, China will allow branching or 51 percent ownership on accession and form wholly owned subsidiaries in two years. Reinsurance is completely open within five years of accession.

investment in the services sector and in production for the domestic market. Foreign investment in telecommunications is essentially forbidden, activities of foreign insurance companies and banks are severely restricted, and distribution and trading rights are very limited.

On the export side, China receives most-favored-nation (MFN) treatment from most countries; the main constraints on its exports that will be affected by accession are quotas previously administered under the Multi-Fibre Arrangement, which will now fall under the WTO Agreement on Textiles and Clothing. China provides export subsidies on some agricultural products (mainly cotton and rice).

China's trade and investment structure has the following characteristics:

- Processing trade, mainly of labor-intensive textiles, apparel, and electronic goods, accounts for about 55 percent of total exports.

About 47 percent of imports consist of inputs for the processing industry and investment goods for FIEs and export
processing enterprises; these imports are largely exempt from tariffs.

- Ordinary trade—conducted primarily by state-owned enterprises
(SOEs) and collectives—accounted for 42 percent of total exports
and about 44 percent of imports in 2000.
- Tariff revenues in 1999 were about $4 billion, or 10 percent of ordi-
nary imports. This is well below the weighted-average tariff of 18.7
percent, suggesting that there are significant additional exemptions
or collection difficulties—including smuggling—in the system.
- Foreign direct investment has been concentrated in manufacturing,
with only 27 percent of inflows directed to the services sector.

The structure of China's trade suggests that WTO accession will
affect only about half of present trade flows, since the export processing
sector is likely to be relatively unaffected in the short term. Moreover,
the impact of tariff reduction may be less than the raw numbers suggest,
to the extent that the protective effect of tariffs has been eroded
through substantial exemptions or smuggling.

The Sectoral Impact

This discussion of the sectoral impact of the WTO accession agreement focuses on the implications for trade in goods and services and foreign direct investment flows, and for the financial sector and financial
stability. Given the limited data and limited basis for extrapolation from
experience in those sectors from which foreign investors are largely
excluded, the analysis focuses primarily on a qualitative discussion of
the affected sectors and their relative importance in the economy, as a
backdrop for the quantitative projections later in the chapter.

On the trade side, as noted above, WTO accession will primarily
affect ordinary trade flows that come in under the regular trade regime.
The impact will depend on the phasing of the agreement, on the
interaction between tariff reductions and the elimination of quantitative
restrictions, and, last but not least, on the extent to which other barriers
to trade remain.[2] However, the main effects expected are as follows:

---

[2]In the short run, protection by local authorities—which is out of the control of central government—may limit the effect of the agreement. In addition, the behavior of
SOEs and state trading organizations may be difficult to change: although the agreement
includes a commitment that SOEs will make purchases and sales on purely commercial
considerations, this may in practice be difficult to enforce, especially given the influence
of local governments.

Table 12.1. Economic Structure of Sectors Affected by WTO Accession, 1995
(In percent)

Sector and Industry	Output as Share of Total	Labor Force as Share of Total	Exports	Imports	Exports as Share of Output	Ordinary Exports as Share of Output	Ordinary Imports as Share of Domestic Use	Ordinary Imports as Share of Domestic Use
Agriculture								
Rice	1.8	11.8	0.0	0.1	0.0	0.0	0.6	0.5
Wheat	0.9	6.0	0.0	0.9	0.0	0.0	7.2	6.6
Other grain	1.4	9.0	0.3	0.3	1.6	1.6	2.0	1.8
Cotton	0.4	2.8	0.0	0.7	0.6	0.6	11.8	7.3
Industry								
Textiles	5.1	1.7	12.9	7.9	21.0	13.4	13.5	0.9
Apparel	2.2	0.7	9.2	0.2	33.8	14.2	1.2	0.0
Automotive	1.5	0.4	0.4	1.6	0.3	1.1	11.1	9.5
Chemicals	7.7	1.9	9.5	14.5	10.6	6.3	14.7	6.2

Source: Li and Zhai (1999).

- Initially, trade liberalization is likely to increase competitive pressures in the agricultural sector, in the automobile industry, and among some capital-intensive producers in the domestic market (including telecommunications and certain petrochemicals; see Lardy, 2002, and Box 12.3 for a summary of market views of gaining and losing industries). Given that these sectors account for relatively small proportions of output, exports, and imports, the impact on growth and the balance of payments may be relatively limited. However, because the agricultural sector is highly labor intensive (Table 12.1), the impact on employment may be more pronounced. Offsetting this would be a modest boost to ordinary exports (due to the lower cost of imported inputs) and diversification into high-value-added agricultural products for export; enterprises in the transportation sector would also benefit.
- Liberalization in the services sector is likely to lead to a considerable increase in foreign direct investment. This would likely be concentrated in the telecommunications, insurance, securities, banking, and retail industries, and to a lesser extent in the manufacturing sector as manufacturing-related services are liberalized. Once liberalization of direct investment in the distribution sector has been completed, there is likely to be a further increase in imports, because the requirement that foreigners use Chinese distributors has been a major constraint on imports.
- Beginning in 2005 the elimination of textile and clothing quotas will result in a substantial increase in textile exports. With textiles

---

Box 12.3. Market Views on Sectoral Winners and Losers

Once agreement was reached with the United States in mid-November 1999 on the terms of China's accession to the WTO, investors moved quickly to reward potential winners and punish potential losers among companies listed on China's two domestic stock markets and in Hong Kong SAR. The initial market reaction was generally favorable for listed firms in trade-dependent sectors (shipping, ports, civil aviation, railways, and coastal expressways) and for exporters of light industrial products (color television sets, textiles, toys, and shoes), but negative for companies in the services and high-technology sectors and for heavily protected primary and industrial producers (agriculture, automobiles, steel, and petrochemicals). In the immediate aftermath of the agreement, share prices of textile issues, port operators, and trading companies rose particularly sharply (by well over 10 percent in some cases), while those of automobile and telecommunications companies dropped significantly (in some cases also by well beyond 10 percent).

However, the price markups of the perceived winners proved short-lived, and profit taking quickly set in, eliminating or reversing most of the earlier gains by the end of 1999. This correction in part reflected the market realization that the benefits—as well as the costs—of WTO accession would take several years to materialize. Market reaction on the domestic A- and B-share markets was also weighed down by underlying concerns about the weak earnings outlook of Chinese corporations, and by the expectation that new listings would rise sharply on the A-share market in the near term as SOEs sought to raise cash to finance restructuring plans. (A-shares are denominated in local currency and available only to domestic investors; B-shares are denominated in dollars and until February 2001 were available only to foreign

---

and clothing already accounting for 4¼ percent of GDP and 22 percent of exports, the impact on growth and exports could be substantial.[3]

- Finally, as the effects of increased competition feed through into efficiency gains, total factor productivity (TFP) growth should rise. Although precise estimates are obviously difficult, cross-country evidence suggests that the impact could be significant:

---

[3]According to Martin, Dimaranan, and Hertel (1999), China's share of the world textiles market could rise from 8½ percent in 1995 to 11 percent ultimately, and its share of the clothing market—where China has a major comparative advantage—from 20 percent to 60 percent. The U.S. International Trade Commission's (1999) estimates of China's share of the U.S. market are similar for textiles, but rather smaller for clothing, where the commission foresees a 20-percentage-point increase. On the other hand, as already noted, China's textile and clothing exports to the United States will be subject to special safeguard provisions.

investors.) In Hong Kong SAR concerns over intensified competition on the mainland as a result of WTO entry, and the continued perception that most China-related companies were not managed to the same standards of transparency and competitiveness as other listed firms, eventually dampened investor sentiment.

There was also significant differentiation among companies within the losing sectors during this period. For example, although many automotive stocks fell sharply, companies with large truck and minibus operations—which are believed to be competitive—or with extensive domestic distribution networks were generally unaffected. Similarly, although agriculture is widely viewed as one of the biggest overall losers from accession, there was little impact on listed agricultural concerns, because the market believed the sector would continue to be protected. Further, although the telecommunications sector has been branded as a loser by many analysts, the share price of China Telecom (since renamed China Mobile) in Hong Kong SAR nevertheless continued to rise because of its strong near- and medium-term prospects. The company was adding new subscribers at a rate of 300,000 a month and seemed likely to remain the dominant player on the domestic market for many years to come. The picture was also mixed within the petrochemicals sector: naphtha and ethylene producers (who already faced low import duties) generally fared much better than polyester and plastic producers (who currently benefit from relatively high duties). Finally, although the steel sector has also generally been considered a loser, the market tended to view producers that had been affected by U.S. antidumping proceedings in the past—particularly those making cold rolled steel—as potential beneficiaries of WTO entry.

annual TFP growth in moderately outward-oriented countries is 2 percentage points higher than in moderately inward-oriented ones (IMF, 1993). Obviously, much will depend on the speed with which supporting reforms in the SOE and financial sectors are undertaken.

The reforms associated with China's WTO accession include a substantial liberalization of the financial system: foreign banks will be allowed to conduct business in domestic currency with Chinese firms after two years, and with retail customers after five years. Restrictions on foreign participation in the securities business, on automobile financing by nonbank institutions, and in the fast-growing insurance business will also be substantially reduced (Box 12.2). Given the extremely small foreign market shares in these industries (at mid-1999, foreign banks accounted for 1.6 percent of bank assets), these represent potentially enormous changes.

With the assets of the Chinese banking system close to $1 trillion, the market share of foreign banks is likely to remain modest for a considerable period. In the initial stages, most foreign banks are likely to focus on servicing the renminbi needs of foreign companies, high-net-worth individual depositors, and perhaps a few domestic blue chip companies. The scope for this business will be constrained by the lack of a deposit base and the limited development of the interbank market. The main risk to domestic banks is that their best borrowers will migrate to foreign banks, thus worsening the overall quality of their portfolios.

With a few exceptions, foreign banks are unlikely to seek to develop retail networks of their own (which are very expensive) or, given the state of the legal and accounting frameworks in China, to start lending to riskier second-tier borrowers. One niche market that may prove attractive to foreign banks is electronic banking for high-income customers. The experience in other countries has been that foreign banks take equity shares in domestic banks (Box 12.4). It is unclear at this stage whether this will be permitted in China, but it has the potential to give foreign banks access to domestic currency and the Chinese banks access to foreign bank know-how and additional capital.

The Macroeconomic Impact

Some tentative estimates can be offered of the overall macroeconomic impact of WTO accession over the period 2002–05. It is assumed that the underlying stance of macroeconomic policies remains unchanged and that efforts at structural reform in the banking and SOE sectors are accelerated. Given the limited data, the estimates are based primarily on the IMF staff's medium-term macroeconomic model, centered on a simple Cobb-Douglas production function and standard trade equations. Although the sectoral analysis of the previous section has been used where possible, the macroeconomic analysis depends importantly on a variety of key assumptions and should be treated as largely illustrative in nature.

Because China's WTO membership became effective only in December 2001, it is assumed that there is little impact on the economy until 2002. Thereafter the main effects (Table 12.2) are the following:

- Between 2000 and 2004 the external current account deteriorates compared with the baseline projection, but it rebounds in 2005 as textile and apparel exports rise sharply. Imports of goods and services are projected to rise by about 8 percent above baseline by 2005, reflecting the impact of the tariff reduction and increased

Table 12.2. Differences Between WTO Accession and Baseline Scenarios

Difference	2000	2001	2002	2003	2004	2005
In real GDP growth (in percentage points)	0.0	0.0	–0.3	0.1	0.6	0.8
In CPI inflation (annual average, in percentage points)	0.0	0.0	–0.6	–0.6	–0.5	–0.2
In current account balance (in billions of dollars)	0.0	0.0	0.2	–5.7	–12.4	–10.5
In change in reserves (in billions of dollars)	0.0	0.0	–0.7	–4.7	–13.0	–2.9

Source: IMF staff estimates.
Note: CPI, consumer price index.

foreign direct investment. Exports of goods and services increase by only 2¼ percent above baseline by 2004. However, exports increase by an extra 7¾ percent (relative to baseline) in 2005 because of the elimination of the textile and clothing quotas. As a result, the external current account deficit deteriorates by $21 billion (1½ percent of GDP) in 2004 but improves considerably thereafter.

- The short-term deterioration in the current account is, however, partly offset by increased foreign direct investment in the services sector, which is assumed to almost double (relative to baseline) to $17 billion. Foreign direct investment in the manufacturing sector, however, initially falls as the reduction in tariff barriers eliminates the rationale for some of the inflows, but it rises above baseline in the medium term. Nevertheless, the overall balance of payments remains in surplus over the period.

- GDP growth is about ¼ percentage point lower than the baseline in 2001, but thereafter it exceeds the baseline forecast by increasing amounts. Initially, the negative impact of trade liberalization on output—modeled by an assumed increase in the depreciation rate of the capital stock due to accelerated corporate restructuring—is only partly offset by the expansionary impact of increased foreign direct investment and higher exports. From 2003 onward, however, GDP growth is raised by faster TFP growth as restructuring begins to bear fruit, and in the later years by an increasing boost from the textile industry as textile and clothing quotas are abolished.

- Although output falls only modestly, labor market pressures could increase in the short run, especially in the labor-intensive agricultural sector. Li and Zhai (1999) estimate that an additional 2 percent of the workforce (mainly in rural areas) will need to be

---

**Box 12.4. Opening to Foreign Banks:
Experience in Other Transition Economies**

The current situation in the Chinese banking sector has some similarities with the prereform situation in a number of transition economies in Eastern Europe, namely, the Czech Republic, Hungary, Poland, and the Slovak Republic. When these countries began to liberalize their banking systems, the balance sheets of the majority of their banks also showed substantial amounts of nonperforming loans, which had resulted from directed lending to SOEs under the command economy. Like China, these countries also lacked a credit culture and had weak bankruptcy laws. Hungary and Poland have since made considerable progress in restructuring and modernizing their banking systems; however, reforms in the Czech Republic and the Slovak Republic are lagging, and state-controlled banks still account for a significant share of banking sector assets.

In Poland and Hungary, foreign banks appeared on the scene in the early stages of restructuring. After an initial cleansing of balance sheets and partial recapitalization by the government, state banks were privatized, and in a number of cases the new owners—often foreign banks—made up the remainder of the recapitalization. When Poland commercialized its banks in 1991, "twinning" arrangements were put in place (with World Bank support) to facilitate the transfer of banking know-how and integrate the banks into the international banking system. In Hungary, the activities of banks with foreign ownership and the privatization of several banks after 1995 greatly facilitated the sound development of the entire banking industry. Competition and efficiency of the sector improved markedly, the range of services expanded, and their quality improved greatly.

---

reemployed in other sectors over the next five years.[4] Although some rural workers with good land will be able to switch to higher-value-added crops, the World Bank's assessment is that those on marginal land could be seriously adversely affected, increasing poverty and urban migration. In urban areas, given the already existing labor market pressures, the scope for reemployment will be limited until textiles and other emerging industries start to pick up.

- At least in the initial period, the reforms associated with WTO accession may widen income disparities. The export-intensive

---

[4]This comprises 13 million workers in rural areas (mainly producing rice, wheat, and cotton) and about 1¼ million workers in urban areas (mainly in the automobile and machinery industries).

In the Czech Republic, subsidiaries and branches of foreign banks have been catalytic in improving the scope and quality of banking services and promoting financial innovation. By rapidly increasing their market share, especially among prime borrowers—mainly foreign and exporting customers—they have been exerting pressure on domestic banks to improve their efficiency. In the Slovak Republic, where banking sector reforms have not advanced as far as in the other three countries, the foreign equity share in the banking sector has increased significantly, leading to increased competition.

In all four countries the entry of foreign banks seems to have had a positive impact on the domestic banking sector, by increasing competition, introducing new knowledge, and providing funds for recapitalization. However, increased competition and new prudential regulations (tighter provisioning requirements, higher capital adequacy ratios) have led banks to become more conservative in their lending.[1] As a result, only large, highly creditworthy borrowers tend to have access to bank credit, whereas small and medium-size companies still face difficulties. For example, in the Czech Republic, branches of foreign banks mainly cater to foreign-owned and exporting companies.

---

[1]This also occurred in the run-up to privatization, when banks cleaned up their balance sheets by reducing their exposure to risky borrowers to obtain funds for recapitalization or to increase the chances of attracting foreign investors. Another important factor in domestic and foreign banks' lending behavior has been the legal framework. Bankruptcy laws in transition economies tended to favor debtors over creditors, contributing to risk aversion on the part of banks.

coastal provinces gain, while the inland provinces, which contain the bulk of the state enterprises and agricultural production, lose. Rural-urban income disparities are also likely to increase.

- The direct budgetary impact of tariff cuts is relatively modest. In the short run, the tariff cuts are likely to lower revenue by 0.1–0.2 percent of GDP, but this loss is modestly offset by the impact of rising imports and reduced smuggling. There will also, however, be additional expenditure pressures due to rising urban unemployment and possibly weakening rural incomes.[5]

---

[5]An increase in urban unemployment by 1 million could cost about 0.1 percent of GDP in additional social services; the rural unemployed do not receive benefits. If agricultural procurement prices are reduced, budgetary subsidies for agriculture (0.8 percent of GDP) will in principle fall, but in practice there may be pressures to maintain rural incomes.

Table 12.3. Estimates of the Domestic Macroeconomic Impact of China's WTO Accession

Source of Estimate	Change in Indicator from Baseline at Indicated Date (in Percent)		
	GDP	Imports	Exports
Rosen[1]	. . .	12 (long run)	12 (long run)
U.S. International Trade Commission[2]	4 (2010)	14 (2010)	12 (2010)
Li and Zhai[3]	1.5 (2005)	26 (2005)	27 (2005)
Zheng and Fan[4]	0.6 (long run)	5.5 (long run)	9.1 (long run)
Walmsley and Hertel[5]	8.7 (2020)	35.2 (2020)	39.4 (2020)
This chapter	1.8 (2005)	8.6 (2005)	7.7 (2005)

Sources: Rosen (1999), U.S. International Trade Commission (1999), Li and Zhai (1999), Zheng and Fan (2001), Walmsley and Hertel (2000), and IMF staff estimates.

[1]Partial-equilibrium analysis based on China's April 1999 offer (close to the U.S. bilateral agreement).

[2]Based on China's April 1999 offer, using China-WTO model.

[3]Appears to be based on China's April 1998 offer; includes full Multi-Fibre Arrangement liberalization by 2005.

[4]Single-country general-equilibrium analysis based on China's April 1999 offer. Analyzes tariff reductions only.

[5]Based on China's August 1998 offer. Analyzes tariff reductions and the removal of Multi-Fibre Arrangement quotas by 2005.

Table 12.3 compares these estimates with those of other analysts. Although the assumptions underlying the various estimates often differ, the projection of this chapter for the impact on GDP is close to the average of the estimates; however, the projections for export and import growth are at the low end of the range. This primarily reflects the fact that some analysts do not distinguish between processing and nonprocessing trade, as well as differences in the timing of the impact of textile liberalization (which some analysts assume will be fully felt by 2005).

Although these projections are obviously very tentative, three broad conclusions that are relevant for policy can be drawn:

- On the central scenario of this chapter, it seems unlikely that WTO accession will lead to significant pressures on GDP growth or the external accounts in the short run.
- If developments were markedly less favorable than expected—for instance, if foreign direct investment did not increase at all—the overall balance of payments would still remain in surplus, although GDP growth would be somewhat slower (about ½ percentage point below baseline over 2002–04).
- In the initial period, before the beneficial effects of faster TFP growth and the elimination of textile and clothing quotas are felt, labor market pressures may increase.

The Impact of China's Accession on Other Countries

China's sheer size means that its entry into the WTO will lead to significant changes in world trade and investment flows. China is already
the world's second-largest economy in purchasing power parity terms, as
measured by the *World Economic Outlook* staff, and the eighth largest in
terms of trade; its foreign direct investment inflow has been the world's
second largest (after that of the United States) in recent years.[6] The
recent increase of foreign direct investment into Hong Kong SAR also
seems to have been linked to China's WTO entry: many foreign
investors have used Hong Kong SAR as a base to ready themselves for
investment opportunities in China.

Countries will tend to benefit from China's WTO accession in proportion to the degree of complementarity between their trade patterns
and China's. Countries whose import and export patterns are similar to
China's patterns of prospective trade growth will be adversely affected
or benefit less. Countries whose export patterns are similar to China's
import demands, on the other hand, will be able to increase exports to
China more than other countries and will compete less with China in
the rest of the world. On the import side, a country that relies on the
world market for the same products as China may have to pay higher
prices for its imports.

China's accession to the WTO is expected to make it more attractive
to foreign investment, especially FDI. This may be detrimental to countries that compete with China for foreign capital. However, countries
that have been competing with China for foreign direct investment often
also invest in China. This is especially true of a number of countries in
East and Southeast Asia. These countries should benefit from increased
and better investment opportunities in China after its WTO accession. If
some of these countries indeed lose FDI inflows, they should be at least
partially compensated by improved returns on investment in China.[7]

The estimates of the impact of China's WTO accession are based on
a simulation of a global general-equilibrium model developed by
the Global Trade Analysis Project (GTAP).[8] This model is best suited

---

[6]Notwithstanding the rapid growth of FDI inflows in recent years, China's FDI per
capita is moderate. Wei (2000) finds that, controlling for its size, China's record in
attracting FDI is less impressive than that of many other countries.

[7]These investment-related benefits will accrue largely to industrial countries and some
of the more advanced emerging market economies. Most other developing countries are
not significant direct investors in China or other markets.

[8]The model and its database are documented in Hertel (1997) and Dimaranan and
McDougall (2001), respectively. The simulation was carried out using RunGTAP, which
is solved with the GEMPACK software suite (Harrison and Pearson, 1996).

Table 12.4. Projected Impact of China's WTO Accession, 2006

Country Group or Region	Welfare Change[1] (In Billions of 1998 Dollars)	Change (in Percent)			
		In GDP	In terms of trade	In export volume	In import volume
Industrial countries	10.4	0.02	0.2	0.6	0.6
Asian NIEs[2]	1.4	0.01	0.2	0.5	0.7
ASEAN[3]	−1.2	−0.03	−0.3	0.0	−0.5
South Asia	−2.9	−0.16	−1.6	−3.0	−5.6
Latin America	−0.3	0.00	−0.1	0.2	−0.2
N. Africa and Middle East	−0.7	−0.03	−0.1	−0.2	−0.7
Southern Africa Customs Union[4]	−0.0	−0.01	−0.1	0.0	−0.3
Rest of Africa	−0.1	0.00	0.0	0.1	−0.1
Rest of world	−0.3	−0.01	−0.1	−0.1	−0.3
Total (excluding China)	6.2	0.01	0.1	0.4	0.2

Source: IMF staff simulation of the GTAP model.
[1]Measured by equivalent variation, an approximate indication of the change in real consumption.
[2]Newly industrializing economies (Hong Kong SAR, Republic of Korea, Singapore, and Taiwan Province of China).
[3]Excluding Singapore.
[4]Botswana, Lesotho, Namibia, South Africa, and Swaziland.

to capture the medium-term static impact of China's WTO accession; it does not include sophisticated modeling of capital markets. The simulated policy changes include tariff reductions and tariff rate quota commitments in agriculture; assumed cumulative productivity improvements of 2 percent in the merchandise sector and 4 percent in the services sector by 2006; and the abolition of Multi-Fibre Arrangement quotas on Chinese textile and clothing exports. The assumed productivity improvement is intended to capture the likely dynamic gains arising from, among other things, accelerated reform, increased technology transfer, and innovation and institutional changes. The simulation results are benchmarked against a baseline projection for 2006, which incorporates Uruguay Round trade reforms.[9]

The results show an overall gain in welfare for the rest of the world from China's WTO accession. The industrial countries and the Asian newly industrializing economies benefit from China's accession (Table 12.4), but the impact is quite small relative to their economies. The underlying factors that determine the benefits to these two groups of countries are quite different. The industrial countries benefit primarily from their own action: removing quotas on textile and clothing imports

---

[9]For a more detailed description of the simulation and a listing of the countries included in the regions used in the tables, see Yang (2002). The remainder of this section also draws heavily on that paper.

from China. Increased export opportunities in China also improve the economic welfare of the industrial countries but are of secondary importance.[10] In contrast, the newly industrializing economies benefit primarily from the expansion of their exports to China, whereas they lose from the removal of the textile and clothing quotas on China, because these economies compete with China in textile and clothing as well as in other labor-intensive goods.

Other regions listed in Table 12.4 tend to lose from China's WTO accession, but in most cases the losses are marginal. Apart from South Asia, no region experiences a change in GDP in excess of 0.03 percent of GDP. Even South Asia suffers a GDP decline of only about one-sixth of 1 percent in 2006, although exports contract by 3 percent. Both South Asia and the ASEAN members (excluding Singapore) suffer from China's increased competition in the textile and clothing industry because of their heavy reliance on exports of these two commodities.[11] The greater competition leads to significant declines in the prices of these commodities. In addition, both regions are projected to be net importers of grain, whose relative price increases because of China's increased import demand. (Table 12.5 shows projections of net exports by region and by industry.) The combined effects of these price changes are reflected in the deterioration of the terms of trade for the ASEAN members and South Asia. The Middle East and North Africa are also estimated to experience a small decline in GDP even though the region is less dependent than developing Asia on textile and clothing exports; its large net agricultural imports lead to a larger decline in its terms of trade than for other regions outside Asia. Despite significant exports to China, the region's large mineral sector hardly benefits from China's accession to the WTO, because China's tariffs on these commodities are already low.

Although the macroeconomic impact of China's WTO accession is small, sectoral effects are substantial, especially in the textile and clothing industry (Table 12.6). All regions except the Asian newly industrializing economies and South Asia experience a decline in textile exports. For the former, textile exports increase significantly, largely because of increased demand by China following the expansion of its clothing exports. On the other hand, South Asia increases textile

---

[10]Although not separately estimated, Japan and some other net food-importing industrial countries will probably lose from increased agricultural imports by China. However, such losses are likely to be outweighed by their gains from increased exports to the Chinese market.

[11]Caution is warranted in applying the regional results to individual countries within a region, as country characteristics may differ substantially.

Table 12.5. Projected Net Exports by Region and Product Type Following China's WTO Accession, 2006
(In billions of dollars)

Product Type	China	Industrial Countries	NIEs	ASEAN	South Asia	Latin America	N. Africa and Middle East	SACU	Rest of Africa	Rest of World
Grain	−0.7	22.4	−3.8	−3.6	−2.5	−1.8	−8.0	0.0	−1.1	−0.9
Other food crops	−14.4	−2.3	−14.9	3.7	−7.5	46.3	−5.7	1.7	8.4	−15.4
Animal products	−7.1	28.5	−6.2	−3.3	−1.1	0.2	−6.6	0.1	−0.7	−3.7
Other agricultural	−5.5	3.1	−2.6	−1.7	−2.1	−0.5	0.4	0.1	4.1	4.7
Mineral products	−2.0	−146.9	−36.8	7.4	−6.0	31.1	110.0	5.5	24.0	13.6
Textiles	7.8	−19.8	18.1	2.2	8.4	−2.6	−4.5	−0.6	−1.6	−7.3
Clothing	23.5	−122.2	4.1	31.0	56.7	2.6	4.8	−0.1	0.0	−0.2
Machinery and equipment	43.0	161.3	42.7	0.5	−18.4	−54.8	−72.7	−13.7	−16.4	−71.6
Other manufactures	54.2	23.3	−20.0	−14.0	−19.4	−15.6	−15.0	7.8	−8.5	7.2
Services	−1.9	11.8	11.2	9.8	−3.3	−8.1	8.6	−0.6	−11.5	−16.1
All goods and services	96.9	−40.7	−8.1	32.0	4.8	−3.3	11.1	0.1	−3.1	−89.7

Source: IMF staff simulation of the GTAP model.
Note: NIEs, newly industrializing economies; ASEAN, Association of South East Asian Nations; SACU, South Africa Customs Union.

Table 12.6. Projected Change in Textile and Clothing Exports and Production Resulting from China's WTO Accession, 2006

(In percent)

Country Group	Exports		Production	
	Textile	Clothing	Textile	Clothing
Industrial countries	–3.0	–16.7	–4.6	–14.5
Asian NIEs	16.6	–24.1	9.3	–11.9
ASEAN	–3.7	–33.1	–12.1	–24.1
South Asia	4.0	–19.9	–2.7	–17.6
Latin America	–7.0	–35.3	–2.4	–5.2
N. Africa and Middle East	–8.2	–30.7	–6.3	–12.1
SACU	–6.7	–23.7	–1.8	–14.8
Rest of Africa	–9.6	–35.1	–2.7	–9.5
Rest of world	–6.7	–35.0	–3.7	–11.7

Source: IMF staff simulation of the GTAP model.

exports because of a large contraction of its clothing exports as well as increased demand for textile imports from China. Clothing exports contract considerably in every region, but only South Asia suffers a significant decline in overall exports as a result, because of its heavy reliance on clothing exports. The effect on production varies significantly across regions. ASEAN and South Asia, the two regions with the highest export dependency in the clothing industry, are affected most.

There is considerable uncertainty over how China's accession to the WTO will affect other developing countries' textile and clothing exports. China will be subject to a special safeguard provision, which could be used to curb its export expansion until the end of 2008. Together with the transitional, product-specific safeguard mechanism and the antidumping provisions based on procedures against nonmarket economies, these contingent protection measures could seriously slow the expansion of China's textile and clothing exports, thus reducing the pressure on other developing country exporters.[12]

The results presented in Table 12.4 do not fully capture the long-term impact of China's WTO accession, particularly in the agriculture and mineral sectors. Despite China's strong market access commitments in agriculture, the short- to medium-term impact on world agricultural prices is likely to be relatively small; however, the long-term impact could be much greater. It is widely accepted that China is losing comparative advantage in land-intensive agricultural commodities, especially grain (Zhang, 2000). Its commitment to relatively low tariff

---

[12]The transitional safeguard will last for 12 years after China's accession to the WTO, whereas the antidumping provisions will be valid for 15 years.

bindings means that this will translate into increased imports of these commodities in the long run. Although some countries that are net food importers may lose from this, net food exporters should benefit. Similarly, China's energy imports have increased rapidly in recent years, and with continued rapid economic growth this trend is likely to continue. This may provide many income-poor but resource-rich countries in Africa and elsewhere with significant opportunities to increase their exports to China.

A more comprehensive assessment of the impact of China's WTO accession would require more detailed modeling of foreign direct investment and services trade. The model used in this study does not incorporate foreign direct investment, and only a few barriers to services trade are taken into account. This tends to underestimate the benefits accruing to the rest of the world from China's WTO accession, especially for the newly industrializing economies and ASEAN, but also for South Asia. India's computer software companies, for example, have potential to invest in China or to export to China. According to a survey conducted by IMF staff, some Asian countries believe that they can increase their exports of financial and entertainment services to China (see Box 1 in Yang, 2002).

Any assessment of the impact of China's WTO accession on other developing countries should also take into account the long-run gains in China's growth prospects. As noted above, WTO accession and increased integration with the world economy will likely accelerate China's growth. It has been shown that China's growth and external opening (as opposed to the expansion of labor-intensive exports alone) in the past have been generally beneficial to its trading partners by improving their terms of trade and expanding the global market (Yang and Vines, 2001). A growing and more open Chinese economy should also play a larger role in smoothing global economic growth, as evidenced by the beneficial effects of China's continued strong growth at the time of the Asian crisis and the recent global slowdown. Such stabilizing effects are particularly important for developing countries, which tend to suffer disproportionately from high volatility in commodity prices.

Conclusions

WTO accession will have important macroeconomic, social, and structural ramifications. In broad terms, accession will support the reform effort under way in China, adding urgency to the further acceleration of reforms. It promises to increase foreign direct investment, remove protection from inefficient industries, and spur the development of the legal and regulatory framework necessary for a market economy.

On the macroeconomic side, the projections reported in this chapter, although subject to large uncertainties, suggest that the short-term impact will be broadly manageable, aided by the improving external environment. It seems unlikely that GDP growth will fall sharply or that a major deterioration in the balance of payments will occur.

There could be an increase in unemployment and a widening of income disparities, which will require further efforts to strengthen the social safety net and to foster more balanced regional development. The authorities' ongoing efforts to encourage private sector development will also assume increased importance.

Perhaps the greatest challenges, however, will occur on the structural side, particularly in the financial and SOE sectors. It is essential that the authorities move ahead rapidly with reforms in these sectors. Because an acceleration of structural reforms will have important fiscal implications, this will need to be accompanied by stronger efforts to bolster the fiscal position over the medium term, including through increased revenue mobilization and improvements to expenditure controls, which are at present very weak and subject to abuse.

China's further integration into the world economy will also require adjustment in its trading partners. Developing countries that compete with China in labor-intensive manufactures will need to diversify their exports, most notably away from textiles and clothing, and agricultural importers may face increases in import costs. There will also be increased competition for foreign direct investment as China opens up further, but there will be opportunities for developing countries to expand their exports and investment in China. To seize upon these opportunities, developing countries need to continue with their structural reform efforts and facilitate the reallocation of resources and strengthen competitiveness.

References

Dimaranan, B.V., and Robert A. McDougall, 2001, *Global Trade, Assistance, and Production: The GTAP 5 Data Base* (Lafayette, Indiana: Center for Global Trade Analysis, Purdue University).

Harrison, W. Jill, and K.R. Pearson, 1996, "Computing Solutions for Large General Equilibrium Models using GEMPACK," *Computational Economics*, Vol. 9, No. 2 (May), pp. 83–127.

Hertel, T.W. (ed.), 1997, *Global Trade Analysis: Modeling and Applications* (New York: Cambridge University Press).

International Monetary Fund, 1993, *World Economic Outlook*, May.

Lardy, Nicholas R., 2002, *Integrating China into the Global Economy* (Washington: Brookings Institution Press).

Li, Shantong, and Fan Zhai, 1999, "China's WTO Accession and Implications for National and Provincial Economies," October (unpublished; Beijing: Development Research Center, State Council).

Martin, Will, Betina Dimaranan, and Thomas Hertel, 1999, "Trade Policies, Structural Change and China's Trade Growth," November (unpublished; Washington: World Bank).

Rosen, Daniel, 1999, "China and the World Trade Organization: An Economic Balance Sheet," International Economics Policy Briefs 99–6 (Washington: Institute for International Economics).

United States International Trade Commission, 1999, *Assessment of the Economic Effects on the United States for China's Accession to the WTO*, Publication 3229 (Washington: United States International Trade Commission).

Walmsley, T.L., and Thomas Hertel, 2000, "China's Accession to the WTO: Timing Is Everything," September (Lafayette, Indiana: Center for Global Trade Analysis, Purdue University).

Wei, Shang-jin, 2000, "Local Corruption and Global Capital Flows," *Brookings Papers on Economic Activity*, No. 2, pp. 303–54.

World Trade Organization, 2001, "WTO Successfully Concludes Negotiations on China's Entry," Press Release 243, September 17 (Geneva: World Trade Organization).

Yang, Yongzheng, 2002, "Entering the WTO: China Is Coming Out" (unpublished; Washington: International Monetary Fund).

———, and David Vines, 2001, "The Fallacy of Composition and the Terms of Trade of Newly Industrialising Countries," revised version of a paper presented at a seminar in the Department of Economics, Oxford University, November 2000.

Zhang, Xiao-guang, 2000, "China's Comparative Advantage in Agriculture: An Empirical Analysis," in *China's Agriculture at the Crossroads*, ed. by Yongzheng Yang and Weiming Tian (New York: St. Martin's Press).

Zheng, Yuxin, and Mingtai Fan, 2001, "The Impact of China's Trade Liberalization for WTO Accession," paper presented at a conference on Greater China and the WTO, Hong Kong SAR, March 22–24.

13

Exchange Rate Policy

NICOLAS BLANCHER

Although China's exchange rate regime is officially described as a managed float, the renminbi has in practice been tightly linked to the U.S. dollar, especially since the Asian financial crisis.[1] This policy was credited with serving as an important anchor of stability, both for China and the region, during this period. However, as the region has stabilized, the question has arisen whether China should allow greater flexibility of the renminbi, particularly in light of continued rapid structural change in the economy, including as a result of World Trade Organization (WTO) accession.

China's External Position

China's external position, resilient during the Asian crisis, has remained strong since then. During the crisis the renminbi appreciated by about 10 percent in real effective terms, and it came under pressure in the thinly traded parallel and offshore nondeliverable forward markets. These developments gave rise to concerns that the renminbi might have become overvalued. Exports did slow sharply in 1998 (Figure

---

[1]Following the unification of the renminbi exchange rate in 1994, the People's Bank of China (PBC) has limited movements of the renminbi against the dollar to plus or minus 0.3 percent around a reference rate. Since the Asian crisis the renminbi has been kept within an even smaller range of plus or minus 0.02 percent. More recently it has been allowed to move slightly outside this narrower range (mainly on the appreciated side).

215

Figure 13.1. Export Growth
(In percent)[1]

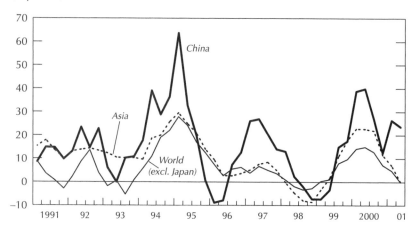

Source: IMF, *Direction of Trade Statistics.*
[1] Change from the preceding quarter.

13.1), but China's export shares held up well in major markets, suggesting that weak external demand, rather than an overvalued currency, was the main reason for the slowdown. The real appreciation reversed itself with the recovery of Asian currencies and the sustained deflation in China in recent years (Figure 13.2), and pressures in the offshore markets have since subsided.

China maintained small current account surpluses (relative to GDP) during 1997–2001. Its export market share has increased steadily, particularly in the United States and the European Union (Figure 13.3). At the same time, China's manufactured exports (which now account for 90 percent of total exports) continued to diversify across sectors, with rapid expansion in machinery and equipment, including electronic goods (Figure 13.4). China's imports have kept pace with the expansion in exports, boosted by the rapid growth of domestic demand, foreign direct investment, and exports.

China's accession to the WTO should support the continued expansion of the tradable goods sector (World Bank, 1997). Initially, WTO accession may have only a limited impact on China's exports; the impact on imports is expected to be more significant as market opening and larger investment inflows are likely to boost imports before export gains materialize. In the longer run, however, WTO accession should contribute to sustained export growth, broadly offsetting the initial import expansion (see Chapter 12).

Figure 13.2. Bilateral and Effective Exchange Rates
(Index, 1990=100)[1]

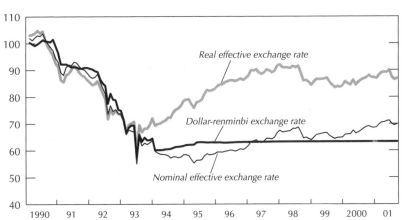

Source: IMF Information Notice System.
[1]A decline indicates a depreciation.

China's overall external position is strong, as shown by the evolution of key indicators of external vulnerability in recent years:

- China's international reserves are equivalent to nine months of imports and more than three times its short-term external debt.[2]
- China's external debt relative to its GDP (as well as to exports) is small and has been declining in recent years.
- China's capital account is relatively closed to debt-creating flows, with most capital inflows coming in the form of foreign direct investment.

The Case for Greater Exchange Rate Flexibility

Although the stability of the renminbi has served China and the region well in recent years, a number of considerations suggest that greater exchange rate flexibility will be beneficial to the Chinese economy going forward, especially after China's accession to the WTO. This assessment is based on the following:

---

[2]In this calculation short-term external debt is measured by remaining maturity and based on the revised debt data categories released by the authorities in November 2001.

Figure 13.3. China's Share of Foreign Import Markets
(In percent of total exports)

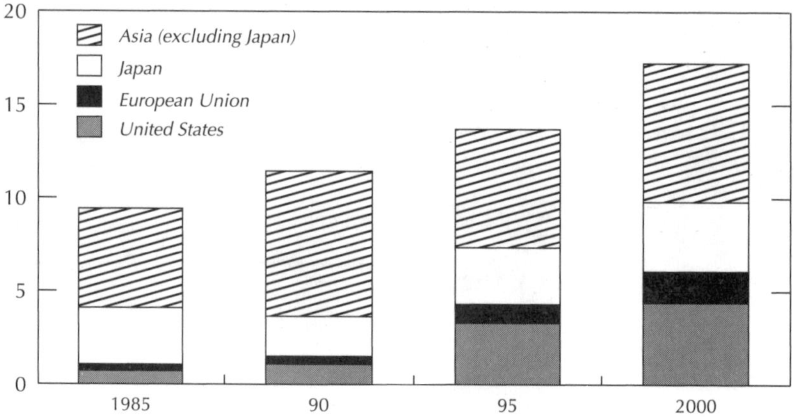

Source: IMF, *Direction of Trade Statistics.*

- The impact of the multitude of ongoing structural changes on the equilibrium exchange rate is difficult to ascertain. For example, further trade liberalization could result in its decline, but rapid productivity gains in China's traded goods sector would put upward pressure on it. Such productivity gains should materialize from continued reform of state-owned enterprises, growth of the nonstate sector, and technology transfers from inward foreign direct investment.
- China's economy does not form an optimum currency area with the U.S. economy, because the two economies are subject to different shocks. However, under the current regime, the volatility of the renminbi's effective exchange rate closely reflects that of the dollar. To better achieve effective exchange rate stability and cope with a greater variety of external shocks, making the renminbi exchange rate more flexible is a prerequisite.
- China has used its control over capital movements to combine a fixed exchange rate with an independent monetary policy. However, capital controls are not watertight, will likely become more porous over time, and are eventually to be removed: convertibility of the renminbi is a stated, and appropriate, long-term policy goal. Preserving monetary independence will thus increasingly require a more flexible exchange rate.
- China is facing a proliferation of floating exchange rate regimes in the rest of the world, especially in Asia. In this context, if the

Figure 13.4. Product Composition of Manufactured Exports
(In billions of dollars)

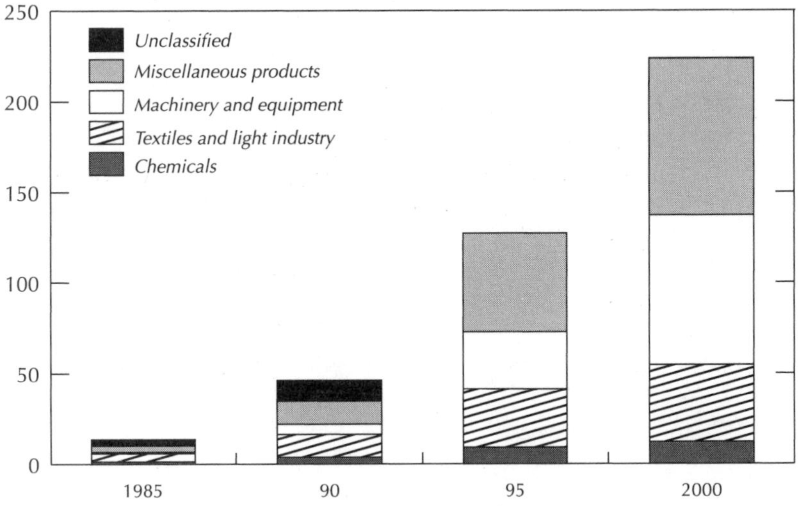

Source: China Economic Information Center.

region is hit by a shock and neighboring countries' currencies adjust, keeping the renminbi stable vis-à-vis the dollar implies that a relatively heavier share of the adjustment burden will fall on China's domestic economy.

- Factor markets in China are not very flexible, and the scope for fiscal policy to help the adjustment to shocks is narrowing. Capital mobility between regions is limited, and wages and prices are not fully market determined, despite progress in increasing their flexibility. The insufficient availability of skilled labor creates bottlenecks in some fast-growing sectors.

- China has a large and relatively diversified economy, which seems well positioned to absorb exchange rate fluctuations. Indeed, China resembles other large economies, which nearly without exception have more flexible exchange rate arrangements in place (Gao, 2000).

- As recent international experience has illustrated, defending rigid exchange rate regimes becomes increasingly difficult with growing capital mobility, and greater flexibility helps reduce the risk of sharp capital flow reversals (Mussa and others, 2000).

These considerations suggest that, from a medium-term perspective, greater exchange rate flexibility would be more appropriate for China.

Furthermore, China's external position allows it to make a gradual move toward greater flexibility from a position of strength.

Modalities and Supporting Measures

Greater flexibility of the exchange rate is desirable, but the move should be gradual and carefully prepared. Current conditions do not support a free float. Instead a gradual move not only would give time for the corporate and banking sectors to adjust, but also would allow the development of China's foreign exchange market infrastructure and regulatory framework (IMF, 1998).

Successful transition to a situation where market forces play a progressively larger role in exchange rate determination requires a comprehensive and well-sequenced set of supporting measures (Ping, 2000). A key priority is to strengthen the foreign exchange market, especially to give market participants greater freedom in handling foreign exchange and hedging against foreign exchange risk.[3] A number of measures are needed to allow for trading to develop and for market participants to use exchange rate flexibility effectively. Key among these are:

- Allowing enterprises greater flexibility to choose the bank with which they conduct their foreign exchange business and further reducing surrender requirements
- Easing restrictions on foreign exchange market entry and increasing the number of instruments available for foreign exchange risk management
- Strengthening the functioning and capacity of the foreign exchange market, for example by introducing two-way quotes, extending trading sessions, and improving settlement procedures.

In parallel, prudential regulation and supervision of banks' foreign exchange transactions will need to be upgraded, in line with international best practice and prudential rules on foreign exchange risks established by the Basel Committee on Banking Supervision. Specifically, foreign currency lending of banks should be monitored closely to ensure that loans are extended only to borrowers with foreign currency earnings, and effective limits should be placed on banks' open foreign currency positions (including off-balance sheet activities). These positions should cover branches of domestic banks operating outside of China.

---

[3]The current foreign exchange trading system (the Shanghai-based China Foreign Exchange Trading System) was established in 1994 as a nationally integrated electronic system for spot interbank foreign exchange trading (Zee, 1999). There is also a small onshore forward market.

Close prudential supervision of the quality and liquidity of banks' foreign currency assets is also essential.

More broadly, greater exchange rate flexibility is part and parcel of China's comprehensive and intertwined market-oriented reforms. In particular, it needs to be supported by further progress in reforming the financial sector, the state-owned enterprises (SOEs), and monetary policy (Mehran and others, 1996):

- *Financial sector reform.* With banks playing a pivotal role in the foreign exchange market, strengthening the banking sector will be key (see Chapter 10).
- *SOE reforms.* To become effective market participants, SOEs will need to strengthen their financial performance and capacity to manage risks, including foreign exchange risk (Chapter 9).
- *Monetary policy and money markets.* With greater exchange rate flexibility, a greater burden will fall on monetary policy to ensure price stability. This points to the need for the People's Bank of China to further strengthen its monetary management, including by fostering the development of the money market and indirect monetary instruments.

Conclusion

Although the policy of keeping the exchange rate stable served China well during the Asian crisis, the Chinese economy would benefit from greater exchange rate flexibility. In particular, in the wake of WTO accession and as China integrates further into the global economy, greater exchange rate flexibility would help China adjust to structural changes and potential shocks, preserve its monetary independence, and limit the risk of sudden capital flow reversals.

Successful transition to greater flexibility requires a range of supporting measures to strengthen the foreign exchange market. It also needs to be accompanied by continued progress in other market-oriented reforms, especially in the banking and SOE sectors.

References

Gao, Haihong, 2000, "Exchange Rate Policy: Possible Choices for China and Other Asian Economies," *World Economy & China*, Vol. 8, No. 4 (July–August).

International Monetary Fund, 1998, "Exit Strategies—Policy Options for Countries Seeking Exchange Rate Flexibility," Occasional Paper No. 168 (Washington: International Monetary Fund).

Mehran, Hassanali, Marc Quintyn, Tom Nordman, and Bernard Laurens, 1996, "Monetary and Exchange System Reforms in China," Occasional Paper No. 141 (Washington: International Monetary Fund).

Mussa, Michael, Paul Masson, Alexander Swoboda, Esteban Jadresic, Paulo Mauro, and Andy Berg, 2000, "Exchange Rate Regimes in an Increasingly Integrated World Economy," Occasional Paper No. 193 (Washington: International Monetary Fund).

Ping, Xie, 2000, "The Convertibility of the RMB and China's Exchange Rate Policies," *World Economy & China*, Vol. 8, No. 4 (July–August).

World Bank, 1997, *China 2020—Development Challenges in the New Century* (Washington: World Bank).

Zee, Winston, 1999, *China Forex Handbook* (Hong Kong: Asian Information Associates).